Great Book of

Shop Drawings
for
Craftsman Furniture

Authentic and Fully Detailed
Plans for 57 Classic Pieces

Robert W. Lang

FOX CHAPEL
PUBLISHING

© 2013 by Robert W. Lang and Fox Chapel Publishing Company, Inc., East Petersburg, PA.

Great Book of Shop Drawings for Craftsman Furniture (ISBN 978-1-56523-812-1, 2013) is a revised version of the book *Great Book of Shop Drawings for Craftsman Furniture* (ISBN 978-1-56523-738-4, 2012), both published by Fox Chapel Publishing Company, Inc., East Petersburg, PA. Revisions include additional detail on blueprints and diagrams. The book is a compilation and update of *Shop Drawings for Craftsman Furniture* (2001), *More Shop Drawings for Craftsman Furniture* (2002), and *Shop Drawings for Craftsman Inlays & Hardware* (2004), all by the same author. The patterns contained herein are copyrighted by the author. Readers may make copies of these patterns for personal use. The patterns themselves, however, are not to be duplicated for resale or distribution under any circumstances. Any such copying is a violation of copyright law.

ISBN 978-1-56523-812-1

To learn more about the other great books from Fox Chapel Publishing, or to find a retailer near you, call toll-free 800-457-9112 or visit us at *www.FoxChapelPublishing.com*.

Note to Authors: We are always looking for talented authors to write new books. Please send a brief letter describing your idea to Acquisition Editor, 1970 Broad Street, East Petersburg, PA 17520.

Printed in the United States of America
First printing

Table of Contents

Table of Contents *continued*

INTRODUCTION

It has been my good fortune to spend nearly all of my adult life earning my living by working with wood. The idea for this book actually came to me quite some time ago, but it was always on the "someday" list. Like most woodworkers, it takes me a while to get around to the big ones.

My first introduction to Craftsman-style furniture was in the late-1970s, and my appreciation and fascination with this style has only grown over the years. At that time, I was still in the "eager-apprentice, soak-up-as-much-information-as-I-possibly-can" phase of my career, and some of my favorite sources were books of drawings of furniture, particularly Ejner Handberg's books on Shaker furniture and Gustave Ecke's book on Chinese furniture. The drawings in those books taught me as much or more about styles, design, and techniques than any of the other sources available to me. I kept expecting that someday someone would produce a book of drawings for Craftsman furniture.

Years passed and the book I wanted to see never appeared and I realized I should go ahead and do it myself. I began by scaling the illustrations in reproduction catalogs, then producing working drawings by hand from that. During the process, I read all I could find about how these pieces were constructed, and took every available opportunity to observe and study actual pieces.

This is more or less the process used to produce these drawings, although it was simplified by the personal computer and AutoCAD software. I scan as many photographs and drawings of original pieces as I can find into AutoCAD, and adjust their size to full scale. Then it becomes a matter of making a mechanical drawing from a perspective image. Details are zoomed in and measured, and then compared to known dimensions from pieces I have measured, similar pieces, or published information. Combined with my experience in the industry, and research on this type of furniture, a relatively accurate shop drawing is then produced.

These drawings are close to the originals but not perfect. There are places where I have had to make educated guesses as to the exact size of a part. Usually my guesses are very close, and many of the pieces in this book that were originally drawn from photographs were later measured and the accuracy of the process was confirmed. In some ways, I think the imperfections are a good thing.

The intent of this book is to give the average woodworker or devotee of Craftsman furniture the ability to produce, for his or her own pleasure, pieces of furniture that represent the style and spirit of the originals. It is not intended to be an aid to anyone attempting to fool the collector's market by passing off new work as antiques. If your intent is to commit such fraud, please look elsewhere for an accomplice. I urge everyone building furniture from these drawings to sign and date their work to avoid future confusion.

The other issue of accuracy comes from the original pieces, which can vary from one example to another. Not everyone measures furniture the same way. An antiques dealer or catalog copywriter without training in woodworking may ignore some of "those funny little marks" between the inches, or may not hold the tape measure squarely. Some consider the height of a dresser to be to the top surface; others measure to a piece of back trim.

The nature of wood and woodworking are also sources of variations. Solid wood expands and contracts as humidity and temperature change. If two identical pieces of furniture leave the factory, they likely won't be exactly the same size after a hundred years, particularly if one has been taken care of and one has been abused. At an auction I saw three examples of Roycroft "Little Journeys" stands. All three tops had different dimensions, varying about half an inch from the smallest to the largest. All were authentic, yet which one was the right size? None matched the dimensions in reference books and auction catalogs.

Factory-made furniture is generally produced in "cuttings"—the amount the manufacturer believes will sell over the next few months. All of the parts for that number of pieces will be milled and stored to be assembled as orders come in. It is common to adjust sizes and make minor changes from one cutting to another, for reasons of appearance, improving productivity or yield, or to utilize a new piece of machinery. If someone makes a mistake and produces a batch of parts that are not quite the proper size, those parts most likely will not be thrown out—they will be used. Many of these pieces were in production for several years, and underwent quite a few minor changes.

While I have tried to be true to the originals, the original pieces themselves don't always match previously published information about them. The answer to the question of "how accurate are these drawings" depends on all of the above factors. They are accurate enough for today's worker to build a very nice, structurally sound piece of furniture, which will be recognized as a Craftsman piece. They are true to the style, and that is not only the best we can do today, but also the best that Stickley himself ever did.

Chapter 1

The Story of Craftsman Furniture

One hundred years ago, society as a whole, and the design community in particular, stood at a crossroads. The world was rapidly changing as new technologies were developed. The notion of what makes a house a home was questioned then, as it should be questioned now. The places where we spend our time and the objects with which we surround ourselves have a significant influence on our comfort, peace of mind, and well-being. Craftsman design fills the need for usefulness and the desire for beauty in a way that expresses the inherent character of the natural materials, and the character and values of the designer, maker and owner. It is a welcome respite from designs whose purpose is to prove the wealth of the owner or to present "newness" only for the sake of following the latest trend.

Good furniture design simply makes sense; furniture should serve its purpose as well as possible, be constructed to endure, and use materials that please the eye and hand. It should bring a sense of calm and comfort to its environment, not disturb or detract from it. Craftsman design expresses integrity and quality in a quiet, dignified manner. It does not shout, but it cannot be ignored. It serves its purpose while providing pleasure to the senses. Good design comes, as Gustav Stickley said, "from the

bottom up." It is based on solid fundamentals, expressed in a straightforward manner.

As Stickley put it:

"In the beginning there was no thought of creating a new style, only a recognition of the fact that we should have in our homes something better suited to our needs and more expressive of our character as a people than Imitations of the traditional styles, and a conviction that the best way to get something better was to go directly back to plain principles of construction and apply them to the making of simple, strong, comfortable furniture that would meet adequately everything that could be required of it." [1]

It is this expression of character that separates Craftsman furniture from other styles, and the values attached to that expression are the foundation of its appeal. This appeal also comes from the bottom up—it matches a desire for things that make sense, that present themselves in an honest way and use the beauty of nature without exploitation. Like the furniture itself, the values and ideals behind the furniture have a timeless appeal to the best aspects of human nature.

Though Gustav Stickley is certainly the main character, the story of American Arts & Crafts furniture also features Gustav's four brothers, particularly his youngest brother, Leopold, who was to become Gustav's biggest competitor. The five brothers were independent and strong-willed men, all successful in the furniture business but unsuccessful at working with each other.

Their father abandoned the family when the boys were quite young; as they came of age, the three oldest went to work at the chair factory in Brandt, Pennsylvania, owned by their uncle, Jacob Schlaeger. In 1884, in Binghamton, New York, Gustav, Albert, and Charles formed the Stickley Brothers Company, which sold (and after 1886, manufactured) furniture. Leopold and John George joined the growing company around 1888.

Gustav left the family business later that same year, and in partnership with Elgin A. Simonds, started a similar business named Stickley & Simonds. Although the partnership lasted only

In 1902, Gustav chose a joiner's compass as his logo with the Flemish phrase "Als ik kan" (To the best of my ability) inscribed within the compass and his signature underneath. Gustav Stickley's shopmark and label offered a guarantee of authenticity, and his personal guarantee of quality.

Shopmark courtesy The Stickley Museum, Fayetteville, N.Y.

a few years, it was revived in Syracuse, New York, in 1894. During the years in between, Gustav held positions with a streetcar company in Binghamton and later was director of manufacturing at the New York State Prison in Auburn, New York.

In the late-1890s, Gustav Stickley and his brothers Albert and Charles were all successful furniture manufacturers. Albert had taken the Stickley Brothers name and moved to Grand Rapids, Michigan. Charles stayed in Binghamton, operating as Stickley and Brandt with brother-in-law Schuyler Brandt. Younger brother John George worked as a sales representative for Albert. Leopold left the family business about a year after Gustav and worked for him both at Stickley & Simonds and at Gustav's independent operation in Syracuse. The three companies became four in 1902 when Leopold formed the L. & J. G. Stickley Company near Syracuse, New York, with John George as his partner.

The three companies operating in the late-1890s were quite similar in size and in the type of furniture that was manufactured—mainly chairs in a variety of styles, including reproductions and adaptations of antique styles. In 1899, Gustav ended his partnership with Simonds and began to develop the furniture designs that became known as Craftsman. Gustav Stickley's efforts went far beyond the manufacture of furniture, he became a publisher and advocate for the Arts & Crafts movement, and had a tremendous effect on American culture, creating a new style that became popular because it spoke to and met the needs of a society in transition.

Across the Atlantic, the Art Nouveau movement in Europe and the Arts and Crafts movement in England were gaining popularity and significantly influencing American design and architecture. Both movements grew from a common root—a reaction to what had happened to the traditions of design and craftsmanship with the industrial age, and the introduction of factory methods for the production of furniture and other objects. The conditions of workers in the factories, and the effects on society of factory-made goods, were important elements of both design movements.

Both Gustav and Albert traveled to Europe in the final years of the nineteenth century, and as thriving manufacturers in an industry dependent on serving the changing tastes of the buying public, they were well aware of trends in style and design. The latter half of the nineteenth century had seen a transition to modern manufacturing methods, but most designs of that time were reiterations of designs from earlier periods, adapted to machine-made techniques. The Art Nouveau and Arts and Crafts designs were among the few new designs in furniture in the previous 50 years.

These trips were essentially scouting missions, searches for the latest trends. Both brothers were greatly influenced by what they saw in Europe and England. Albert returned to America ready to hop on the English Arts and Crafts bandwagon, while Gustav returned ready to hitch up his own horses and drive the American Arts & Crafts movement in a new direction.

Albert established a warehouse in England in the hopes of establishing an export business, and hired T.A. Conti to design and produce inlays, and David Robertson Smith to design furniture. Conti was working in Grand Rapids in 1900, and Smith came to Michigan in 1902. The inlay designs produced by Stickley Brothers and the Quaint line of furniture were apparently the work of Conti and Smith. There is little evidence of Albert being involved in design work beyond the role of owner of the company—he was astute enough to recognize trends in design and style, and wise enough to hire competent designers, but he was not the creative force that his brother Gustav was.

After dissolving his partnership with Simonds, and touring Europe and England, Gustav returned to Syracuse and worked at developing his new designs. His new furniture was first marketed by the Tobey Company of Chicago, a distributor of furniture produced by others, as well as a manufacturer. Dissatisfied with this arrangement, Gustav began marketing his own work. His new designs and the style he developed became popular, and his company became successful—as did those of his brothers and numerous other competitors.

The first decade of the twentieth century belonged to Gustav Stickley. *The Craftsman* magazine was launched in October 1901, and within a few years Gustav expanded his reach into architecture and home construction. Furniture remained the backbone of the business, but Gustav expanded operations to also produce linens, rugs, and metalwork, including lamps, hardware, and accessories. This continued expansion eventually became his financial undoing. Following all of his interests, and developing enterprises devoted to each of them, Gustav created an operation that was too complex for one person to manage.

When Gustav Stickley first began his experiments with Arts & Crafts furniture,

Stickley's furniture as it was presented in the first issue of The Craftsman magazine.

he tried many variations before settling on the designs that went into production. These early pieces were not the squared-off designs associated with him today, but featured curves and decorative carvings based on plant forms. He soon decided it was better to start with a structural idea rather than with an ornamental one. That philosophy is at the core of Stickley's designs: an eloquent expression of a purely functional item, with the structural elements themselves becoming the ornamentation.

Stickley's strength as a designer was his sense of proportion. Simple furniture is not simple to design, and with decorative elements nonexistent or kept to a minimum, a successful design must make the most of those elements that do exist, show the materials to their best advantage, and be balanced. While the scale of many pieces often appears monumental when viewed in isolation, the overall scale of the furniture is often on the small side, which keeps the furniture from overwhelming its environment.

At first glance, Craftsman furniture is intriguing because it is so well proportioned and makes such good use of the material. But a quick glance is never enough. It invites a closer look, to examine the exposed joints, to take a good look at the details. This furniture makes friends with its user. Chairs invite you to sit and relax, and once seated you discover interesting details you might not have noticed before. Bookcases and

china cabinets provide a safe and secure place to keep things, and by their nature let you know that what is inside is rather special.

Rather than being overpowering, this furniture invites the viewer to look closer and to use it for its intended purpose. Tables provide a welcome place for family and friends to gather, and desks give a sense of taking care of necessary business without being ostentatious. All of the elements are quite simple, but the way they are combined makes all the difference. The quality of the joinery and finish must be executed as flawlessly as possible for these designs to be successful.

Gustav Stickley, while an innovator in design, did not work single-handedly, and his work does show influences from designs that were seen in England prior to the introduction of his Craftsman furniture. Although Stickley's daughter Barbara, maintained that Harvey Ellis was the only person to ever collaborate with or design furniture for Stickley[2], a letter from the architect Claude Bragdon mentions another architect, Henry Wilkinson, working for Gustav designing furniture in 1900.[3]

After Gustav Stickley, the most influential designer of the period was Harvey Ellis. Gustav employed Ellis briefly before his untimely death in 1904. Ellis is usually described as an itinerant architect, and his addiction to alcohol caused his early death. Ellis and Stickley met in 1903, with Ellis going to work for Stickley in May or June of that year. At the beginning of the next year, Ellis was already dead, but Stickley's 1904 catalog featured many Ellis designs, notably inlaid chairs and cabinets that never went into full production, a bedroom suite (Nos. 911, 912, 913, 914), the No. 700 series of bookcases, and china cabinets, servers, and delicate small drop-front desks. The addition of arched elements, subtle curves, and purely decorative elements added a touch of lightness and grace to Stickley's previous work. These pieces are some of the best-proportioned and most elegant furniture ever made.

In addition to these furniture designs, Ellis also wrote articles, designed houses, and drew illustrations for *The Craftsman* magazine. It is generally reported that Ellis was hired for his skill and training as an architect. But Ellis' talent for furniture design and the number of pieces attributed to him make it hard to believe Stickley was interested in his furniture designs only as an afterthought. Furniture production was always the largest part of Stickley's business, and faced with the ever-increasing number of companies copying his work, Stickley needed new, fresh designs to stay ahead of the competition. Harvey

Ellis strongly influenced Gustav Stickley's furniture, and many of the pieces that are considered the "best" examples came from or were strongly influenced by Harvey Ellis.

The temptation to attribute designs for specific pieces to individuals is strong, and many writers have done so. But there simply isn't enough evidence available to do that. Some design elements attributed to Harvey Ellis appeared before he came on the scene, while others appear in pieces that didn't come into production until well after his death. It is likely that Ellis, and others employed by Stickley, supplied the themes for these pieces, while Stickley's draftsmen worked out the details and possibly applied the themes and design elements to other pieces.

Harvey Ellis had a remarkable influence on Stickley's designs, but this influence is often overstated. As Stickley's daughter, Barbara, put it:

"Gustav took care of Harvey, but he also recognized Ellis' design genius . . . (and) above anyone else at the United Crafts, Harvey understood Gustav's ideas about furniture." [4]

Before settling in on his Craftsman designs, Stickley experimented with Art Nouveau designs, the best known of which are the tea tables based on stylized plant forms. There were also notable china cabinets that featured applied curves on the panels, a shape quite similar to the corbels that would appear on later pieces. The rarely seen early pieces indicate clearly that subtle curves and delicate pieces were a part of Stickley's design vocabulary before Ellis arrived on the scene.

Stickley's bungalow chair, produced in 1900, is remarkably similar to chairs shown in Ellis' renderings and raises the question of who was influenced by whom. Stickley's final designs, produced at the end of his career in 1915 and 1916, show a versatile and talented designer fully capable of producing work in a variety of styles.

Stickley and Ellis' work showed influences from English Arts & Crafts designs, notably those of Voysey, Ashbee, and Mackintosh. The two men shared interests and leadership in the Arts & Crafts movement, had common interests and influences, and recognized the importance of the philosophy behind their new designs. While Stickley employed Ellis, Ellis was also extremely independent and able to explain his designs as logical solutions to common problems. Their brief working relationship seems to be more the collaboration of equals rather than of a hired hand doing his employer's bidding.

Harvey Ellis arrived in Syracuse in late spring 1903, with a considerable reputation as a talented

Image courtesy University of Wisconsin Digital Collections

Many of the pieces attributed to Harvey Ellis, including this sideboard, first appeared as illustrations in The Craftsman (October 1903).

designer and leader of the Arts & Crafts Society in Rochester, New York. He also carried a significant amount of baggage, due to his alcoholism, and the effect that his addiction had already had on his career. The chaotic effects of his drinking had played a role in Ellis' career from the beginning.

After a six-month stay at West Point, Ellis traveled to Europe and then served a brief apprenticeship in Albany, New York, with architect H.H. Richardson. In 1879, he opened an architectural practice in Rochester with his brothers, Charles and Frank. In 1885, reportedly after a disagreement with brother Charles, Ellis headed west, working first in St Paul, Minnesota, for Leroy Buffington and J. Walter Stevens, and later in St. Louis, Missouri, for George R. Mann.

The work produced during this period, both actual buildings and architectural renderings, showed a talent for design and a mastery of technique. His pen-and-ink and watercolor renderings, reportedly executed without the aid of drafting instruments, are among the finest work ever produced. Architectural renderings are usually thought of as technical works, but in addition to mastery of lines, Ellis brought a wonderful sense of composition and detail.

Many of his designs were never constructed, but were significant for the era, notably two designs for Buffington—a 29-story office building, and a prototype for the now-common suburban bank branch. Some notable structures that were built include the Mabel Tainter Memorial Theater in Menomonie, Wisconsin, Pillsbury Hall at the University of Minnesota, and the John L. Merriam residence.

Ellis' obituary[5] reflected the view of his peers in the architectural community:

"The drawings and designs of the late Harvey Ellis...came just short of influencing western work more strongly than that of any other designer, before or since his time...No one else could do such striking things and yet avoid the bizarre."

What kept Harvey Ellis from becoming a truly great architect was his erratic behavior, typical of an alcoholic, and described by his friend, Claude Bragdon, a few years after Ellis' death:

"To paint an authentic human portrait glowing colors will not suffice: it is the shadows that tell the story, and one black shadow, already outlined, I must proceed to block in at once. During the major portion of his life Harvey Ellis was the slave of drink.

"During the period he worked for Eckel and Mann of St. Louis, he did not know the amount of his salary. When he found his pockets empty, he went to them for more money, and got it—he left all keeping of accounts to them. Buffington found it necessary to deal with him on a somewhat similar basis. He gave Harvey, at the end of every day, amounts varying from a quarter to several dollars; and whatever the sum, in the morning it was gone. The prize money, which he won in the first New York Grant Monument competition, he dissipated (with the help of boon companions) in three days. He seldom sold a picture, because he could not endure the patronage of the rich buyer, while if a true connoisseur expressed a liking for one of his pictures Harvey usually insisted on making him a present of it." (6)

It is a common misconception that an alcoholic or other addict isn't capable of producing quality work. In reality, they are often able to produce quality and quantities of work well beyond the norm. What suffers most is the alcoholic's relationships with other people, particularly employers, and with themselves. Here is Bragdon's description of Ellis' work:

"One may praise without qualification Harvey's architectural pen-drawings. They are everything that such drawings should be: unlabored, economical of line, brilliant, beautifully balanced, with far more of color and body than is usual in pen-drawings. His early experience as an etcher doubtless accounts for his mastery over this difficult medium." (7)

In 1893, an economic downturn led to a slowdown in building and architecture, and Ellis returned to Rochester. He also did something he had never been able to do: he began a ten-year period of sobriety. As Bragdon describes it:

"...he rose from his besotted bed and for a period of ten years did not touch alcohol until, a few months before his melancholy death,

weakened by disease, he sought its aid to give him strength for his daily task." (8)

In 1929, Bragdon wrote:

"Ellis quit drinking and left architecture to escape from the 'work-a-day world' to return to Rochester...[where] the only things he seemed to care for were to paint cryptic, unsalable pictures, under a still north light, with plenty of time and plenty of cigarettes and to talk about everything under the sun except himself to anyone who would listen." (9)

During this period, Ellis did little architectural work, but it isn't clear if it was due to a slow economy, or personal reasons. He was active in the Arts & Crafts movement, helping to found the Rochester Arts & Crafts Society in 1897, and became that organization's first president. In late-1902, Gustav Stickley was planning a major exhibition of American and European Arts & Crafts to be held in Syracuse. Stickley selected Theodore Hanford Pond to organize and serve as chairman of this exhibition. It was likely Pond who introduced Ellis and Stickley. (10)

At the close of the exhibition in Syracuse, it was moved to Rochester and shortly afterward Harvey Ellis arrived in Syracuse to work for Stickley. The exact date of Ellis' employment is not known. The Arts & Crafts exhibition closed in Rochester at the end of April 1903, and the first publication of Ellis' work in *The Craftsman* appeared in the July 1903 issue. Given the amount of material by Ellis in that issue, it seems likely he began to work for Stickley soon after the exhibition closed, and that he arrived with a good deal of the published material in complete, or near-complete form. Gustav Stickley introduced his readers to Harvey Ellis as follows:

"The illustrations and text of A Craftsman House Design, and An Adirondack Camp, are from the pen and pencil of an artist and writer new to the pages of our magazine: one whose practical qualities, originality, and artistic accent cannot fail to make him welcome in our present issue, and eagerly awaited in the future." (11)

In addition to the two house designs, there were articles on a Man's Dressing Cabinet and A Child's Bedroom that are evidently the work of Ellis. The dressing cabinet was presented as a do-it-yourself article, later reprinted in *Making Authentic Craftsman Furniture,* and the illustrations in the bedroom furniture article carry Ellis' signature, a stylized "H" and "E" enclosed in a circle. Ellis' illustrations usually contained design motifs similar to those that eventually appeared on inlaid Craftsman furniture, not only on furniture but also on curtains and other linens, patterns in art glass windows, and as stenciled wall decorations.

LaMont Warner was Gustav Stickley's head draftsman and furniture designer from 1900 to 1906. He has been credited with design of the No. 634 five-leg cross-stretcher table (pp. 99-102). The trumpet stretchers on this table also appear on smaller tables. It is not possible to say authoritatively whose idea was whose. My guess is much of the design work was collaborative, with Gustav supplying creative direction and general ideas, while Warner, his staff, and production people generated details and final designs.

Mary Ann Smith's *Gustav Stickley: The Craftsman* outlines Stickley's design process, as described by his grandson Peter Wiles. Gustav explained the design concept to his workman verbally, waving his hands to indicate the general shape and features of the piece. The workman built the piece and showed it to Stickley who inspected it, again indicating changes by waving his hands. Another model would be built incorporating the changes. This process continued until Stickley approved the design, which then went into production. Only at this point would measured drawings be made.

Although Wiles would have been too young to have witnessed this first-hand, I see no reason to doubt it was Stickley's method, at least in part. However, there is a contradiction between Wiles' second-hand account, and Claude Bragdon's description of Wilkinson's work. Wilkinson's role as a designer is unclear. Were the ideas his or interpretations of Stickley's ideas? Quite likely, the designs were a collaborative effort.

Many of the pieces of furniture designed for Stickley by Harvey Ellis first appeared as renderings in *The Craftsman*, and there would be several stages of drawing and prototype-making between concept and final production. When and where someone else picked up the work of Ellis is unknown, as is the actual role of anyone involved.

Stickley's ability to communicate design ideas verbally could also be used by others in preparing drawings for the production of prototypes. In addition to the architects who worked on *The Craftsman*, Stickley also employed a number of designers and draftsmen, notably Peter Hansen, who later worked for L. & J. G. Stickley, and LaMont Warner. Some sources have attributed designs to Hansen and Warner, but these attributions seem based solely on the fact they were present and *could* have produced the designs.

I believe most of the design ideas came directly from Gustav Stickley, but that the process of taking any design from idea to production was quite likely a collaborative effort. Stickley was involved in all the details of all the work that bore his name, be it the furniture, the magazine or house designs. It is not likely that a significant manufacturer, with decades of experience in the industry, would develop prototypes without any drawings or sketches in the early stages of the process. It is also unlikely, given the number of different pieces manufactured by Stickley that each piece depended on building a complete prototype, without any drawings.

Gustav Stickley was a very busy man, involved in many projects simultaneously, and he seemed quite able to plant the seeds of ideas that others would bring to completion under his direction. In the development of his furniture designs, it is likely the cabinetmaker building the prototype, the draftsman finalizing the production drawings, and everyone else in the process, would have some input. Stickley had a talent for attracting like-minded people, and as a good leader, seemed able to assign projects and accept the results with minimal intervention.

This is evident in the editing and publication of *The Craftsman* and in the preparation of architectural drawings. Stickley is credited, and in the case of the architectural drawings, many had his signature of approval, but there is no evidence of drawings prepared by Stickley himself. This does not mean the designs are not his creations. It would not have been possible for one individual to do all of the detail work associated with conveying his ideas. I think it reasonable to assume the development of the furniture and inlay designs involved a similar process. Stickley outlined his ideas and his team refined the designs and prepared them for production.

One of the main means of communication in furniture making is sketches, often hurriedly drawn and rarely saved, but nonetheless crucial to the process. There is always some degree of give-and-take in the process of bringing a design idea to finished form, and the scale of Stickley's operation suggests a team effort would have been necessary. Stickley would not have come close to achieving what he did, if he did not have the ability to listen to those he trusted to carry out his ideas. It is tempting to give credit to Stickley alone, but it must be remembered that he had highly skilled, talented help. It is also tempting to give credit to those who worked for Stickley, but this should only be done if there is strong evidence of significant influence.

Stickley moved his offices and showroom to New York City in 1905. He purchased land

Most of Harvey Ellis' work in The Craftsman was architectural designs and illustrations.

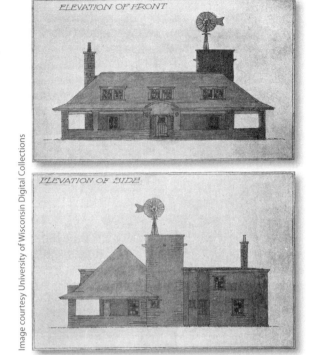

Image courtesy University of Wisconsin Digital Collections

in New Jersey, and called it Craftsman Farms. He planned a large house for his residence and planned to establish a school there. He moved his corporate headquarters to a large, expensive building in New York City in 1913 and included showrooms for his furniture, other manufacturers, his architectural and publishing offices, and a restaurant featuring meat and vegetables raised at Craftsman Farms.

Eventually, he was spending much more than he was taking in and, in late-1915, Gustav was forced into bankruptcy. He briefly worked as a consultant, and then joined in an ill-fated venture with his brothers before retiring in 1918. His final 24 years were spent living with his daughter and grandchildren. When Gustav retired, Leopold and John George took control of Gustav's factory and other assets. They continued as the L. & J. G. Stickley Company, which still operates, although not owned by the family. Albert and Charles continued into the 1920s with their companies.

Leopold Stickley had left his brother's company in 1902 to start his own operation, financed in part by a loan from Gustav. At first, he made products sold under other names, but in 1904, Leopold's own line of furniture was introduced. Focused solely on one business, and aided by brother John George, who was considered one of the best furniture salesmen in the country, Leopold was more successful financially than Gustav. When public tastes changed around World War I, he switched from Arts & Crafts furniture to reproductions of early American furniture. Leopold himself ran the company until his death in 1957.

Gustav Stickley and his brothers literally grew up in the furniture business, manufacturing reproduction and other popular styles of chairs, as well as marketing the work of other manufacturers. Each brother was talented and successful. However, as with their first attempt at working together, their business relationships were on-again, off-again. Their independence and strong wills helped them to achieve business success, but apparently prevented them from working together in groups of more than two.

One of Gustav's challenges was the vast number of competitors who freely adopted his designs, including those companies owned and operated by his brothers. Similar shop-marks and similar names added fuel to the fire. Gustav's catalogs emphasized how his furniture was marked, and he occasionally took the opportunity to remind the public that *"some of the most persistent of these imitators bear the same name as myself."* [12] Gustav Stickley was among the first to produce this style of furniture, and one of the most successful manufacturers of his day. The number of companies that copied his work attests to his design leadership. But Stickley's impact was broader than his furniture.

Gustav Stickley was also a leader of the Arts & Crafts movement, seeking to promote a better way of life based on ideals from the past adapted to a changing society. While others were trying to sell furniture, Stickley was looking at the changes that were making a tremendous impact on the way people lived and worked. The last 20 years of the nineteenth century brought new ways of manufacturing, communicating, and day-to-day living. The technological revolution at the turn of the twentieth century was lighting homes, powering factories, and speeding up the pace of everything. The telephone was becoming common and automobiles were beginning to replace horses for transportation.

Stickley questioned whether people should use the new technology to do the same things faster and cheaper, or whether new technology should be used to do things differently, to improve the quality of life for all. Quality of life was important to Stickley, and he saw both the home environment and workplace as ideal places for people to establish values of honesty and integrity. He saw cheap, poorly made furniture as a threat to American values. He felt that if people would surround themselves with simple, pure, humble, and honest objects, those qualities would become an inherent part of their daily lives. Driven by his ideas more than by a desire for personal wealth, Stickley couldn't stop with furniture making. He became a publisher, an educator, and a designer of homes and virtually everything that went into them.

Gustav Stickley's designs, and those created by Harvey Ellis and produced by Stickley's factory, are what everyone else at the time copied and are most of what is being reproduced today by the L. & J. G. Stickley Company and other manufacturers. William Morris and John Ruskin in England had sown the seeds for the Arts & Crafts movement. Architects in England and America, notably Charles Rennie Macintosh, Frank Lloyd Wright, and Charles and Henry Greene, were working on similar designs, derived from the same philosophical framework. But it was Gustav Stickley who popularized the style.

The basic elements of Stickley's designs— simple forms, lack of ornamentation, and high quality—expressed construction that had been seen earlier in the work of the Shakers, the English Arts & Crafts designers, and to some extent the designs of Charles Eastlake. Stickley's expression of these ideals was, however, quite different in the materials he used, in his structural composition, and in the joinery elements he emphasized. His sense of proportion, and the way in which he combined simple elements, was flawless. Gustav Stickley's designs simply "look right." They serve their purpose superbly and make a positive statement about quality without being showy or ostentatious. His designs fit the user, the home, and their purpose, expressing the philosophy behind the designs without making it more important than the specific use of the furniture.

Leopold Stickley is also credited with all of the designs that came from his factory, and even though Leopold didn't have the demands on his time that his older brother did, it seems sensible that the L. & J. G. Stickley designs were also not the work of one man alone. According to Leopold's widow, he "roughed out" the designs[13] so others could complete them. Peter Hansen was Leopold's chief designer after 1909, but it is unknown who held the position prior to that date. Because so much of Leopold's work derived from Gustav's, the question of who designed what becomes even harder to resolve.

One of the few truly original designs to come from L. & J. G. Stickley is the "Prairie" Sofa and Chair (Nos. 220 & 416, pgs. 147-153), which featured elements that were never included in any of Gustav's designs. The wide arms supported by corbels and paneled sides combine to form furniture pieces, which, by a combination of architectural elements, become a part of their environment. Like the best Craftsman designs, these pieces blur the lines between "house" and "furniture," replacing both with "home."

Charles Limbert, a Michigan manufacturer, also was willing to experiment and innovate with designs, although some of his construction techniques have not passed the test of time. Limbert's best designs were well proportioned and included curved work, unexpected angles, and the use of empty space in cutout areas as a design element. Though much of Limbert's work was derivative of other designers, his original designs stand on their own merits.

The Roycroft shop produced excellent work in small quantity. Founded by Elbert Hubbard following a successful business career, Roycroft's primary mission was to revive printing. Hubbard's main interest was writing and publishing— furniture production was a sideline. Hubbard was prominent in the Arts & Crafts movement, but his influence in furniture design was negligible. Much Roycroft furniture reflects English Arts & Crafts design rather than American. Bruce Smith's *Furniture of the Grove Park Inn* documents the history of Roycroft furniture making.

World War I and the beginning of the Roaring Twenties signaled the end of the popularity of Craftsman furniture. Wallace Nutting charmed the country with his romantic version of Colonial America, and a craving for glitz and glamour replaced the desire for simplicity. Reproductions from earlier times again became popular with the public, and Art Deco design became a major influence in art and architecture. With its emphasis on form and material, Art Deco can be seen as stemming from the Arts & Crafts movement. Curves replaced straight lines and structure and joinery were no longer emphasized. Comfort and purpose took a secondary role to overall design, and the desire to appeal to the wealthy replaced the desire to appeal to everyone.

Between the 1930s and the 1960s, America struggled to find furniture it was comfortable with and could live with for more than a few years. After World War II, many attempts were made to produce designs based on new materials such as plastics and plywood. With few exceptions, these new styles appealed only to the manufacturers, who were trying to cut costs to the minimum. Older styles were recycled in and out of fashion during these years.

In the late-1960s, people again began to question the role of technology in daily life, posing the same questions Gustav Stickley had asked many years before. Shaker furniture and the work of individual designer/craftsmen gained in influence and popularity. Like an old friend, Craftsman furniture was waiting patiently to be noticed again, enduring because of the way it was made—too good to throw away, and too strong to disappear. Its timeless quality speaks to our desire for comfort and purpose in the home.

During the 1970s and 1980s, interest in the Arts & Crafts movement blossomed in woodworking, furniture making, glass, ceramics, and other crafts. By the mid-1980s, manufacturers recognized the revived interest and began reproducing Craftsman furniture, along with derivative designs. Collectors of antique furniture began offering higher prices for original pieces. Today, the Craftsman style has a permanent place in our design vocabulary.

There is a trend among writers on the Arts and Crafts movement to force history into neatly defined periods and to speculate wildly on the characters involved, making great leaps on the flimsiest of evidence. Often there is no evidence, and motivations are assigned to the players based on what *could* have happened, or what *must* have happened, based on the author's wholly subjective opinion, or connections to the collector's market. There has also been a trend to downplay the importance of Gustav Stickley, in favor of his imitators and employees. History has always been written by the winners, and from a distant viewpoint. The history of this period has at times suffered at the hands of some writers.

My efforts have been based on the desire to help preserve the important details of Stickley's designs from the point of view of someone with at least a bit of knowledge about furniture making, and of the process of bringing designs to tangible form. The characters involved and the events that occurred form a fascinating story. Where the facts are incomplete, and the motivations of the characters are unknown, I avoid speculation and trust readers to form their own opinions and draw their own conclusions.

If Gustav Stickley were merely a successful furniture manufacturer from the late-nineteenth and early twentieth centuries, we would not be interested in his work today. During his lifetime, hundreds of men operated successful furniture companies but only a handful are remembered today and a good

portion of those shared Stickley's name. To pretend their financial success and common last name make them the equal of their older brother misses the legacy of Gustav Stickley. To identify their imitations of his designs, and their shortcuts to production, as important design elements reflects poor understanding of the processes of designing and making furniture, and what is important in Stickley's innovative designs.

Gustav Stickley is important because in addition to being a successful manufacturer, he was an innovative designer, publisher, and spokesman for the Arts and Crafts movement. He was the leader who was followed, the provider of the platform for other innovators of the time. In the end, he was the one who lost everything he had achieved financially, while preserving his dignity and quality of character.

The Craftsman magazine is often described as a promotional vehicle for Stickley's furniture company, but it was in fact the voice of the American Arts and Crafts movement, and an attempt to provide ways for a changing society to improve social values and moral virtues. Designs for furniture and houses were important in *The Craftsman* but nearly always in the context of a much larger picture: how homes and the objects within them affect the lives of the occupants, and the affect of neighborhoods and neighbors on society as a whole. I think the current appeal of these designs is rooted in our need for the ideals Gustav Stickley championed—lasting value, honesty in character, and a healthy relationship between a home and its occupants.

Perhaps if we surrounded ourselves with excellent designs, expertly crafted, we would come to recognize the good qualities in ourselves, and insist on them as a necessary part of all aspects of our lives.

The more I study the work of Gustav Stickley, the more convinced I become that the reason for the revival of interest in his work is that we have a genuine need for the intangible things his designs reflect, that we have the same needs that these designs were originally intended to serve. Craftsman designs were the reflection of an ideal, and the ideal is what is most important. My experience has been that the study and reproduction of these designs has caused the ideas behind the designs to become an important part of how I think and view the world around me. My hope is that those who enjoy my work will also find these values rubbing off in their own lives.

Chapter 2
Interpreting the Drawings

The drawings in this book have been prepared the same way drawings are prepared in the furniture industry. In the industry, before any wood is cut, the builder takes time to thoroughly review the drawing to be certain that his or her interpretation agrees with what is shown, and that individual techniques, preferences, and methods will produce the piece shown. Then the maker prepares a list of parts, taking into account the available materials, joinery details, and any changes that may be necessary due to these variables.

The cut lists presented in this book are what I would use in my workshop. You may work differently from me, so you should check my cut lists with care, or better yet, devise your own lists from the information given in the drawings. If you are not certain what size to make a given part, please take the time to figure it out before you cut any wood. Building a nice piece of furniture takes some time, and any time spent at the beginning of the project to understand what is to be built and how it will be built will be rewarded in the end.

The drawings include a plan view (straight down from above), elevations (looking straight at the piece from the front or side), sections (looking straight at an imaginary slice taken through the piece), and details (either three-dimensional views, or close-up two-dimensional views). Technical drawing gives a highly accurate, although somewhat unrealistic view of the three-dimensional world. Because our eyes are used to looking at three-dimensional objects, a technical drawing can be confusing, because it does not show perspective. In plans and elevations, the point of view is from a true 90° angle to the object and what is seen are the outlines of what is closest to the observer.

Imagine a large pane of glass placed in front of a piece of furniture, upon which the image is somehow projected. Objects parallel to this piece of glass appear in the drawing at their true length. A line that is perpendicular to the glass would appear as a single point, and a line at any other angle, or a curve, would appear to be shortened or otherwise distorted. The three-dimensional views in this book are also prepared as mechanical representations, with parallel lines remaining parallel rather than converging as they would in real life. Because there is no foreshortening, these sometimes appear to be distorted.

Section views show the details on the inside. Imagine a hamburger, a stack (from the bottom up) of bottom bun, lettuce, tomato, meat, cheese, onion, pickle, mustard, ketchup, and top bun. If you look at the sandwich directly from above, all you will see is the top bun. You know that it is round, and you can measure its diameter, but you can't tell how thick it is, or what is underneath. If you look at it directly from the front or side, you will see the edges of the bun, the meat, and perhaps a little bit of cheese or lettuce sticking out. You can measure the height and the width, but you still don't learn what is inside and you can't see that the bun is round—the edges could represent a rectangular slice of bread rather than a round bun.

The two drawings together give you a good idea of the shape and size, but you still can't tell what is inside. Is there a big slice of onion, or is it chopped in tiny pieces? Did they forget the pickle, or is it above or below the meat? If you slice the burger and then look at the edge, you will get a good look at what is inside. This is the principle behind a section view, and all of the views together help you to know how the hamburger is built. If you are having trouble visualizing what a piece of furniture is like, try looking at all the views. Something that doesn't make sense in one view usually will be shown clearly in another.

Some conventions and terms will help you interpret the drawings. Dashed lines usually represent something that is behind, or hidden by, what is in the drawing. If we are looking at the leg of a dresser where a crossrail joins it, and we see some dashed lines going into the leg from the rail, then we know that part of the rail is tenoned into a mortise in the leg. If a solid line continues out the other side of the leg, then we know that the mortise goes completely through the leg and what we are seeing is the end of the tenon on the rail.

In section views, our imaginary pane of glass goes through the middle of the object *cutting* the parts it intersects and giving a clear view of the parts beyond. In section views, some areas will be filled in (hatched). This means the filled part lies on the plane of the imaginary glass. In these drawings, arcs or splines (squiggly lines) represent solid wood, and patterns that are more regular represent plywood, although it remains the maker's option as to what material to use. Glass is represented by its own pattern. In a section view, a dashed line represents something that is in front of the cutting plane. Many of the plan views in this book are sections, or views with the top removed, with the outline of the top indicated by a dashed line.

Extension lines and dimension lines, both of which are noticeably thinner than the lines of the actual parts of the furniture, indicate dimensions. Extension lines approach, but do not quite touch, the point on the drawing that the dimensions refer to. Dimension lines have arrowheads that either point to the extension line, or in some cases point directly to an object. Dimension lines are kept off to the edges of the drawing so that they don't interfere with the actual drawing, with extension lines connecting them to the object. Occasionally, there may be confusion about where an extension line is actually pointing, but if you lay a straight edge on the extension line you will be able to see where it leads.

One of the challenges of doing drawings in this small format is to provide enough dimensions to build a piece without covering most of the page with dimension lines, arrows, and numbers. Generally, a dimension for a part is given in only one view of a drawing, hopefully in the view where it makes the most sense. The width and depth of a desktop, for example, will be located in the plan view, and the thickness of the top will be in a section view or an elevation. If it seems that a needed dimension is missing, try looking for the same object in a different view.

There will be times when it's necessary to do a little math. If there are a number of parts making up an overall dimension and the overall dimension is given, not all of the dimensions for the parts will be given. Take, for example, a plan view of a dresser. There is an overall width of the top, the width from the outside of one leg to the outside of the other leg, the width of the legs, and the widths of all the parts in between. If the parts are symmetrical, only one will be dimensioned. If you know the overall width of a paneled back, the width of one outer stile, and the width of the center stile, you can reasonably assume that both outer stiles will be the same width, and you can calculate the width of the panels in between. This is done both to keep the drawing from becoming cluttered and to ensure

that the maker understands the drawing. It also ensures that if there is an error in the drawing or dimensions, the maker will be able to catch it and compensate for it. If the dimensions don't seem to add up, study the drawing and carefully add and subtract the sizes of the parts. Check and double-check before you go cutting up your material.

The dimensions in the drawings don't necessarily reflect the total sizes of the parts. Dimensions are shown from finished surface to finished surface. Where there are openings for doors and drawers, for example, the dimensions shown are for the size of the opening. On frame-and-panel parts, the dimensions shown are for the exposed areas. The maker needs to decide how deep to make the grooves for the panels and tongues, how much of a gap to leave around doors and drawers, how much to add for tenons. This depends on many factors; personal preference, species of wood, time of year, or type of climate. You may not have access to a planer, so you decide to use the wood you have that is $^{25}/_{32}$" thick instead of ¾". There is nothing wrong with that, but if you have six rails in between seven drawers and each rail is $^{1}/_{32}$" oversize, you will have to compensate for the extra $^{3}/_{16}$" somewhere. You may not like dealing with thirty-seconds so you decide to fudge things a little. Again, there is nothing inherently wrong in doing this, but you need to consider it before cutting anything.

The pieces of furniture in this book are very adaptable, and examples of originals show variations not only in sizes but also in the material used for various parts. Some production runs were made using solid, V-grooved and splined, or ship-lapped backs, while in other years the same pieces were manufactured with plywood or paneled backs. Some items were shown in catalogs with paneled sides, yet the only known examples have solid or plywood sides. You may be a purist, and nothing but a hand-cut dovetailed drawer in solid maple will be acceptable. Or, you may prefer biscuit-joined plywood drawers. This book gives you a place to start, and the information you need to make your own decisions.

Preparing a cut list, deciding how to join one piece of wood to another, what order in which to assemble, and considering the consequences of all of these decisions are part of learning how to organize a bunch of pieces of wood into an attractive piece of furniture. Understanding and interpreting what is shown in a drawing, and translating that into a finished piece of furniture,

is a major part of learning the entire process of building furniture.

The way that you measure, mill stock, and make joints will all affect the size of the parts needed to build this furniture. For details that cannot be seen in the original pieces, such as unexposed mortises or grooves in panels, I have used my own judgment based on my experience. You might not agree with my decisions, and for this reason many of the smallest dimensions in this book are not given, leaving the reader to decide whether panels should be set in a ⅜"-deep groove or a ½"-deep groove. All of the information needed to generate your own cut list is in the drawing, but each maker must be responsible for determining the finished size of all of the parts.

CUT LIST GUIDELINES

Let's use the No. 913 Dresser on page 187 as an example of how to prepare a list of parts.

In this book, the following conventions are used when discussing thickness, width, and length. When referring to pieces of wood, these terms reflect the direction of the grain. When referring to the piece of furniture as a whole, they refer to the piece's normal orientation in space, and apply no matter what view of the drawing we are looking at. This may seem like a minor point, but adopting a standard and sticking to it avoids much confusion. When looking at the drawings, the whole piece is 50" high, 36" wide, and 20" deep, the way it appears when looking at the front elevation. By keeping these terms consistent, regardless of the view, we can generate a more accurate cut list and avoid errors and parts with the wood grain going in the wrong direction.

For individual parts, width is always the direction across the wood grain, and length is always the direction with the grain. The top of the dresser is ¹³⁄₁₆" thick, 20" wide, and 36" long, even though the width of the dresser is determined by the length of the top. A drawer opening is 4⅜" high by 13²⁵⁄₃₂" wide. The drawer front that goes into the opening is 4⅜" wide (minus the desired gap around the opening) by 13²⁵⁄₃₂" long. This convention, when adhered to, keeps the grain running the right way for all parts. In the example above, we know that the grain on the drawer front runs horizontally. If the dimension were stated the other way—13²⁵⁄₃₂" wide by 4⅜" high—it would indicate the grain runs up and down. The depth of a drawer is the distance from the front to the back, not from the bottom to the top. The drawers in this piece of furniture are

all the same depth, but the second drawer up from the bottom is the tallest one.

I start by making a list of the major components, such as the top, the sides, the back, the front rails, and the drawers, leaving room on the paper to list the parts that make up these components. For this dresser, I will have:

- One top—which may be composed of one or more pieces of solid wood or plywood. There is also a backsplash across the back of the top.
- Two sides—composed of legs, stiles (frame parts that go up and down), rails (frame pieces that go horizontally), and panels.
- One back—which may be frame-and-panel construction as shown, solid-wood planks, or plywood.
- Several front rails and one center stile.
- Nine drawers and drawer fronts.

In addition, there are a dozen knobs or drawer pulls, and some way must be provided to slide the drawers in and out, either on purchased hardware or on guides fabricated from wood.

Looking at the drawing, I know the finished top is ¹³⁄₁₆" thick, 20" wide, and 36" long. I probably don't have a piece of wood that wide, so the top may be composed of two, three, or even four pieces of wood, and if gluing up for width, the individual pieces should be a little wider than necessary to allow for preparing the joint.

I start my list with the largest pieces first because they will have the greatest impact on the finished piece of furniture. That way, when digging through a stack of lumber, I will be looking for the widest, most attractive pieces first. I may decide to use some lumber for the top that is already planed to ¾" thick. This decision won't have a tremendous impact on the appearance of the finished piece, but I must keep in mind that the ¹⁄₁₆" I've just eliminated from the top thickness has to come from somewhere. I would most likely let the overall height be a little shorter, but someone else might decide to lengthen the legs. If this is done, somewhere in the height, the dimensions noted in the drawing will change. Making these decisions now, and noting where the changes will occur, will avoid much frustration later on.

Having determined the parts and their sizes for making the top, I move on to the other parts that appear in the front elevation. Once again, the question of thickness arises when looking at the rails between the drawers. These are stated to be ¹³⁄₁₆" thick, but I might reasonably decide to use some ¾" thick stock. If I do, then I must recalculate the vertical layout where these pieces meet the legs, or I will end up with a $\frac{5}{16}$" discrepancy.

At this point, it would be helpful to take a scrap piece of wood, cut it to the length of the finished leg, and do a full-size layout. When changing the thickness of any component, it's safest to work from the middle of each joint rather than from the spaces between the parts. By laying out full size, locating the midpoints—and from them the edges—you will end up with a full-size layout to help you visualize the relationships and be better able to plan your work.

A calculator that can add and subtract in fractions is a tremendous help. I use a "Construction Master," which works to sixty-fourths of an inch. Some of the other brands available will only work to one-sixteenth of an inch, and this isn't fine enough for quality work. This calculator is also available as an "app" for smart phones. If you decide to ignore all of these $\frac{1}{32}$" differences, their feelings will get hurt and they will all get together and travel to one point of your project to rally against you. You won't know what point at which they have gathered until you find yourself trying to put something together that just won't fit. It will be off by the sum of all the little discrepancies that you ignored.

The section view gives the width of the rails, and the plan view gives the distance between the front legs, which is the given length of the rails. The rails will be that given length, plus whatever is needed to make the joints between the rails and the legs. The drawings show tenons on the rails and mortises in the legs, but without exact dimensions. The builder must decide on joint details and must account for whatever effect that decision will have on the finished length of the parts.

After determining the sizes of the rails between the drawers, I can list the drawer fronts themselves, with the drawer boxes appearing as a sublist. Knowing the sizes of the openings for the drawers, either from the drawing or from calculations that include any changes, the width and length of the drawer fronts can be determined. The desired gap around the drawer front must be considered at some point, and will be based on the species and cut of wood used, atmospheric conditions both in the shop and in the furniture's future home, and the preferences of the maker.

Returning to the list of major components, the pieces for the sides can be determined by studying the drawing, listing the various parts, laying out to full size, and deciding on and noting the joinery details and how these will affect the overall sizes. The side view of the dresser tells me the exposed portion of the stiles on the side panels is 4½" wide; however, by looking at the plan I can see that the rail fits into a groove cut into the leg, so it must be made wider to allow for the tongue. Here is yet another case where the individual maker must decide how to join the stile to the leg, and the effect that decision will have on the overall width of the stile. This same caveat applies to the sizing of the rails, and the panels that make up the sides of the case. The drawings show what the outcome should look like, but the reader needs to determine for himself the final sizes of the component parts.

The back is not shown in elevation anywhere, but the sizes for all of the parts can be determined from the top and side section views. The method of making the back should be determined, the overall size established, and then the sizes of the component parts figured.

After the list of all of the parts is completed and double-checked with the drawing, then the process of fabricating parts and building the furniture can begin. It is beyond the scope of this book to cover all of the techniques and options for milling joints and assembling furniture. If you are new to woodworking, the Bibliography lists few resources for this information. If there is a woodworking club in your area, attend some meetings and get to know other woodworkers.

Many community colleges and high schools offer woodworking classes. These can be a tremendous resource for meeting other woodworkers, learning from the instructors, and for access to machinery and tools. The chapters that follow discuss some of the various techniques used in the Stickley workshops, with tips for either duplicating these techniques or using alternative techniques that were not available in the early 1900s. The furniture presented in this book is generally straightforward and simple. However, there is no place to cover up less than perfect work. The results you achieve will depend on your experience and the time and care you devote to your project. If you don't feel confident in your abilities or your personal safety, take some time to develop your basic skills before attempting a large project.

Building any of the pieces of furniture in this book can be an opportunity to learn much about the process of woodworking, as well as about excellence in design. It is also an opportunity to learn new things about yourself and the way you think and work.

Chapter 3
Materials & Hardware

Quartersawn white oak has a unique grain structure that gives it quality and character ideally suited for Craftsman furniture.

The most common wood used in Craftsman furniture was quartersawn white oak, although many pieces were also originally made from mahogany and a few were made of bird's-eye or curly maple. The current line of reproductions being manufactured by L. & J. G. Stickley is also available in cherry, a wood that works well for this style of furniture. Virtually any fine cabinet wood will work, as one of the key elements of these designs is the role that the grain, texture, and figure of the wood is allowed to play. The individual's taste, budget, and sense of history will all be involved in the decision of which species to use and whether or not to build entirely from solid wood or a combination of solids and veneers.

I would avoid the softer woods, such as poplar or pine, which won't hold up well, and plainsawn red oak, which, despite its wide use, is too coarse and unstable for fine furniture. This furniture deserves not only your best effort but also the nicest materials you can obtain.

Quartersawn white oak is not commonly available, and it's not inexpensive. This method of sawing does not give the yield that comes from plainsawing and therefore the price is higher. You may have to do a bit of digging to find it, depending on where you live. I'm fortunate that I live close to the Frank Miller Lumber Company of Union City, Indiana. They are the major sawyer of quartersawn white oak in the United States, and the original source of most of this material. The company website, at www.frankmiller.com is an excellent source of information.

One of the benefits of quartersawn wood is that it is more stable, and less likely to move seasonally. Because of the grain orientation, seasonal changes in dimension are reduced along the width and more pronounced in the thickness of the material. In most of the case designs in this book, the grain direction of the sides and horizontal members are aligned, and these pieces can be made entirely of solid wood.

If you haven't worked much with solid wood, it will be worthwhile to read *Understanding Wood*, by R. Bruce Hoadley. Solid wood differs from many materials, particularly other materials used for precise work. One of the biggest challenges in woodworking is doing precision work with a material that keeps changing in size in response to changes in the humidity of its environment. This movement can be reduced to some extent by the finish applied, but it cannot be eliminated. Attempts to ignore wood movement or to restrain it will inevitably end in failure. It is a powerful force of nature and it can be understood and accommodated, but not stopped.

Seasonal wood movement varies from species to species and the selection of species used in a piece of furniture will affect many decisions that must be made during the building process. Woods considered suitable for fine furniture generally are reasonably stable once dried. The biggest mistakes I have seen people make, and I myself have made, involve rushing into the building process without allowing the wood enough time to reach equilibrium with the temperature and humidity of the shop. Likewise, it is folly to perform the work in an environment that is quite different from the environment where the finished piece will be placed.

Kiln-dried wood is often thought to be insurance against wood movement, but once the wood comes out of the kiln it will take on moisture from the atmosphere until it reaches equilibrium with its environment. Air-dried wood and kiln-dried wood stored in the same conditions will eventually come to the same moisture content.

A good moisture meter is not cheap, but it will let you know the state your wood is in when you receive it and when it has been conditioned to your shop environment, as well as help you spot any "wild" boards that are either unusually wet or dry. Without a meter, you are left to guesswork. Where I live, the summers are humid and the winters are cold and dry, so there is quite a swing in relative humidity as the seasons turn. Your area may be quite different, but you should be aware of what is likely to happen and be prepared to work with the wood, not against it.

When you work with wood that has not been conditioned to the shop environment, the newly cut surfaces will have different moisture contents and are likely to warp or twist as the wood seeks equilibrium. Even if the wood does not warp, it will change noticeably in size in a short period. Joints cut from damp wood recently brought into a dry shop will shrink overnight and not fit the next day. The opposite effect will occur with dry wood brought into a damp shop. I have learned to be patient, to wait a few weeks, and to compare the moisture content of lumber brought into the shop with similar pieces that have been there for a while before I start building.

The biggest problems with wood movement will occur in the widest and thickest pieces, particularly solid-wood tops and case sides, and wide doors and tall drawer fronts. Woodworkers over the centuries have learned how to allow for wood movement and the original makers of Craftsman furniture mostly followed these techniques.

Here are the main points about working with solid wood:
• Plan the gaps around doors and drawers according to the season, your shop environment, and the environment where the finished piece will be placed.
• Fasten tabletops or other wide pieces of solid wood in a way that allows for the expansion and contraction that will occur.
• Don't force the wood into place with clamps. If you straighten out a crooked piece of wood by bending, eventually it will "remember" that it prefers being crooked, and will someday return to that state, even it has to crack to do so.
• Make joints that fit snugly. No glue will successfully fill gaps in joints for very long. The piece may hold together long enough to get it out of your shop, but eventually it will fail.

The other important factor in working with solid wood is to buy it from a reliable supplier, preferably from stock that has been on hand for a while. If your dealer has accepted a load of wood fresh from the kiln and passed it directly along to you without waiting for it to settle down, you could experience problems with wood movement.

If wood bends as you cut it, or splits as you near the end of a rip, it has been "stressed" or "case hardened" during drying. This means the surfaces of the lumber were dried too quickly, shrinking the cells so much that the moisture on the inside cannot readily escape. Be especially careful during all cutting operations in case this happens, and if it does, be prepared for more problems later on. If your supplier won't replace the wood (go ahead and ask, but don't hold your breath), cut parts enough over-size so that you can re-straighten them if need be, and let them adjust to the shop environment for a few weeks between rough and finish milling.

VENEERS AND PLYWOODS

Veneers and plywoods were used in original Craftsman pieces, and there is no reason not to use them in reproductions. For paneled backs, dust panels, drawer bottoms, and the side panels of some cases, plywood is clearly a good choice. It is less susceptible to seasonal changes than solid wood, it is stable in thin sheets, and it can be less expensive than solid wood.

Furniture-quality plywood can be difficult to find, and your local lumberyard or big-box home center probably won't have what you are looking for. Companies that specialize in supplying woodworking hobbyists charge a premium for this type of material. The best source will be a company that supplies professional cabinet shops and architectural millwork companies. They will have access to a variety of cores, thicknesses, and species, though they may not like to make small sales to individuals. A local cabinet shop may be willing to order some for you, but remember their time is money, so don't waste it, and offer some compensation for their efforts.

Particleboard and medium-density fiberboard (MDF) are the better choice for veneer substrate materials than regular plywood, which is known as *veneer core* in the industry. The quality of particleboard and fiberboard cores has improved greatly during the last 30 years, while the quality of veneer core material has steadily gone downhill. In particular, it has become thinner than its nominal size as a way for producers to save material costs. Don't believe stories about "metric" sizes— ¾" plywood barely measures $^{11}/_{16}$" for the same reasons that 1-pound coffee cans now weigh in at 13 ounces. The "new convenient size" saves money for the producer.

The cores are not only thinner, they are not of the same quality material that formerly was used.

Poplar and mysterious species from around the world have taken the place of birch. Thickness will be inconsistent throughout the sheet and the coarse grain of the core will likely telegraph through the veneer during finishing, creating a rough surface on what was once a smooth panel. Some plywood is also laminated before being thoroughly dry, which makes it likely to warp. Imported plywood cores are especially prone to this kind of stress, and will often bend while being cut. If you do use veneer core plywood, be sure to mill any joints in a way that will ensure a consistent thickness in the joint.

Particleboard and MDF have been the subject of much engineering work and most of the problems that used to be associated with these materials are no longer present. MDF will have a smoother, more consistent surface than particleboard, but it does tend to split when fasteners are used on the edges. These materials will warp if treated differently on opposite sides, so if you do your own veneering, be sure to veneer both sides. Veneering or otherwise sealing any edges that are exposed to the air is also a good idea to prevent the panels from warping.

For thin panels, such as ¼"-thick drawer bottoms or back panels, veneer core is probably the better choice because it is stronger than particleboard. For drawer bottoms in bedroom cases, aromatic cedar plywood is a nice touch, although it can be hard to find.

A central wooden runner was a typical guide in Gustav Stickley's drawer.

HARDWARE

Reproductions of original hand-hammered copper hardware are available, but expensive. There are Mission-style pulls and strap hinges that are less costly, but they're also not as nice. Wooden knobs, turned or sawn square with a pyramid shape, are an alternative to metal pulls.

Original pieces were shown in catalogs and manufactured both ways, probably to offer an alternative in pricing because hand-hammered copper hardware was as expensive a century ago as it is now. Both looks are authentic.

Hinges on the original pieces were heavier than today's standards. Butt hinges on originals tend to have longer leaves than today's hinges, and the barrels are of a larger diameter. Doors on the originals generally are still swinging nicely after one hundred years, so the choice of hardware should go to the nicest available.

A center-mounted dovetail-shaped rail on the drawer's bottom usually guided drawers on original Craftsman pieces. Reproductions by L. & J. G. Stickley use both this center guiderail and rails in the sides of the drawers. Modern metal slides can be used, though purists will cringe. Accuride makes the most reliable slides; their model 3832 is a good choice for a full-extension slide. European manufacturers Grass, Mepla, Blum, and others offer bottom-mounted ball-bearing glides that are hidden when the drawer is open, making these more acceptable (and more expensive) than the Accuride. Before starting construction, be sure you understand how mechanical slides mount and how their use affects the size of drawer fronts and boxes.

Mirrors on bedroom cases swing on a fitting designed especially for that purpose, and the hardware used on the original Craftsman pieces was the same as used on most other furniture manufactured at the time. These fittings are available from mail-order suppliers of woodworking materials and reproduction hardware.

The patina and texture of hand-hammered copper hardware complements the surrounding wood.

Chapter 4

Woodworking Techniques

This is a book about furniture construction, but not a basic woodworking text. Different methods will be discussed, in the context of this style of furniture and in specific pieces, but the reader without much experience would benefit greatly from practice in basic joinery before attempting a major piece of furniture. There is no substitute for practical experience. The Bibliography (page 325) contains a list of books I have found helpful over the years. In addition, in many geographical areas it's possible to gain experience through woodworking classes or clubs.

Woodworking is not something to approach lightly, given the inherent danger of the tools involved. Never attempt a technique that doesn't feel safe, and practice different techniques on scrap wood before embarking on the real project. Seek the advice of experienced woodworkers as needed, and if you get the feeling that something you are about to do is risky, it probably is. Stop and examine ways to work safely before proceeding.

A large part of the preparation for building furniture is consideration of which technique to use to make each joint. There really isn't a *right* or *wrong* way; there are simply a variety of choices based on a maker's tools, skills, and experience. There are many different ways to accomplish any task, and one of the pleasures of learning to work with wood is the discovery of the ways that work best in any given situation.

The simplicity of Craftsman furniture designs could lead one to believe it is simple to make. This simplicity, however, carries with it a need to truly master basic skills, and to apply them with care and forethought. There are no moldings to cover gaps, and with exposed joinery, there is no place to cover up errors. An exposed, keyed mortise-and-tenon joint makes a statement about its maker. Like a sports team that wins the championship due to mastery of the basics, someone who has the patience to master the fine points of joinery and the confidence to let it show will make a successful piece of Craftsman furniture.

The choices I make about the techniques to use can vary widely depending on whether I am making furniture to sell, for my own use, or simply for the experience and the opportunity to learn something new. Sometimes the choice is to use machinery, and sometimes it is to do the work by hand. Usually it is some combination of the two. I am always amused by those who claim some sort of moral superiority for using a hand technique over a machine. Each method has advantages and disadvantages, and either can be appropriate in some circumstances and not in others. The choice of which to use is simply personal preference based on the job, the tools, and the available time. Knowledge of several different methods gives the builder more options.

Sometimes the right choice is a hand plane or scraper, and sometimes it is a plunge router. It is definitely worthwhile to have the ability to hand plane and scrape a solid-wood top to a flat, level, and smooth surface, and it is a pleasurable, gratifying experience. It is also a lot of work and it takes time. If that time is not available, and if my old-time woodworker ego doesn't need to be stroked, I would choose to use a wide-belt thicknessing sander. In another situation, I might choose a quiet afternoon, a physical workout, and a pile of shavings on the floor.

My preferences are simply that, and I encourage readers to explore all the available options and adopt the ones that are most suitable. There are as many ways to make a mortise and tenon as there are ways to skin a cat. The trick is to find a few that you are comfortable with, that succeed most of the time, and that make your woodworking more enjoyable. We learn and develop our skills by trying things we haven't tried before; we won't learn anything new and we won't grow when we decide that there is only one right way to accomplish any given task.

JOINERY DETAILS

The only photograph I have seen of the inside of Gustav Stickley's Craftsman Workshops shows joiners at work, some nearly completed bookcases, and a desk. The floor is nearly covered with plane shavings, and light streams into the room from a row of windows above the workbenches. It would be easy to imagine that these men had made the furniture entirely by hand, from start to finish. Stickley's factory was, however, quite modern for the period, and was equipped with early versions of most of the machinery commonly seen in furniture factories of today. The men in the picture assembled and fitted pieces from parts that came to them cut to size, likely with the mortise and tenon joints already machined. Their job was to assemble the pieces, and fine-tune the fit and finish of the joints, the doors and drawers, and drawer fronts.

One of the difficulties of production furniture-making is that no matter how carefully and accurately parts are cut, wood will move slightly from day to day, and parts that fit perfectly yesterday might not go easily together today. Wood just doesn't cooperate with precision machining techniques, and it takes a keen eye and a practiced hand to produce truly excellent work. A little adjustment here and there is usually necessary, both in a home workshop and in furniture factories. The joiners in Stickley's factory had the luxury of practicing the most skilled and most demanding parts of their trade without having to perform the heavy, unskilled labor.

Gustav Stickley was not against the use of machinery, in fact he saw it as a way to relieve the worker of drudgery. His written objections to machine-made furniture were mostly aimed at issues of style and quality—furniture that pretended to be something it was not, with useless ornamentation covering up shoddy work. At the turn of the twentieth century, the attitude of most woodworkers toward powered saws, joiners, planers, and shapers was likely one of welcome relief. Gustav Stickley's production methods used the skills of his workers for the details that needed the human touch, and efficiently used available machinery wherever it was appropriate.

We tend to romanticize handwork without looking at the reality of what is involved in doing it. In my own work, I try to judge what is the most appropriate and efficient method. I don't find any pleasure in working harder than necessary for the sake of authenticity, if the results come out the same. Nearly every project

Joiners at work performing final furniture assembly and fitting in Gustav Stickley's factory in Eastwood, N.Y.

in *Mission Furniture—How to Make It* (originally published as articles in *Popular Mechanics* magazine during the period) begins with the advice to have someone with machinery cut and plane the wood.

Stickley designed his furniture for production in a factory setting, and many of the changes that occurred from one year's production to the next reflect ways of producing the pieces more efficiently, or less expensively. The details left to be done by hand reflect a wise use of available resources, both machine, and human. Efficiency in production makes equal sense to the owner of a factory, a small modern shop with one or two furniture-makers trying to earn a living, and to the hobbyist trying to make something for his own enjoyment in his scarce leisure time.

Many of the fine details of Craftsman furniture cannot be shown in mechanical drawings. Their execution provides evidence of different sets of hands on the originals, as well as an opportunity for today's woodworker to develop his own skills and style.

Edges and corners are generally given a very slight chamfer—what I would call a broken edge. The chamfer is not large enough to call attention to itself, but it's no longer a sharp corner either. There is considerable variation in both the size and the shape of this edge-treatment in the original examples. Sometimes the edges have more of a radius than a chamfer, and the size of the chamfer or radius can vary from nearly nothing to an eighth of an inch.

These variations occur both in types of pieces—chairs tend to have more of a radiused edge than casework and tables—and between

Edges are gently chamfered or rounded in original pieces. Variations in individual pieces indicate that this work was done by hand.

The treatment of through tenons also shows variations from piece to piece.

A typical Craftsman door is set back slightly, and is often hinged to a thin strip set back from the front of the case.

two examples of the same piece. The differences could be the result of wear over time, but I believe different departments in the factory, and different individuals, had their own distinct way of doing things. Some workers prefer a tiny crisp chamfer cut with a stroke or two of a plane, while others prefer a softer and more rounded edge developed by lightly sanding the corner. Neither one is right or wrong—choose the method or look that works for you.

Exposed tenons, and especially keyed tenons, exhibit more evidence of handwork, and more variations in the execution of these details. Generally, there will be more of a chamfer or radius on these exposed joints than on the rest of the piece, and again, these are sometimes seen chamfered, and sometimes rounded. In the drawings, I show these larger details as I found them on the individual piece I studied. There will likely be another example of the same piece, done a little differently. The worker building a reproduction is once again left to make a decision based on his or her own preferences.

Drawer and door fronts are set back slightly—no more than one-sixteenth of an inch—from adjacent frames. Horizontal rails are often set back by a similar amount from vertical stiles or legs. I have shown these setbacks in the drawings, and have included dimensions where space permits. Where dimensions are not given, the reader can safely assume the setback is slight.

Another place where details are often not shown precisely is in small joints, such as front rails on case pieces, and the joints between elements in glass doors or case sides. Rails were originally mortised and tenoned, but the reproductions currently manufactured by L. & J. G. Stickley use a hidden dovetail joint, an idea said to have been developed by Leopold Stickley in the 1920s when the factory switched to reproductions of early American furniture.

LAYING OUT & MAKING PATTERNS

One of the traditional ways of taking the step from drawing to building is the story pole, essentially a full-size representation of important details from the drawing. This is an excellent way to work out joinery details, and to transfer measurements from one part to another without repetitiously measuring. The exact form of the story pole will vary depending on the size and complexity of the piece to be built. A stick of wood, ¾" by 1¾" is commonly used, but in some cases, a wider piece may be more appropriate, up to a piece the actual size of a finished part. I tend to use ¾"-thick Melamine covered particleboard because lines drawn on it are easy to see, pencil lines can be erased with a damp rag, and I usually have some around. If I had to buy a 4' by 8' sheet to use only for story poles, I would probably switch to the traditional stick of hardwood.

I usually make three separate story poles, one for height, one for width, and one for depth. The stick representing height may show details for the front of the piece on one surface, and details for the side on the adjacent surface. For complicated cases, there may be two distinct sticks, one representing drawer or door locations on the front of the finished case, and the other showing details of the paneled sides. Often it is helpful to draw a full-size plan view or a section on a piece of light-colored plywood or Melamine board to aid in visualizing the work, and to check things as the work progresses. When laying out parts, dimensions can be transferred directly from the story pole to the workpieces.

Story poles are cut to the exact length of the finished piece of furniture, so the locations of intersecting pieces and joints can be marked out full size. Take your time, and work carefully and precisely. I write notes on the stick, and mark with an X areas that will be removed. When parts have been cut to size, say four legs for a dresser or desk, the parts will be clamped together, and the locations for intersections and joints transferred from the story pole with a square. This saves a good deal of time and reduces the possibility of a mathematical or measurement error. If the piece is ever to be made again in the future, all of the layout work is already complete, saving a step in the production process.

As the work progresses, story poles can be used to check subassemblies and parts to be sure that the plan is being followed, and that the work is as it should be. Changes and corrections can also be noted directly on the pole for future reference.

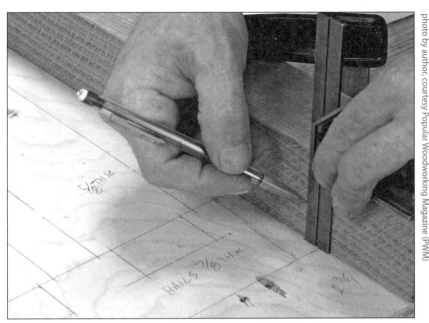

A full size pattern is useful for laying out the joinery in a complex piece of furniture.

A story pole is used to layout joints on several pieces at once. This ensures all parts have joints in identical locations.

photo by author, courtesy Popular Woodworking Magazine (PWM)

Author photo, courtesy PWM.

SOLID-WOOD TOPS & PANELS

Solid-wood tops are included in nearly every piece featured in this book, except, of course, chairs. Many of the case pieces have solid-wood sides, made of several boards glued edge-to-edge. The original makers faced the same decision today's woodworker must make—how to make a wide piece from narrow boards.

Except for the work of L. & J. G. Stickley, which used splines, most tops and panels were made by butt-joining the pieces. The advantage of using splines, or the modern alternative—biscuits—is not a matter of adding strength, but a method of keeping the pieces aligned during glue-up. As long as the edges are square and smooth, an edge-grain-to-edge-grain butt joint is extremely strong and stable. Battens clamped above and below the pieces being joined, in addition to the clamps holding the parts together, will keep the pieces nice and flat as they are assembled. It is worth extra effort at this point because removing material after glue-up isn't much fun.

Much has been written about orienting the boards to be glued to prevent cupping. One popular theory is that alternating the planks so that the bark side is up or down on every other piece will prevent the top from warping. The important issues in making a solid-wood top, however, are appearance and longevity—you want the top to stay together forever. A solid-wood top on a nice piece of furniture should appear to be a single board. If stable, seasoned stock is used and care is taken in design and construction, it doesn't matter which way the boards face. I begin a furniture project by gluing up the top or other wide panels.

The easiest way to match parts for a top is by taking as many pieces as possible either from a single board or from boards cut from the log in sequence. By doing this task first, all of the available lumber can be examined and compared. My approach is to go through the lumber stack, picking out candidates for the top, and setting them aside after sketching or noting the rough sizes on the surface with chalk or a lumber crayon. Cut long pieces to a rough length, and mill to a consistent thickness, and arrange the pieces in different ways until an acceptable appearance is found. I then draw a triangle on the surface to maintain the desired orientation.

I prefer to joint the edges just before glue-up. Even though I am confident in the squareness of the jointer's fence and table, I alternate the face of every other edge against the fence. This ensures that even if the edges are slightly out of square, the angles will be complementary and the resulting joint will be flat across the faces. It is easier to make a perfect top from perfect pieces, and my preference is to have the edges as straight as possible. Some woodworkers plane a slight hollow in the edges so they must be forced together by clamps. In my experience, wood stressed during glue-up will eventually relax and crack at the joint. If the stock is at equilibrium with the shop environment and milled carefully, the parts used in the top will not need great pressure and can be expected to stay together.

I usually glue up a panel an inch or so wider than what I need, and several inches longer. I alternate clamps above and below the surface so they are pulling as close to the center of each board as possible. I check to make sure I haven't put any kind of bow or twist into the top, and I'm also careful about how much glue I use.

As a young apprentice being instructed in gluing, I jumped into the conversation about thirty seconds too soon and said, "The glue should squeeze out so I know I've used enough, right?" The journeyman instructing me looked me right in the eye and replied, "The glue should almost squeeze out so you don't make a mess you'll have to clean up later on." I thought he was nuts and way too picky, but I have, over the years, become just as nuts and just as picky. I don't like to waste glue any more than I like to waste any other material, and cleaning up a lot of glue squeeze-out is messy and can get glue in places you don't want it and won't be able to see until it ruins your first attempt at putting on a finish. Judging the amount of glue to use isn't that difficult, it just requires practice.

In this original cabinet, the side is a glued assembly of three random width pieces.

If I do have any squeeze-out, I make sure to remove it before the glue dries hard. I use an old scraper or the back of a wide chisel to get it off, not a wet rag, which often just thins the glue out and spreads it all around. Leaving beads of glue on the surface will slow down the drying process, and weaken the joint at that point. The other big problem with leaving squeeze-out on the surface is that you eventually must remove it. A thoroughly dry bead of glue is incredibly hard. Popping it off with a chisel is likely to remove some wood along with the glue. Trying to take it off with a hand plane is hard on the edge of the iron, and it is easy to tip a sander balanced on a bead of glue and gouge the wood.

After the glue dries, smooth the wood and cut to finished size. With the top the right size, level the glue joints and make the entire top smooth enough for finishing. Finding a wide-belt sander large enough to send the completed top through is best. Many shops will let you use theirs for a reasonable price. A decent hand plane in capable hands is the next most efficient choice.

A belt sander is an option but doesn't offer any advantage in efficiency or quality over the plane and scraper. It can take more skill to guide a belt sander to good results than a plane, and the chances of doing some damage with the belt sander are higher. Factor in the noise and dust of the belt sander versus the good workout from the plane and scraper, and make your choice.

With the top complete except for the final finish sanding or scraping, how is it held down to the rest of the furniture piece? Most of the original examples featured in this book were attached with "table irons"—figure-eight-shaped pieces of metal that are screwed down to a rail on one end and up to the top on the other.

They are available from woodworking hardware suppliers. These allow the top to be pulled down flush, and will shift as the wood in the top expands and contracts. The side that attaches to the rail needs to go in a counterbored hole that partially intersects the inner edge of the rail. The best way to make this counterbore is with a Forstner bit, because it leaves a flat bottom and will cut neatly through the edge of the rail.

Avoid the temptation to be cheap by using a spade bit. The cut through the edge of the rail will be ragged, and more important, the pilot will leave a hole too large for the screw to grab. After making the counterbore with the Forstner bit, drill a separate pilot hole for the screw into the rail. Be extremely careful when drilling the pilot hole that goes up into the top. If the top is around

Tops were typically fastened with "table irons", figure 8 shapes held with screws.

Square the sides of the recess so that the figure 8 fasteners can swivel.

Table buttons

¾" thick, there will not be many threads in the screw that will be able to grab. Use a tapered bit and be careful to match the depth of the hole to the length of the screw.

The alternative to table irons are shop-made table buttons. These small blocks of wood have a rabbet on one end that slips into a groove on the inside of the rail. They work well, but require more effort to make. When attaching the top, remember it will expand and contract and the movement cannot be restrained or prevented.

LEGS

Many of the legs in Craftsman furniture are too thick to be made from a single piece of wood. As attractive as the face of quartersawn white oak can be, the edge grain tends to be downright ugly, particularly when seen next to a beautifully flecked surface. On tabletops or case tops, the edge doesn't have enough surface area for this difference in appearance to be a real aesthetic problem. Square legs, however, are another story. The leg looks funny if the quartersawn rays do not appear on adjacent surfaces, even though it isn't possible to have rays on both the face and the edge of a single board. Gustav Stickley laminated legs, gluing two or more pieces together to achieve the desired thickness. The solid faces show quartersawn figure, and the edges of the legs were veneered with material around ⅛" thick.

This method works, and if the thick veneered edges are chamfered back to the glue line, the joint is barely visible. The risk to this construction is that the seasonal wood movement of the laminated pieces might eventually cause the veneered faces to crack.

Unlike plainsawn wood, quartersawn pieces will expand and contract more in thickness than in width. Many of the original Gustav Stickley pieces I have seen exhibit some cracking. Usually it is rather minor, occurring for an inch or two near the bottom of the leg, or near the top. I can't honestly say how long it may take the cracking to develop, or if it will occur at all. I've used this method without dire consequences, but who is to say what may happen over the next 90–100 years. Many original pieces were stored for extended periods in basements or attics, harsh environments that magnify issues of wood movement.

Thin, commercially available veneer is a seemingly reasonable solution, but riskier than thicker, shop-made veneer, because it can cause problems. The first is in finishing—if the work is stained or dyed, the veneer and the solid wood will each take the stain differently, and there's liable to be a difference in color or shade between the two surfaces. This is not insurmountable,

Thick veneers on two sides of a laminated leg allow quartersawn grain to be visible on all sides.

The thick veneer is beveled back to the glue line, hiding the joint.

but it will require some extra effort to match the coloring on both types of surfaces. The same problem will also occur when fuming—the tannic acid content of the solid wood and of the veneer will be different, and the chemical reaction will color the pieces differently. This is not the end of the world, but some amount of toning or shading will be necessary. The second problem, which is more troublesome, is that of wood movement between the solid material and the veneer. This movement won't match the seasonal movement of the veneer, and it is quite likely that thin veneer eventually will crack.

In other woods, such as mahogany, bird's-eye maple, or cherry, the difference in appearance between the face and edge grain is not as great as it is in quartersawn white oak, and laminated legs could look good without veneering. If thick enough solid stock is available, the only reason not to use a solid piece, provided that the wood is thoroughly dry and at equilibrium with its environment, would be the difference in

Quarter sawing yields less lumber than plain sawing, but the grain is more consistent and more stable.

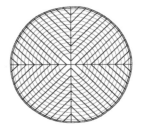
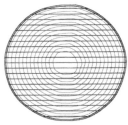

appearance between the quartersawn face and the edges.

Leopold Stickley came up with a solution that was both elegant in appearance, and eminently practical for production in a factory setting—legs made from four pieces of wood joined at each corner with a mitered rabbet. This allows the use of thinner stock, and provides face grain on all four sides. These joints could be simply mitered, but the rabbets keep the miters from sliding out of alignment during gluing. A similar joint can be made with a lock miter shaper cutter or router bit.

Figure 1 shows his method of quadralinear construction, and one of the pieces. This method eliminates the two problems mentioned previously. The leg is all solid construction, the core can be filled with another piece of wood if there has to be an exposed tenon, and with the machinery available then, as well as today, it is relatively simple to produce.

The same visual effect can be achieved if the pieces are simply mitered, but with Leopold's ingenious system, the joints can be clamped together without the tendency to slide apart that simple miters have. Also, all four pieces are machined identically—there are no rights or lefts or fronts or backs to keep track of, so the set up work for milling needs to be done only one time for any number of legs.

These legs were originally milled in the factory in one pass on a shaper or molder, using custom made knives. Those machines were in use in factories of the period, but are not common for the average woodworker of today. This joint can be cut on a table saw, and there are several alternative ways to make a joint that is just as easy to assemble and with the same finished appearance. The key to success in any of these methods lies in careful stock preparation, and being sure that the position of the stock does not change as the wood moves past the cutter. Due to

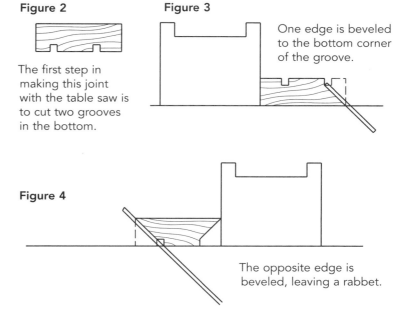

Figure 2

The first step in making this joint with the table saw is to cut two grooves in the bottom.

Figure 3

One edge is beveled to the bottom corner of the groove.

Figure 4

The opposite edge is beveled, leaving a rabbet.

the nature of this joint, any error will result in a gap twice as large as the deviation. For example, if you try to make a long miter cut on a board with a bow of 1/32" over its length, the result will be a 1/16" gap in the finished joint. Similarly, if the board should rise up slightly while moving past the saw blade, a gap of twice that distance will result. Careful stock preparation, machine set-up, feather boards, hold-downs, or a power feeder will go a long way toward ensuring the successful milling of this joint.

Figures 2, 3, and **4** show the sequence of cuts to make this joint with a table saw. First, two grooves are milled in the back face of the board. Note that these grooves are offset; the exact distance will depend on the thickness and width of the wood. The groove that is closest to the edge could be the width of the saw blade, but I generally cut it with the dado head since that will be in the saw for cutting the other groove. Next, a miter is cut from one outside corner to the bottom corner of this groove. Lastly, the opposite edge is mitered, leaving a flat-bottomed rabbet. Take great care when cutting this last miter, since the flat surface that is left to bear against the saw table is rather small. If a feather board is used, locate it away from the fence so that it bears on the flat of the workpiece. Use a push stick, which should also bear on the middle of the board. Pressure on the board close to the saw fence will cause that edge of the board to tip down, ruining the cut.

These illustrations are drawn assuming a left-tilt table saw, and are shown from the infeed side of the saw. If using a right-tilt saw, the fence

Figure 1

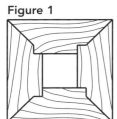

Leopold Stickley developed the quadralinear leg, four solid pieces with a mitered rabbet.

Figure 5

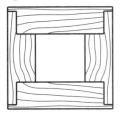

An alternate method is to cut deep rabbets, leaving a narrow exposed edge.

Figure 6

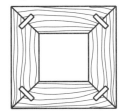

Simple miters can be held together with splines. Splines aren't needed for strength, but they prevent the parts from slipping during assembly.

positions and angle of the blade will be opposite of that shown. These cuts could also be made on a shaper or a router table.

Some alternative methods are shown in the following illustrations, and it should be remembered that simple miters also can do the job. The biggest drawback to simple miters is they tend to slide while being clamped during assembly. One method I use to glue together long miters is to place all four pieces face up on the bench, with their long edges touching. Apply clear packing tape along the length of each joint. After the tape is applied, flip the assembly over, add glue, fold the pieces together, and then tape the final joint. This works well if the parts are carefully cut, and with modern glues, the joint will be more than strong enough.

Figure 7

A lock-miter cutter can also be used, but it is expensive and can be tedious to set up properly.

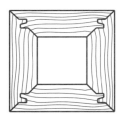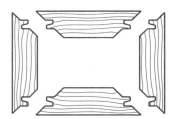

Taper jig consists of a plywood sled with screwed-down blocks to hold the workpiece in place.

Figure 5 shows a stepped rabbet joint. This method avoids the cutting of miters, but it should be noted that the glue line will be offset from the corner, and not directly on the corner as in the mitered joints. If the edges are slightly rounded or beveled, the glue line will disappear where the edge of the bevel meets the face of the leg.

Figure 6 shows a miter joint reinforced with splines running the length of each joint. Biscuits could also be used. The advantage of splines or biscuits is to keep the parts aligned while also adding some strength.

Figure 7 shows a lock miter joint. Available as a router bit or a shaper cutter, this joint is a good alternative to the authentic joint, and is probably the most efficient alternative, particularly if a shaper with a power feeder is available, and enough pieces are made to justify the time spent setting up the cutter. Setting up this joint may take some time, but once done, a sample can be kept for future set-ups. The pieces should be rough-cut oversize to 45° so the router or shaper is only milling the joint, not removing the entire edge of the board.

Once assembled, the leg can be treated as a single piece of wood, although it would be prudent to insert a carefully sized core piece wherever joints occur. Whatever method is used, acceptable results will come only if all the pieces to be milled are truly straight, flat, and square, and they are kept flat to the machine table and tight against the fence during milling.

Craftsman-style legs often are tapered on one or more edges. The most reliable way I have found to taper legs is to cut them slightly oversize, either on the band saw or with a jig on the table saw, and then remove the saw marks with the jointer or a hand plane. For cutting on the table saw, I use a sled of plywood a few inches wider and longer than the leg as the base for a jig. One edge of this is run through the blade, and the fence is kept in the position used for this cut. The cuts are laid out directly on the leg, and these marks are then placed on the freshly cut edge. Blocks of scrap are then screwed down to the plywood sled to hold the leg from behind and on the side that is not being cut. With the saw blade raised to cut the full thickness of the leg, the jig is pulled back behind the blade, the leg placed upon it, held down with a toggle clamp, and the sled is pushed through the blade with the other edge pushed against the fence as in a normal rip cut. This jig can be put together quickly, and works better than the adjustable tapering jigs that are available commercially.

FRAMES AND PANELS

Much of the furniture in this book features frame-and-panel construction for doors, case sides, or as an alternative to a plank-constructed back. These are straightforward tongue-and-groove constructions, without any decorative molding. There are some variations: In some pieces the legs take the place of the stiles, and in others, the stiles have a tongue on the outer edges that fits into a stopped groove in the leg. At the corners, a long tenon (sometimes reinforced with a cross-grain dowel), fits into a mortise deeper than the groove provided for the panel.

Many of the original panels were veneered, a reasonable alternative to solid wood for these relatively thin, wide panels. Most of the drawings show ½"-thick plywood with a tongue worked around the edges for the panels. These could easily be replaced with a piece of ¼" plywood, the way paneled backs are shown in the drawings. The cost difference between ½" and ¼" material is minimal, and I find it easier to rabbet thicker panels to fit a ¼"-wide groove.

The thinner plywood will have a greater tendency to warp, and the quality and thickness of the core can cause problems in appearance and require a slightly different technique for making the grooves. Most dado setups cannot mill a groove narrower than ¼" wide, and nominal ¼"-thick plywood is undersized enough so that there will be a visible gap between the frame components and the panel itself. The easiest solution is to use a stackable slot-cutting setup in a router table to mill the grooves, instead of a dado head setup on the table saw. These cutters are available in increments of ⅟₃₂", so a good fit can usually be achieved. Alternately, grooves can be made with two passes with a standard table saw blade.

Making good panels is mainly a matter of starting with good parts and working precisely. All surfaces should be square, true, and of a consistent size. Saw marks from ripping the stock for stiles and rails should be removed before assembly. If these pieces are ripped slightly oversize, they can be sent through the thickness planer up on edge, in groups of several pieces. Ganging the pieces in this way helps keep them from tipping on their way through the planer, and will ensure the size is consistent.

The grooves or rabbets can be cut in a number of ways, the important point being that the parts are held tightly against the fence and the table surface during cutting. Featherboards and other hold-downs not only increase safety, they increase accuracy by keeping the stock where it should be for cutting. Care taken at this stage will be appreciated at the next stage, when the joints must be cleaned up. It's a good idea to make practice joints on scrap wood and to save parts from a successful joint as an aid in setting up the next time.

In gluing up frames and panels, many workers make the stiles and rails slightly oversize so they can trim the entire panel to size after assembly. In my opinion, this practice complicates the process and encourages sloppy work. For the panel to look right in the end the joints need to be assembled tight and square and any trimming should leave parts that are parallel to each other at the same exact width. If I am capable of working that precisely, I don't need to leave extra to be trimmed for the sake of trimming. The exception is paneled doors, which I make to the size of the opening, and then trim to achieve the desired gap around the edges.

Some pieces have a single flat panel for the side, instead of a framed panel. A number of pieces were shown both ways in catalogs, and this is always an option whenever a frame-and-panel side is shown. These panels can be made from solid wood, or you can use a veneered panel instead, either made from a sheet of hardwood plywood, or veneered by the maker. Both sides—back and front—of the panel should be veneered to equalize the movement of moisture through the panel.

Dust panels below and between drawers were occasionally used in some of the originals, but not in others. To avoid complicating the drawings in this book, they have not been included in any of the pieces. If these panels are desired, it is a simple matter to construct a four-sided frame with the front rail as shown in the drawings, and a piece of ¼"-thick plywood trapped in a groove in all four pieces.

Frame and panel backs were typically used in Craftsman case pieces.

BACKS

The earlier pieces of Craftsman furniture usually had backs made up of individual planks, chamfered on the long edges and joined together with splines at each joint. As time went on, these were replaced in the manufacturing process with either frame-and-panel backs with thin veneer panels or with thicker plywood backs as a single unframed panel. The drawings show different styles in different pieces, but these should not be taken as hard and fast rules. The maker will need to decide which style and method should be used.

The advantages of a single-piece ¾"- or ½"-thick plywood back are simplicity of construction and overall stability. There is only one piece to be cut to size, and seasonal wood movement won't be a factor. If the back is exposed, as in the case of an open or glass-door bookcase or china cabinet, the appearance won't be as nice as a framed panel or plank back.

Solid-wood backs require a bit of planning regarding seasonal wood movement and a few steps in construction to accommodate this movement. An alternative to the splined back is the ship-lapped back. In either case, some space should be allowed for the wood to either expand or contract, depending on the season of construction. This will vary with the wood species, and local environmental conditions. R. Bruce Hoadley's *Understanding Wood* provides some methods for calculating this movement in various species. If using a splined back, the splines themselves should be of the same species as the wood of the planks, as there will

be times when they will be exposed to view, however slightly.

If the V-groove appearance of the splined back is preferred, the edges of the shiplapped pieces can just as easily be chamfered. The advantage of the shiplap is there are fewer pieces to make and fit. The disadvantage is that if any of the individual planks start to bow, they will not be held in place by the adjacent plank. The back pieces should not be glued to each other, or to the case itself, except along the long edges at the cabinet sides. Each individual plank should be fastened top and bottom with one fastener in the center of the plank. This fastener can be either a nail, which will bend slightly as the wood moves, or a screw. This keeps each plank in its relative position, but leaves it free to expand and contract in width. If the back were glued together to form one piece, as in a solid top, the total movement could force the case sides apart. Keeping the planks separate will show slight gaps between them during the driest season. These gaps will then expose either the splines or the shiplap on the neighboring piece.

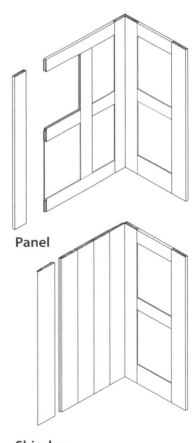

Panel

Ship-lap

MISCELLANEOUS CASE JOINTS

In several pieces, the legs form a part of the frame-and-panel structure either by replacing the stiles, or by having the stiles joined to the legs. The joints for these are shown clearly in the drawings, but the reader should be aware that grooves in the legs for this purpose will have a definite stopping point near the end of the panel toward the bottom of the piece. I make these stopped grooves with a spiral cutting bit in a router rather than with a dado head in the table saw. Either method makes an acceptable groove, but the dado head will leave a substantial ramp where the groove stops, and it will need to be cleaned out by hand or dealt with in some other manner. It would also be wise not to carry the groove completely to the intersection of the rail, but to stop it ¼" to ½" further up, and take a notch out of the tenon in the corresponding rail. This will ensure that none of the groove is exposed after assembly.

In pieces where there is a single wide piece of wood between the legs, the reader is again advised to consider using a veneered panel product rather than solid wood. Many original pieces of this form were actually veneered, and the ones that used solid wood can often be identified by the cracks that have formed over time. Solid wood can successfully be used, but the carcase must be constructed so that the movement of the solid sidepieces is not restrained by another component.

Rails between doors and drawers are shown to be joined by mortise and tenon to either a vertical stile or, more often, to the front leg of the case. This is authentic construction, but the sizes of the joints shown in the drawings reflect my own preferences. An alternative to mortises and tenons, and probably a superior method to the original construction, is to put a dovetail on the ends of the rails. The dovetail will fit a corresponding socket either routed or cut from the backside of the leg or stile. This is the method used by the current L. & J. G. Stickley Company for their reproductions of Craftsman furniture. Once set up, milling these joints is a little faster than making the mortises and tenons, the need for clamping the case during assembly is reduced, and there is a mechanical advantage should any parts shrink over time.

Rail to leg joints.

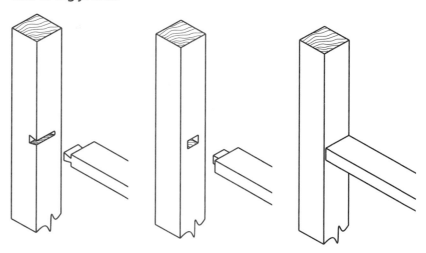

MORTISE & TENON

If nothing else, making Craftsman-style furniture will provide an opportunity to practice woodworking joints, and in some pieces, an opportunity to practice, practice, practice making joints. For mortises, I prefer the hollow chisel mortiser. A good plunge router, with the right bits and jigs, is nearly as fast but for me, it is too noisy, dusty, and hard to hang on to for any extended period of time. For tenons, I prefer to cut the cheeks with a jig on the table saw, and to cut the shoulders by hand. When it comes time to fit the joints, I find it easier to fit the tenon to the mortise.

The shoulder cuts can be made on the table saw with the miter gauge, or on a sliding compound miter saw with the blade set to the proper height above the saw table. I prefer cutting shoulders by hand because I can get a smoother cut with a backsaw than by machine, and the cut is visible as I make it. Knife in the cut lines, use a bench hook, and practice on some scrap and you will find that it isn't difficult. For cheek cuts, I either use the band saw, or a jig on the table saw.

Marking joints with a knife will create a guide for the saw, and leave a clean edge on the tenon shoulder.

Author photo, courtesy PWM.

With a bit of practice, hand cut shoulders are faster and have cleaner edges than cuts by machine.

The tenon jig is made from ¾"-thick Baltic birch plywood, with a replaceable hardwood fence, and an adjustable hold-down clamp. Construction of this jig is simple; it is basically the shape of a small letter h with the inside of the bottom of the h sized to fit over the fence of the saw. The width of the horizontal piece is the only critical dimension in the whole jig, because it must be sized so that the jig will fit over the saw fence and slide freely, but not so tight it will bind. With this jig, the saw can be set accurately in the first place, then adjusted to remove a small fraction of the tenon, with the table saw's fence mechanism utilized for making fine, precise adjustments.

The height of the short piece should be close to the height of the fence, but it is better if it is

wide enough so that the horizontal piece does not touch the top of the fence at all. This way, the bottoms and insides of the two vertical pieces are the only points of friction, and they can be sanded smooth and waxed.

The other dimensions of the jig are not critical. A width of 8" and a height of 12" are good starting points for the tall upright piece, but these can be adapted depending on the work at hand. A handle in the center of the horizontal piece provides a way to push the jig past the saw blade. The fence is solid wood, and should be thick enough to back up the cut to reduce tear-out, and wide enough to allow for secure fastening of the hold-down clamp. It should be held to the tall vertical piece with screws only, as it will need to be replaced periodically. It can be attached at an angle to make the cuts on angled tenons. For safety, attach a tailpiece to the jig to cover the saw blade as you push the jig over the saw table.

In setting up to use the jig, the height of the blade is set first, before the fence is locked down. I mark the depth of the cut (height of the blade) directly on the workpiece, and clamp it in the jig. Placing the jig over the saw fence, the fence is then slid toward the blade. The blade is then raised, and the height is judged by the line on the workpiece. The distance from the fence to the blade can also be set to lines drawn on the workpiece. I make the initial setting a little wider than it should be, and then use the scale on the saw fence to get the exact size. This is a good way to fine-tune the cut because an error on the first attempt won't ruin the workpiece. Make the cut on the side away from the fence, so that any scrap is not caught between the blade and the fence. If, in fitting the tenon to its mortise, you discover the tenon is too thick, return the piece to the jig, adjust the fence, and take an equal amount off both sides.

Usually a combination saw blade works well for this operation, but in the case of an extremely long tenon, it can be helpful to switch to a ripping blade, as this is actually the type of cut that is being made. Before turning on the saw, and adjusting the fence and blade for the actual cut, be sure the jig slides freely along the fence, and the workpiece is securely clamped to the jig. Make sure the blade insert for the saw is perfectly flush to the tabletop, so that the work piece or the jig does not catch on the insert.

After making the adjustments, clamp the work to the jig, and with the right hand on the handle over the fence, push past the blade to make the cut. I carefully slide the jig back past the blade so

Tenoning jig for table saw

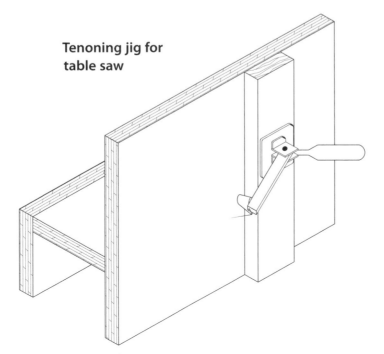

that I am removing and turning the workpiece at the infeed side of the saw.

One of the hallmarks of Craftsman furniture is the through-mortise-with-exposed-tenon joint. In some pieces, the tenon extends far enough to allow the cutting of a second mortise that holds a wedge-shaped key that locks the joint. Through mortises really aren't any more difficult to make than hidden mortise-and-tenon joints—the difference is similar to singing in the shower and singing in front of an audience. Any mortise-and-tenon joint must be precisely made if it is to serve its function over time, but when the joint is exposed, extra care needs to be taken because the appearance of the joint is so important to how the entire piece looks.

The problem is there is a built-in limit as to how far one can go in making these surfaces smooth before the fit of the joint becomes too loose. How much to take off to make the joint smooth depends on how the joint is cut in the first place, and there are numerous options. Many of the keyed tenons are too long to be cut with a tenoning jig on a table saw. These cuts may be made with a well-tuned band saw, and the option of cutting them by hand should be considered. In any case, the quality of the work at this point takes precedence over speed, and it would be worthwhile to make a few practice joints to find a technique that works for you.

There are also numerous methods for cutting the mortises, and again, exposed joints will require a great deal of care. Whatever method is used for the actual cutting, cut in from the finished side as well as the hidden side to avoid tearing out the grain.

In some pieces, the through tenon extends and is held together with a wedge.

A hollow-chisel mortiser is an efficient method for making joints.

Author photo, courtesy PWM.

My first choice for mortising is a hollow chisel mortiser. Low-priced, bench top hollow chisel mortisers have become available in the last few years, and are a welcome addition to a shop making this sort of furniture. Dedicated mortisers perform better than drill-press attachments, but the smaller versions are underpowered and must be used at a pace that doesn't force the work. The more expensive floor models not only offer more power, but also a cross-slide table, which securely holds the work and moves it back and forth in a straight line. While this machine will greatly speed the work, the quality of the cuts made are dependent on the quality of the chisels and bits used and the way they are sharpened and maintained.

Even when optimally tuned, hollow chisel mortisers tend to be a little uneven, showing marks at each place the chisel is plunged in. Exposed mortises will probably need a little bit of handwork with either a chisel or a file to get nice crisp edges. I find that a plastic laminate file works well. When using a hollow chisel mortiser, it is important to stagger the cuts so that the bit and chisel are either completely embedded in

Exposed mortise and tenon joinery is typical in Craftsman furniture.

Author photo, courtesy PWM.

A piece of scrap below the tenon allows the mortiser to be used for making the keyed mortise.

The angle for the wedge can be cut by eye. Look from above down the back of the chisel and tilt the chisel until the bottom edge of the mortise is in line with the chisel back.

Be careful when driving in the keys—the end of the tenon can break, as seen in this original example.

the wood or are taking a cut with two sides in the wood. Trying to continue a cut with three sides in the wood will cause the bit to lean in the direction of least resistance, and will damage the bit and chisel.

A plunge router equipped with a fence or some other sort of guide is a good alternative for making mortises and useful for other tasks as well. For mortising, a 3hp model is preferable to a 1½hp model. The collet should be long enough to hold the bit securely. A spiral up-cut bit will give the best results.

If routing the mortise, I remove most of the waste by making multiple, light passes because this reduces the stress, strain, and noise produced by this operation. The router will leave rounded corners, which need to be cleaned up by hand with a chisel. A chisel with a flat back is essential. By starting the cut with the chisel angled and resting on the flat part of the mortise cut by the router, the working end can be swung into the corner and then brought straight by tilting the handle end toward the vertical, and then working down. Of course, the mortises can be made entirely by hand, drilling out most of the waste with a slightly smaller bit in the drill press.

The angled mortises that receive keys need some handwork to angle the side that matches the wedge. Generally these wedge-shaped keys are cut at an angle of between 5° and 10° but the exact angle is not as important as getting a good match between the mortise and the wedge. It is easier to lay this out if the top of the mortise is made ¹⁄₁₆" to ⅛" larger than the bottom, depending on the thickness of the material. Or the layout can be made on the wedge itself, making the top perhaps ¼" larger than the bottom, and then simply transferring the angle from the wedge to the edge of the tenon that is to receive the angled mortise.

Make a square mortise first—the hollow chisel mortiser can often make this in one pass. Place a piece of scrap under the tenon for support. Make the angled cut with a chisel. Score the two sides from the existing end of the mortise to the layout line. Place the end of the chisel on the line, and aim it at the bottom edge of the mortise. A few taps with a mallet are all it takes to make this cut.

While this joint is sturdy, the weak point is at the end of the tenon that has the angled mortise cut into it. It is quite possible to split the wood at this point by using too much force to drive the wedge home. Make sure the pieces are well matched, and listen as the wedge gets tight. It will make a different sound when it seats. Locate the end of the mortise ¹⁄₁₆" or so behind the face that the back of the wedge is against. This will enable the wedge to pull the joint together and keep it tight if the wood should happen to shrink.

On the originals, all the edges of both the exposed tenon and the wedge are either rounded or chamfered, these cuts tapering down to the corner where the tenon comes through the side of the case. Often the wedge will have a slight notch cut about 1" down from the top. This notch is more decorative than practical, even if it looks to be a surface for knocking the wedge out of its seat. The small protrusion is easy to break off. Leave the wedge an inch or two longer than necessary, and trim it to length after fitting.

Pegged mortises are common, trimmed flush with the surrounding surface. The biggest problem in using this method may be finding a dowel of the right size and species. Few woodworking suppliers carry them, but if a lathe is available, they can be turned in the shop. Sorby makes a sizing tool that fits on a parting tool that works well for this purpose because it can be set to size directly on the bit to be used for drilling the peg hole. Dowels can also be made by driving an octagonal blank through a succession of four or five holes drilled in $\frac{1}{32}$" increments drilled in a piece of $\frac{1}{4}$" thick steel, ending up with a hole the desired size. The edges of the steel will shave the wood to the proper size, and stock that is split to rough size rather than sawn will perform better.

In timber framing, draw-boring is used to pull tenons tight, and hold them in place as wet frame elements shrink. The technique is to drill the hole in the tenon slightly closer to the shoulder of the tenon than the hole in the mortise, in order to use the dowel to force the joint together. This is not necessary in furniture made from dry material, and it can either crush the wood at the edge of the hole in the tenon or make the dowel so difficult to drive that it may split. Clamp the joint tightly together and then drill through the assembled joint and tap in the dowel.

Dowel construction might seem to be an alternative to mortise-and-tenon joints, but I do not recommend it. Dowels never expand and contract at the same pace as the surrounding wood, and eventually either the dowel or the hole becomes out-of-round. When this happens, the surface area of the two parts of the joint is reduced to nearly nothing, and the joint will come apart. Nearly every antique I have seen with failing joints has been of dowel construction, and nearly every mortise-and-tenon joint I have seen has remained secure.

The back edge of the second mortise is behind the surface, allowing the wedge to pull the joint tight.

The chamfered edges of the key taper away from the intersection.

Mark the key to finished length after assembling the joint.

Pare the end of the peg flush with the surrounding surface. A saw is used for initial trimming close to the surface.

The first edge of a laminated curve can be surfaced on the jointer.

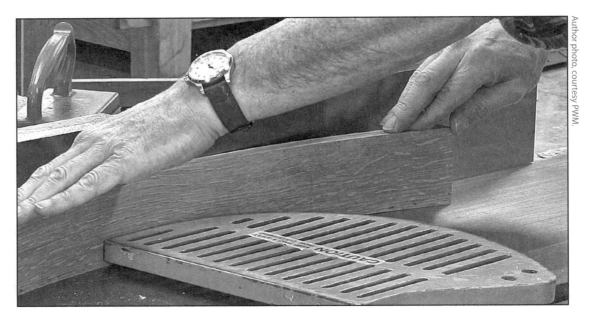

Author photo. courtesy PWM.

CURVED PARTS

Curved aprons, case sides, and corbels can be laid out from the drawings. Long arcs, such as front aprons, start about ½" from where the end of the arc meets the leg, after cutting the curve the intersection between this small flat and the start of the curve is rounded slightly. This is to keep the end of the apron at a defined width. If the arc went right to the end of the part, it would terminate in a point, and sanding or otherwise smoothing the inside of the curve would reduce the height of the part at that point. It is usually easier to cut tenons or other joints before cutting the curve. Dimensions for the radius are usually given in the drawings, but it is not always convenient to draw the arc with a trammel or beam compass.

Measure using the dimensions in the drawings to find the high point of the curve. Transfer that measurement to the part, and plot out the points of the curve. Bend a thin strip of scrap across these points (this may take three hands), to draw the curve, which can then be cut with a band saw or jigsaw.

For chair legs, or other parts that are curved, it is a good idea to go a step further, and make a full-size pattern of the part. This is particularly helpful when making chairs, because they are usually made in multiples, and the layout can be complicated and time-consuming. The pattern for chair legs can also incorporate templates for routing mortises, so that in use the chair leg can be cut slightly oversize, attached to the pattern, and then trimmed to finish size with a router and a flush-cutting bit. A second router with a

guide collar can then cut the mortises for the joints. If using this method, remember to size the mortise openings in the pattern according to the guide collar. I usually write the collar and bit combination on the pattern, to avoid confusion later.

Some curved pieces shown in the drawings include a 1"-square grid as a layout aid. By re-creating the grid full size, you can locate the intersections of the curved line and the grid, and develop a full-size pattern of the part. Once these points are located, a thin strip of wood can be bent across the points, and the curve drawn by running a pencil along the edge of the curved strip.

Parts that are curved in plan, such as table aprons or chair backs, were often cut from solid stock, one of the few areas where some original makers used a technique that won't hold up over time. This leaves weak "short grain" near the ends that is likely to break. These parts are better made by steam bending, or by lamination, from solid stock, five or six pieces ⅛" to ³⁄₁₆" in thickness. For table aprons, nominal ⅜" thick "bending ply" or "wacky wood" is available from some sources. It is made from lauan or Philippine mahogany and is of inconsistent thickness, with a rough surface that will need some filling and sanding before veneering. Birch plywood door skin at ⅛" thick is a better choice, but involves more work, because there will be more pieces.

To laminate a curved part, make a form from particleboard or plywood in the correct radius—subtract the thickness from the out side radius given in the drawing, and make the form a few inches longer than the planned end of the arc. Cut the plys about ¼" wider and a few inches longer than necessary. Apply glue evenly to each ply and clamp to the form. Liquid hide glue, or reactive polyurethane glue is preferred for this work rather than yellow glue. These glues have a longer open time and produce a more rigid glue line, reducing the tendency of the curved part to spring back toward its original straight form.

After the glue is thoroughly dry, one edge can be run over the jointer, and the curved piece can then be ripped to final width. Be extremely careful when doing this. Keep the convex face tight to the jointer fence, and watch where your fingers are. When ripping, keep the face down on the saw table at the front edge of the blade, and again be aware of where your fingers are as you make the cut.

Curved rails on the backs of chairs were usually steam-bent on originals. This is a rather involved process, and most contemporary workers favor laminating these types of parts. If you keep the slices for a lamination in the order they were cut, the glue lines are hard to detect. A form is also used for steam bending, and a strap along the length of the curve will hold the wood fibers together as the wood dries back out.

No matter how the curve is formed, the joints (usually tenons) will need to be worked after the curve is formed. This represents a challenge, but not an insurmountable one. If the layout can be made accurately, it is easiest to cut the shoulders by hand. I make a pattern from a straight piece of wood, then locate the tenons by tracing the pattern on top of the curved part. After cutting the shoulders by hand, I usually make the cheek cuts at the band saw.

To cut the shoulders by machine, a jig of some sort must be devised to safely carry the curved piece past the cutter used to form the tenon. Scrap plywood or particleboard cut to the shape of the radius can be attached to a sled that rides either on the surface of the machine table or vertically along an extended fence. The important thing is to be sure the work is held securely, and there is no danger of it shifting while being cut. The problem with machine joinery techniques on curved parts is that the part will need to be presented to the cutter four times to make each tenon shoulder, each with a separate set up. If configuring and building jigs for cutting takes longer than it would take to cut the joint by hand, there is no advantage to making this joint by machine.

DOORS

Doors are mainly frame-and-panel construction, similar to the panel construction discussed earlier. On some pieces, the doors are solid slabs. With a solid door, more consideration must be given to wood movement, as solid wood will gain and lose some width over the seasons. This would be another place where a veneered panel might be better than a solid-wood slab. If made from solid wood, the wood must be well seasoned and stable, and a decision must be made regarding the size of the gaps around the perimeter of the door in regard to the environment during construction.

It is important that the door be flat, the corners square, and the edges parallel both to each other and to the opening. Techniques for construction and trimming to final size have been covered previously under the topics of frames and panels and solid-wood tops. I make doors and drawer fronts to match the size of the openings, and then trim them to fit.

Shoulders on door joints are offset to align with the rabbet for the glass.

Author photo, courtesy PWM.

Lap joints connect the mullions and muntins within the door frame.

Most of the doors on the pieces in this book are set slightly behind the edges of their openings. These details are noted in the drawings, but could be easily overlooked. Sometimes a thin strip of wood is added to the inside of the leg or stile to carry the hinge. The back of this piece lies in the same plane as the back of the door, and provides space for the hinge barrel on the outside of the door. It may be necessary to cut a small recess for the hinge barrel on the leg or stile if this piece is not present.

Once the locations for the hinges have been determined, careful layout is critical. I mark the lines with a sharp knife, and then use a laminate trimmer or the smallest router available to waste out most of the hinge mortise. The smaller router is easy to balance and control on the edge of the door, and if it is difficult to keep the base of the router flat, a piece of extra stock can be clamped flush with the edge of the door to give the router a wider bearing surface. Guides and stops can be set to limit the router cuts to the exact size of the mortise, but my preference is to use a fence to obtain a straight edge at the back of the cut, and to rout the ends freehand, stopping the cuts about ⅛" from the layout lines. I set the depth of the cutter directly from the leaf of the hinge by inverting the router, with the power cord unplugged.

The gains for the hinges can also be cut entirely with a chisel. The knife marks from the layout provide a place for the edge of the chisel to rest. If the mortise does not go entirely through the edge of the stile, the cuts on the long, narrow edge that is left must be delicately made, for it is remarkably easy to split this piece off the stile, and remarkably difficult to glue it back exactly where it belongs. I use the widest chisel possible to minimize the number of cuts that must be made. The condition of the back of the chisel is as important as the condition of the edge. If the chisel back is nice and flat, it will be guided by the flat surface left by the router, pushed gently in toward the relief cuts previously made down from the layout lines.

If the mortise is carefully made, the hinge should sit in it firmly, and the locations for the screw holes can be marked and drilled with the hinge in place. If these holes are not drilled dead center in the holes in the hinges, the screws will pull the hinge out of position. Self-centering bits (Vix-Bits) work well, provided the drill is held firmly in the countersink and at a

Glass doors and case sides are joined in a similar fashion to panels; however, instead of grooves, the back sides of the frame members have a rabbet for the glass with removable stops behind the glass. Most of these pieces are small, and with a rabbet on the back to accommodate the glass, there is not much room left for a tenon. Line up the edges of the mortises with the edges of the rabbets as shown in the drawing above. The corners of the stops are mitered, and the stops are held in place with small brads. Muntins and mullions on glass doors or case sides should be mortised and tenoned to the adjacent stiles and rails, and either mortises and tenons or half lap joints are appropriate at their intersections. Some early examples had mitered joints at these points, but this method of production did not remain in use for long. It does make for an attractive glass door, but it is more demanding to construct.

Hanging doors is intimidating to many, but it is mostly a matter of working precisely and carefully on a small scale. In most of the original pieces, the doors are hung on good-quality butt or strap hinges that are longer and heavier than those commonly used today. In these pieces, the doors still swing smoothly after 100 years of use. Don't expect good results from sloppy hardware, and give yourself plenty of time to get it right the first time.

90° angle to the hinge. The only drawback to the Vix-Bit is that it doesn't drill a tapered hole. A self-centering punch is also available, which will mark the location for the hole for drilling with a tapered bit of the appropriate size.

Setting the hinges is the time to find the screwdriver that you haven't used since you got your battery-powered drill. Finesse rather than force is essential, for the screws must be seated carefully if they are not to be damaged or stripped in their holes. If brass screws are provided with the hinges, they should not be used the first time the hinge is set because the soft brass is easy to damage. Instead, use a steel screw of the exact same size to cut the threads for the brass screw. Use a bit of beeswax—not soap—to lubricate the screw and make it easier to turn. Soap will attract moisture from the surrounding wood to the screw location. Beeswax can be obtained from any hardware store in the form of a toilet bowl ring at a small fraction of the cost of beeswax sold specifically for lubricating screws. One toilet ring can supply your needs for life. I keep a glob from the ring in an empty 35 mm film canister.

On the edge of the door opposite the hinges, some means must be provided to keep the door from swinging in too far. Generally, this is done by either gluing a thin strip of wood the proper distance behind the door at the top or bottom or on the long edge, or by cutting a rabbet into the edge of the stile.

Gluing in the extra strip is easier, because it can be put off until near the end of the project and thus can be located exactly based on the actual size of the hung door. While the rabbeted stop looks a little nicer, its location must be determined at an early stage of construction, whereupon any necessary adjustments become difficult to make.

Any hardware used to keep the door closed or locked should be as carefully located and set as the hinges. If the door does not swing properly or does not look right in its opening it is possible to make some adjustments, but these are time-consuming and the results are not always successful. A veneer or paper shim can be placed behind a hinge to move it into the opening, but if much movement is required, it will show on the stile side of the hinge. Screw holes can be relocated, but the old holes must be filled as completely as possible with slivers of wood and glue. Allow the glue to dry completely or else the screw in the new hole will drift into the old hole.

DRAWERS

One hundred years from now, when your great-grandchildren are admiring the furniture you made, they should be as impressed with how nice the drawers are as your spouse will be today. Because of the many possible methods of building and hanging drawers, the details in the individual drawings have been left vague, usually indicating only the overall size of the finished drawer. In the original pieces, drawers were mainly joined with half-blind dovetails at the front. The backs were dovetailed or dadoed into the sides and the bottoms were set into grooves in the sides. This is standard, quality construction and is highly recommended.

Maple is a good choice for drawer stock, but I will often use cherry, walnut, or quartersawn oak that contains sapwood or is otherwise not attractive enough to use as a primary wood. Poplar could be used, but it is rather soft and won't wear well. It also moves more than the harder woods, as does plainsawn oak. Bottoms are commonly made from ¼"-thick plywood—birch or maple will match the drawer sides, and aromatic cedar plywood, although hard to find, will add a nice touch to bedroom furniture.

It is important to take great care in the construction of the drawers and the openings. The front must be securely attached to the sides and some form of dovetail joint is preferred because it provides a mechanical connection as well as a glue joint. This joint bears the weight of the drawer, its contents, and whatever resistance there is to movement every time it is opened or closed. You may cut the drawer dovetails by hand or with a router jig. Of the common router dovetail jigs, I like the Leigh jig because it allows for variable spacing of the tails and pins, making for attractive joints. Set-up time is an important factor in using a router jig for drawers because it can take longer to set the jig and make test cuts than it can to dovetail a few drawers by hand.

Backs of drawers don't have as much force constantly applied to them, so a dado into the drawer sides works well, although many people prefer a dovetail at the back as well as the front. Bottoms need to be set in grooves with small wooden fillets or a bead of hot glue to reinforce this joint. This reinforcement not only will keep the bottom secure, it also helps to hold the drawer box itself square. If the bottom of the drawer back ends at the top of the groove for the drawer bottom, then the bottom can be slid into place after the drawer is assembled. This makes finishing the drawer box much easier. After

Half-blind dovetails were typical joints at the front of drawers in original Craftsman pieces.

the box is assembled and finished I put corner clamps on the front two corners to keep it square, slide the bottom in place, and glue in the fillets. The back of the bottom is then either screwed or nailed to the bottom of the drawer back.

For drawers to slide in and out effortlessly, they and their openings must be square and parallel. Even with commercial slides, this is the most important factor in how well the drawer works. There are ways to fudge and adjust after the fact, but it is much easier to fit a square drawer into a parallel opening than it is to correct a problem later on. Usually the drawers on the original pieces slide on a centered wooden guide rail running from the front rail to the back of the case, with a matching guide block on the bottom of the drawer. In other pieces, the drawers slide directly on the bottom edges of the drawer sides, guided by blocks added to the case at the sides to prevent side-to-side movement.

The center guide method works well, but its attachment to the front rail tends to work loose over time, and it must be carefully squared front to back. Rails attached to the sides of the case

should end up square to the front if the case was properly assembled, and they can be shimmed from behind if needed. Using the bottoms of the drawer sides as runners wears the parts of the case they run on, eventually forming grooves in the front rail and causing the drawer front to jam.

I prefer to hang drawers from their sides, on wood rails that ride in a shallow groove ploughed in the drawer side. These grooves need to stop behind the front edge of the drawer side so they won't show on the finished front nor interfere with the front joints. While these grooves can be made on the table saw, routing the groove keeps the bottom flat and consistent. Centering the groove vertically on the drawer side makes the set-up easy. On a typical ½"-thick drawer side, I make the groove ⅛" to ³⁄₁₆" deep, and the width depends on the height of the drawer.

The runners themselves need to be made from a durable, stable wood. Quartersawn walnut and cherry are ideal. If cut from thick stock, they should be given some time to reach equilibrium with the shop atmosphere before final milling. To mount the runners vertically, I set them centered in the drawer opening and set the distance from the front with an adjustable square. Then I use the square to locate the front edge of the runner on the inside of the case. When the drawer is slid in to its opening, the end of the runner stops the drawer just inside the opening. Two or three countersunk screws attach the runner to the side of the case. This makes it easy to remove and adjust the runners.

Sizing the runners can be tricky—if they are too big the drawer will stick, but if they are too small the drawer will be sloppy. I find that making the runner ¹⁄₃₂" narrower than the width of the groove is about right, and that the distance between the two runners should be between ¹⁄₃₂" and ¹⁄₁₆" more than the distance between the bottoms of the grooves in the drawer sides. If the drawer sticks or binds, rub colored chalk or crayon onto the runners, and slide the drawer into place. Remove the drawer and the chalk marks will show where it rubs. The high spots can then be planed or sanded down. Paraffin, paste wax, or Teflon-based spray lubricants (such as Top Coat) will keep the drawer sliding smoothly.

DUST PANELS

Some people are surprised by the absence of dust panels in between drawers in case pieces such as dressers. This is generally the way this furniture was originally manufactured. Dust panels can be added by building a frame behind the front rail, and adding a thin panel inside the frame. This will impart some strength to the case, though in most pieces it will be overbuilding a structure that is already very sturdy.

One design element that could use improvement is the absence of a rail above the top drawer in case pieces. Gustav Stickley liked to have the top of the drawer directly under the case top, and his many imitators followed his lead. Visually it is an important element in his furniture, but in many original examples that I have seen, the unsupported top sags over time, either dragging at the center of the drawer or pulling loose where it is supported at the sides of the case. This condition can be improved by adding a hidden rail behind the top of the drawer front. This will provide both a means of support and a way to attach the top to the case, and the only real impact is to reduce the height of the drawer by the thickness of the rail.

RIGHTS & LEFTS

Most of the pieces in this book have parts that will only go in one place, for example, a dresser or other case piece will have four legs that are identical in size and shape, but the joints cut in each will be on opposing sides depending on the orientation of the piece. These should be marked in some way so that you don't end up with two left front legs, and no right front legs. I mark legs on the bottom or top with simple designations in pencil, indicating not only which piece is which, but also which face of the part is the front. In general, the nicest face should be on the front of the furniture. After the joints are laid out and cut, it should be obvious which piece is which.

Triangles can be drawn across several pieces of a subassembly, or a group such as four legs, in order to maintain their orientation. I was taught that the triangle's point always faces up, or always faces to the right. I also add a line parallel to one or more of the legs of the triangle if there are more than one identical assemblies. I usually draw these with chalk or a lumber crayon so I don't have to worry about removing pencil lines later on.

ASSEMBLY

Building a piece of furniture with many intricate parts can be intimidating, but putting together a box is simple. When planning what steps to take to put a piece of furniture together, I try to look for the box, that is, to look at the piece as subassemblies rather than as many individual parts. A chair or a case piece can usually be seen as having two sides, plus a front and a back. Sides usually can be put together as units, so that final assembly is greatly simplified. In the drawings that contain exploded views, I have tried to show subassemblies as I would put them together. My inclination is to put sides together first, although with chairs it may be preferable to assemble the front and back first. Once the glue has dried, treat the subassemblies as single pieces during the next stage of assembly.

I generally use yellow glue, which doesn't have a very long open time. If a piece is particularly complicated, I use a slow drying formula, or liquid hide glue so I don't have to rush. When putting furniture together, I try to have as many of the parts as I possibly can nearly ready to finish before final assembly. I sand parts to the next to the finest grit so that once the piece is put together, the intersections of adjoining parts are the only places where there might be some work to be done, and a final hand-sanding is the only sanding left. It is easier to completely sand individual parts, and sanding before assembly reduces the risk of cross-grain scratches.

If the joints are worked carefully and accurately, then any work beyond the final glue up will be kept to a minimum. If the back of a piece can be added as the very last step, it will make finishing of the entire piece significantly easier, because the inside can be reached from the front or back, and there will be fewer inside corners with which to deal.

When the time comes for the final assembly, I begin with a dry run to be sure all of the joints fit properly, and that I have all of the clamps, pads, and anything else I may need close at hand and ready for the final glue-up. The best way to ensure the final assembly goes well is to be very careful when making parts, and in putting together subassemblies. Sizes of parts should be double-checked, and joints should be test-fit. Panels and other subassemblies need to be put together square and without any twists or bows from improper clamping. If these early steps are done well, then problems at the end will be minimized.

Two elements of assembling furniture that are often overlooked are the necessity of having a flat and level surface upon which to do the final assembly and to have a way of holding the work square during assembly. Right-angle clamps hold corners together nicely and I usually apply them to hold the parts in alignment while clamping or fastening. In many shops, the table saw is the only flat surface, and if you are not too sloppy with the glue, it makes a good work surface for this all-important stage of furniture-making.

Original examples of Craftsman furniture demonstrate good, sound construction techniques. I have raised a few minor points regarding things I have seen fail in original examples, but it should be remembered that these are minor, usually cosmetic flaws in furniture that is one hundred years old. Overall, this furniture teaches us a wonderful lesson in technique, as well in as design and proportion.

In original pieces with a fumed finish, the color is consistent. The rays should not "pop."

FINISHING

Oak Craftsman furniture with its original finish is most often a light or dark brown, the light being close to the natural color of the wood mellowed with age. Medium Walnut Watco Oil or American Walnut Minwax stain come close to the darker color. Most stains with walnut in their name are close in tone with white oak. In quartersawn material, the problem is in coloring the rays and the surrounding grain evenly. In authentic Craftsman-style furniture, the quartersawn grain is subdued; it shouldn't "pop." The easiest way to accomplish this is with fuming or with aniline dyes, or dye-based stains, or with multiple steps of staining and glazing.

There were several colors available from the factory so if you are trying to match the original colors, a color photograph magazine will help. A satin sheen is appropriate, whether it is achieved with oil and wax, shellac, lacquer, or other finish. The finish should not be allowed to build up too thick on the oak, so that it leaves a somewhat textured, but not filled, finish.

Fuming is a good technique for coloring quartersawn white oak, but it must be remembered that ammonia can be toxic. Household ammonia is too weak to be effective but 26% ammonia can be obtained from companies that make blueprints, and while you are there, please note the blurry demeanor of the employees who breathe ammonia fumes all day. When working with ammonia, wear gloves and goggles and a proper respirator, not a dust mask. Don't use metal containers, and never mix ammonia with any other chemicals.

Fuming will be most successful if all the wood in the piece comes from the same log, because it is a chemical reaction between the ammonia and the tannic acid in the wood that causes the color change. The tannic content varies from tree to tree. An airtight tent is quick to put together from plastic sheeting and scrap lumber. Place the tent over the completed piece with a bowl inside, carefully pour a small amount of ammonia into the bowl, seal the tent, and leave it for 12 to 48 hours. A test on some scrap from the project will show you how long it takes to achieve the desired color. Unevenness of color can be touched up with alcohol-based aniline dye. Mixing the dye with clear shellac will allow layering in the color for a close match.

Fuming will leave the piece dull and gray. A coat of either amber or garnet shellac will warm this color, and move it to a nice brown. A dark wax, applied after the shellac is thoroughly dry, will fill the open pores in the wood and darken the color. The appearance of this will be close to that of original pieces. Nearly the same color and tone can be reached with Lockwood's Fumed Oak aniline dye, followed by shellac and dark wax. Water-based dyes will raise the grain. If you use water-based dyes, raise the grain first by dampening the wood with distilled water and follow by sanding with 180- or 220- grit sandpaper. Shellac and dark wax applied over the dye will complete the finish, and be close to the look of a fumed finish. Always experiment on scraps before committing to a finishing routine.

Fuming can also be used to age brass hardware. Soak the hinges or other hardware in lacquer thinner for an hour or so, then scrub with an old toothbrush to remove any finish. Place the hardware in a small plastic container, so that it is off the bottom, and place a small dish with a little ammonia in it and seal the lid. A clear container will allow you to see inside to judge the amount of oxidation on the metal. The time it takes will depend on the strength of the ammonia, an hour or two with 26% ammonia, or several hours with janitorial (10%) or household (5%) ammonia will oxidize and age the brass. When you remove the hardware, buff with a soft rag.

Mahogany pieces were not colored heavily, just a bit of brown to come very close to traditional mahogany finishes. Some pieces that were finished quite dark now appear nearly black. The maple pieces are not common, and the examples I have seen were in curly maple with a dark brown, rather muddy looking color.

The old catalogs list a "silver gray" finish on maple, which Stickley describes as being achieved by brushing on a solution of vinegar that has had rusty iron soaking in it for a few days. I haven't seen an original example of this, and I have never tried this treatment on maple, but I have successfully ebonized walnut with this same solution. Use white vinegar and any rusty scrap metal or steel wool, which will degrade quickly in the solution. As the metal soaks it releases iron oxide into the solution, which will react with chemicals in the wood in different ways in different species. Do not let the rusty metal soak in a sealed container, because gas forms during the process and can build up and cause an explosion.

The color of the solution won't change, but it will cause a chemical reaction when applied to raw wood. Strain through a coffee filter, then brush on the wood, or apply with a rag. The color change will occur within five to ten minutes.

Original examples in maple have a dark finish, and are rarer than oak.

UPHOLSTERY

In the drawings in this book, upholstered seats are shown without much detail. While this could be attributed to laziness on my part, there are good reasons for this fuzziness. The original pieces of furniture used several different types of cushions—some of them appear to be changes in manufacturing methods over time, while others likely were optional ways of ordering the furniture. Also, the seat cushions are the least durable part of old chairs and settles, so original examples are often seen either with the cushions missing entirely, or with some sort of replacement cushion or support. If you are making chairs or settles, you will need to make your own decision based on your own desire for comfort, and your skills and budget.

Upholstering is a distinct trade from woodworking, and I will confess that I am far from an expert. Slip seats on dining chairs are relatively simple to produce, and are not very demanding. Large cushions on settles and Morris chairs, with their necessary supporting structure, are more involved, and I think the best advice for the do-it-yourselfer is to either take a class on techniques, or hire someone competent to perform this work. I will review the basic methods and materials, and leave a more detailed description of how to do it to those more experienced than me. Van Dyke's Restorers (800-558-1234, www.vandykes.com) is a good source both for supplies, and for reference material. Local community colleges and vocational schools often offer classes in upholstery, and this would be a good way to learn the fine points, and to get access to needed tools and machinery capable of sewing leather and other upholstery fabrics.

The simplest cushions are found in dining chairs. Usually these were a slip seat—leather wrapped around a padded wooden frame, attached to the frame of the chair itself by screws from below, usually through corner blocks. Occasionally, the frame and padding was attached to the chair before the fabric, and the leather was fastened to the outside of the chair frame with decorative tacks. Morris chairs, large easy chairs, and settles had a greater variety of cushions, and exhibit more changes over time with new technologies and production methods.

Slip seats are simple to make. A hardwood frame, of pieces ¾" by 1¾" to 2", is made to fit inside the frame of the chair itself, with an allowance around the edges for the fabric. A piece of plywood could be used, but the open area in the inside of the hardwood frame will allow air to circulate through the padding and fabric. It also looks nicer if anyone ever peeks under your chair.

If you use an open frame, place webbing across the opening to keep the padding from falling through, and to provide support in the middle of the seat. Padding comes next, and depending on the choice of materials, it can be either glued or tacked in place. It is easiest to wrap the fabric around the seat if it is placed good side down on a clean bench or table. Place the padded seat on top of the fabric, wrap the edges of the fabric around the edges of the frame, and tack or staple it down.

Working opposite edges will make it easier to pull the fabric evenly, and to get it tight without distortion. Where the fabric meets at the corners on the underside, it is best to fold it so that adjacent edges meet at a mitered edge. After tacking down both sides, the excess fabric can be trimmed so that there is no bump at the corners. If you use your wife's good scissors, put them back before she finds out that you borrowed them. The completed seat can then be attached to the chair frame, and this is generally done by screwing from below through corner blocks or cleats.

The earliest versions of Gustav Stickley's larger chairs and settles used a woven cane support attached inside the frame of the chair, with a loose cushion on top of that. Some chairs had a canvas or leather sling, secured to the chair frame at the inside front and back. Both the cane and the sling supports have a bit of give to

them, resulting in more comfort than the slip seat provides.

Unfortunately, neither cane nor slings last forever, and chairs made this way are most likely to be missing their original supports. Later versions of chairs and settles had eight-way tied coil springs, either in a wooden frame that attached inside the chair frame, or directly attached to the chair frame. One of Leopold Stickley's innovations was a drop-in spring unit, an idea apparently borrowed from the fledgling automobile industry. This was a metal frame containing springs, wrapped and upholstered, and dropped-in the finished chair frame.

An upholstered seat functions much like the suspension system of a car, and high quality seating comes from a balanced combination of both spring support and cushion materials. The main function of cushions is to provide comfort by compressing under load, and by keeping the body separated from a hard surface. The main function of springs is to provide support, yet be flexible enough so that when weight is shifted the point of support also shifts, and the cushion is not forced to take the entire load.

For maximum comfort, and for long life of the cushions, springs are the best but most expensive choice—either coil springs supported by webbing, or the more modern sinuous wire springs (also known as "no-sag"). Cushions can also be supported either by a piece of plywood or by wooden slats, and this method is often used by antique dealers to replace missing upholstery. Cotton-filled futon cushions can be ordered to size at nearly any store that sells futon mattresses. Slats are preferred to plywood, because the spaces between slats will allow air to circulate through the cushion. This is the least expensive, simplest-to-construct option, but it is also the least comfortable, and shortest lived. The problem with this method is that the chair or settle will feel stiff, and the futon or other cushion material, taking the full load of the sitter, will become compressed. As time goes on, the seat will get harder and harder. This can be minimized by regularly turning the cushions. Wear on the fabric covering will also be greater with this method than with springs.

Modern flexible webbing is better than slats. Run the webbing from front to back and side to side, weaving the pieces in alternate directions over and under, as in a basket weave. Sinuous wire springs are a step above slats or webbing. These zigzag shaped springs are easily attached either to the chair frame, or to a separate frame, and are usually covered with a stiff fabric. The cushion then rests on top. While they provide decent support, they are not as comfortable or as long lasting as coil springs. They are a relatively inexpensive option, and function best in smaller seats.

Properly tied and supported coil springs are the most expensive choice, as well as the most comfortable and longest-lasting method for supporting seating. Jute webbing is attached in a crisscross pattern and a coil spring is attached with staples at each intersection of the webbing. Each spring is then tied with heavy twine either to the frame or to adjacent springs. A stiff fabric decking may be applied, as with the sinuous springs, and a cushion placed on top. Alternatively, layers of different padding materials may be placed directly over the springs, with the final layer of leather or fabric as the layer that shows. When a load is placed on any one spring, it compresses, and the tying causes all the neighboring springs to also compress. This allows the seat to be quite comfortable, moving slightly with the sitter. It also spreads the load, resulting in longer life for both the springs and the cushions.

There are a number of choices for cushion material. One hundred years ago, the choices weren't as numerous nor as comfortable. Horsehair, excelsior, and cotton batting were common, not only in Craftsman furniture, but also in other upholstered furniture of the period. Foam cushions did not come into use until the 1930s. Modern upholstery foams function better than the earlier alternatives, and are available in a range of densities and thicknesses. The biggest drawback to foam cushions is that they usually take 24 hours or more to return to their uncompressed state. As time goes on, foam cushions tend to stay compressed and the seat gets harder and less resilient. Good quality cushions are usually a combination of materials with the foam wrapped in polyester or cotton batting. A layer of down adds a considerable measure of comfort, as do small, wrapped coil springs inside the cushion.

Leather was the first choice of fabric on the originals and is a good choice today, although it is expensive. It is extremely durable, looks good in combination with wood, and is very comfortable. Original cushions also were covered with heavy canvas, and today there are a variety of upholstery fabrics available that will work well with this style of furniture.

In the drawings, I have left the details vague, in most cases showing only ledger strips inside the frame to support any type of cushion.

Many times existing pieces bear no trace of their original upholstery. Pieces that were in production for several years were likely to have used different methods and materials in different years. Attempts to be authentic in building a reproduction will need to be tempered by the realization that 100% historical accuracy may not be possible. In my opinion, strict authenticity usually should take second place to issues of comfort and durability.

Building one of the large chairs or settles from the drawings in this book represents a considerable investment both in materials and in time. While those of us who work with wood tend to think that the purpose for having one of these pieces in our homes is so that others may admire our skills, the rest of the world is looking for a comfortable place to sit and relax. The best way to admire a Morris chair is while seated in it. I think it is unwise to scrimp on materials at this point, and I have no problem in hiring someone else to do the upholstery. I have enough trouble getting the wooden parts to work without diving into materials and techniques that aren't as familiar to me.

Most of the furniture designs in this book use either a loose cushion, or can use a removable frame for springs to support the seat cushions. This is how the original furniture was made, and it is an advantage to today's woodworker. All of the wooden parts can be completely finished, then the springs or other seat supports can be installed at the very last step. This is far easier than trying to work around upholstery during finishing, and it nearly eliminates the risks of damaging the finish while doing the upholstery. The fact that these are two distinct processes makes it easier to have the work done by two distinct people.

These designs also lend themselves to trading up at some later date. If you are on a tight budget, you can use a futon, or a foam cushion supported by simple wood slats that rest on cleats inside the frame of the chair or settle. These parts are in no way permanent; replace them later with a drop-in frame with spring supports. In fact the wooden structure, if carefully made, will last many times longer than any of the upholstery, no matter what choice you make initially.

Chapter 5
Inlays

In January 1904, readers of Gustav Stickley's *The Craftsman* magazine were presented with an article titled "Structure and Ornament in the Craftsman Workshops." It described a new line of furniture featuring inlaid designs in veneers and various metals. This furniture had been announced six months earlier, and throughout 1903, *The Craftsman* had featured inlaid furniture from English manufacturers and designers, along with renderings of inlaid furniture in articles written by Harvey Ellis. In October 1903, a photograph of an inlaid piano appeared in *The Craftsman*, a preview of the inlaid furniture.

While the addition of ornamental elements was a departure from Stickley's previous designs, the inlays fit perfectly with the furniture, a logical and natural addition rather than an unnecessary frill. It was in keeping with design trends of the period, and added a note of elegance and grace to Stickley's furniture. It was an example of Stickley's ability to absorb influences from other sources, and incorporate them in something new.

The Craftsman inlays, and the furniture they adorn are generally attributed to Harvey Ellis. There are good reasons to support that attribution, but not a lot of hard evidence. The furniture and the inlays clearly show the hand of Ellis, but the influence of Gustav Stickley is also evident. Did Harvey Ellis produce these designs in response to Gustav Stickley's waving hands and verbal directions, or did he approach his employer with completed drawings, and the suggestion to add thinner elements and subtle curves to the existing Craftsman style? Clearly, other hands and other voices also were involved in the process; what exists today are published renderings and finished pieces of furniture, the many steps in between, and exactly who took them, has not been preserved.

Today these designs, the result of the collaboration between Gustav Stickley and Harvey Ellis, are generally seen as the high point of Craftsman design. Most of the furniture pieces were also manufactured without the inlays, excellent designs in their own right.

What the inlays add is a note of color, a lyrical element, and a graceful flourish. *The Craftsman* article explains:

"...this ornament, like that of the Greeks, appears to proceed from within outward. It bears no trace of having been applied. It consists of fine markings, discs, and other figures of pewter and copper, which, like the stems of plants and obscured, simplified floral forms, seem to pierce the surface of the wood from beneath..." [14]

The inlays do appear to be a natural element of the furniture. Much like the blooms on a dogwood tree in spring, they simply appear, bringing an inspiring touch of beauty. These elements are neither necessary nor expected, but their presence perfectly fits the overall design.

At the time, however, the inlay designs were not commercially successful, and they weren't considered important for very long. According to Stickley's daughter Barbara:

"I don't think the inlay furniture was ever put on the market. We displayed it at merchandise marts and made samples to show in stores, but it was never put in production" [15]

The rarity of the original pieces has made this furniture somewhat of a holy grail among collectors and others interested in Craftsman furniture. Rarity alone cannot account for the tremendous interest in these pieces. The excellence of the designs, and the way that they relate to the total design of the furniture pieces, ensure them a place of importance in American design history.

It is difficult to explain why these designs were not successful when they were introduced. Stickley's other furniture designs were copied outright or adapted by hundreds of other manufacturers. The most likely explanation is price. Craftsman furniture, despite its appeal to the common man, was never inexpensive and the additional costs of the marquetry may have pushed the price to where demand was insufficient to support production.

It is also difficult to definitively answer many questions about these designs and the people responsible for them. What today is considered a major element of Stickley's furniture was but a brief episode at the time, and rarely does anyone make much of an effort to preserve detailed information about less-than-successful enterprises. The facts are sketchy and incomplete, and many of these questions will likely never be answered definitively.

The six months between the announcement of the new designs and the presentation of several finished pieces is actually a short period, given the realities of publishing deadlines, preparation of prototypes, and finding a source for the production of the inlays. Gustav Stickley's company was large enough and diverse enough to own its own sawmills and kilns, and to produce metal hardware and leather and other upholstery in house. Production of the inlays used in Stickley's furniture, however, was contracted out and most, if not all, was produced by the firm of George Jones of New York City.

The July 1903 issue of *The Craftsman* brought together Gustav Stickley, Harvey Ellis, the Art Nouveau movement, and plans for inlaid Craftsman furniture. The magazine featured this announcement for "The New Models of the Gustav Stickley Furniture":

...are receiving favorable criticism for their qualities of originality, chaste design, beauty of line and color. They are the result of a deep study of the principles of the new art movement, considered as a revolution against the historic style, and a return to nature as the true source of inspiration for all constructive effort.

They are lighter in effect and subtler in form than any former production of the same workshops. They have also an added color element introduced by means of wood-inlay, in designs of great delicacy, founded upon plant forms that are obscured and highly conventionalized.

A short article in the same issue, without illustrations, introduced readers to George Jones, the artisan who would bring the ideas of Stickley and Ellis to tangible form. Here is an excerpt:

The artistic work, as distinguished from the commercial product, is now executed in at least one studio in the United States. But the workmen who are there engaged are not native Americans, because the traditions of the craft are preserved only in France and in Holland, and are not to be acquired, save by thorough apprenticeship.

The American studio, to which reference has already been made, is under the charge of Mr. George H. Jones, a young craftsman who has worked in marqueterie for ten years, during which he has obtained most unexpected and beautiful results, and has gained an entrance for his productions into the most artistic interiors of the country.

A visit to his studio is time most profitably spent, since it acquaints one interested in the present revival of the handicrafts with the skillful and thoroughly honest methods of a workman who gives his energies and labors to the creation of beautiful things, rather than to the accumulation of wealth at the expense of art and truth. As a single example of his care and fidelity may be cited the device used by him in opposition to the less expensive and more mechanical methods of some of his rivals. This is the production of shadows by his scrupulous selection of woods, which he matches together in a delicate gradation of shades, or, more artistically still, by varying the direction of the fibers of his veneers. The processes rejected by him are the browning and shading of the wood by the use of hot sand, and the abuse of dyes and acids, with which to produce striking color-effects. [16]

Jones, born in 1865, had purchased an existing marquetry business in 1893; it is possible he may have been an employee. Not much is known about his work other than a few magazine articles, and his own advertising in trade journals. His advertising was simple and effective—bold headlines stating:

JONES! THE MARQUETERIE MAN

Unfortunately, these ads were not illustrated, and as a supplier to the furniture industry, his work is undocumented except by the designs produced for Stickley. He was apparently well regarded within the furniture trade, and an article in *American Cabinet Maker and Upholsterer* noted:

He saws his own veneers, originates his own designs, finishes his own work...The same man who saws the inlay saws the ground that is to receive it. The artist who originates the design assembles the woods and indicates every detail...master of color who achieves his rich and varied tints with acid baths and dyes he prepares himself. [17]

The execution of the Craftsman inlays is excellent, and the selection of veneers and use of grain direction for visual effect is quite striking. The addition of metal, usually pewter and copper, adds a touch of elegance. There are records of Stickley receiving orders from Jones starting in the summer of 1903, and the logical assumption is that Jones' firm produced most, if not all, of the inlays.

Again the question of exactly who did what arises. Did Harvey Ellis prepare drawings for the inlays beyond the illustrations that were published in *The Craftsman*? Was there an unknown draftsman employed by Stickley who detailed Ellis' rather sketchy designs for production? Were some of the designs the work of Stickley himself, or of other designers on his staff? Are any of the designs actually the work of Jones or his employees? There are some significant differences among the designs used in Stickley's furniture that suggest at least the influence of other hands, but these questions cannot be answered with certainty.

In the first group of drawings for the Stickley/Ellis inlays (pages 268-293), most of the curves are sections of ellipses, while the curves in the patterns on pages 294-299 are either arcs of circles or irregular curves. I attribute these differences either to the style of the draftsman making the final working drawings, or to the craftsman who actually made the inlays. Most of the patterns with elliptical arcs are combinations of veneer and metal, and are likely the work of Jones.

In much of the second group, the inlays are all metal. This variation suggests there were at least two layout artists or craftsmen involved, and could be the work of either a second inlay specialty firm, or of artisans at Stickley's factory. This does not mean, however, that Harvey Ellis was not the originator of the initial designs. Finally, there are two examples that are entirely veneer (pages 291 and 300) in a significantly different style from the other inlay patterns. David Cathers tries to make the leap that this difference means there was another designer for these patterns [18], but I believe that there is enough similarity to the work of Ellis to attribute them to him, because there is no real evidence of another designer.

Harvey Ellis resumed drinking heavily at some point near the time that he went to work for Stickley. In December 1903 he was hospitalized, and he died on January 2, 1904, just as the inlaid furniture appeared in finished form in the pages of *The Craftsman*. What effect his drinking had on his ability to perform his work, and on his relationship with Stickley, is not known. Claude Bragdon, who was also working for Stickley in the summer of 1903, describes Harvey Ellis at work in a letter:

"I've just had a chat with the same old Harvey, making the same old beautiful watercolors in the same old madden-ing-ly simple and easy way...I see Harvey every day." [19]

Alcoholics are also frequently workaholics and in the summer and fall of 1903, Harvey Ellis produced a tremendous amount of work for Gustav Stickley. Those six issues of *The Craftsman* include complete designs for several houses and a church, articles and illustrations for several interiors, furniture and drapery designs, articles on design principles, and on the Spanish Missions of California. After his death, the January 1904 issue of *The Craftsman* contained another house design, with the rendering, exterior elevations and plan in the style of Ellis, while the interior elevations and furniture illustrations appear to be by another hand. In March and June of 1904, articles on linen designs were published that appear to be the work of Harvey Ellis.

Motifs similar to those seen in the Stickley inlays are everywhere in the published illustrations by Harvey Ellis, appearing as decorative murals on walls, and designs on art glass, curtains, and table linens, as well as on furniture. Even if much of this material had been prepared by Ellis in Rochester, before he came to Syracuse, organizing and preparing it all for publication would have been a daunting task.

Hugh M. Garden in a tribute to Ellis after his death wrote:

A glutton for work when it had to be done, he was nevertheless incredibly lazy. The greater the task, the faster his nimble wits and fingers; always with the desire to have done and get back to the paths of his restless and insatiable fancy. [20]

Until we perfect time travel, we will likely never know the exact process by which the initial designs became finished pieces. The evidence that exists today is not solid enough to identify everyone involved, or to clearly define the role that anyone may have played. The differences I see between the patterns could well be differences in style of whoever prepared working drawings for the production of the inlays, much in the same way that there were distinct differences in style among the various draftsmen who worked on architectural drawings for Stickley.

Harvey Ellis clearly was the originator for most of the design motifs, but how far beyond that his role extended will remain a mystery. George Jones, the manufacturer of most of the patterns, also likely had a significant role in their creation, and may have been responsible for some of the inlay designs, or in the translation of illustrations to completed patterns ready for production.

Many of the furniture designs were produced for several years without the inlays. Around 1909, as Stickley was getting ready to move to Craftsman Farms in New Jersey, a few inlaid pieces were produced, mostly in maple. The bed in Stickley's daughters' bedroom was one of these pieces. It isn't clear if these pieces were only produced for his personal use, or if Stickley's intent was to revive the inlaid furniture line in the lighter maple instead of the original darker oak. If this was his plan, it didn't meet with enough demand to justify putting the inlaid furniture into regular production, and the maple examples of inlaid furniture are rarer than the oak.

The strength, beauty, and timelessness of these designs accounts for our interest in them from this vantage point, more than one hundred years after their creation. Gustav Stickley and Harvey Ellis were largely forgotten for more than sixty years. After Ellis' death, a few tributes to him were published in architectural magazines, but the inlay designs were not mentioned, and the furniture he created received only passing attention. We never know what part of our work history will judge as important, or if we will be remembered at all. The recent revival of interest in Gustav Stickley's work has quite naturally led to a rediscovery of Harvey Ellis, usually only for the furniture and inlays produced during his short stint with Stickley.

In February 1904, *The Craftsman* published the following obituary of Harvey Ellis, an excellent summation of his career and of his important contribution to Gustav Stickley's work:

In the death of Mr. Harvey Ellis, which occurred on January 2, The Craftsman *lost a valued contributor to its department of architecture. Mr. Ellis was a man of unusual gifts; possessing an accurate and exquisite sense of color, a great facility in design, and a sound judgment of effect. These qualities were evidenced in his slightest sketches, causing them to be kept as treasures by those fortunate enough to acquire them.*

As a teacher, Mr. Ellis was very successful, while many of his fellow students, among whom are several eminent painters of the country, have acknowledged their debt to him lying in the counsels and criticisms that he gave them.

As an architect, Mr. Ellis showed style and distinction: his ability having received public recognition through the award of the first prize in the design competition for the tomb of General Grant. Mr. Ellis was, further, a connoisseur of Japanese art, the principles of which he assimilated and practiced. Altogether, he is to be regretted as one who possessed the sacred fire of genius. [21]

The arts and designs of any culture reflect the values and character of that culture. The inlay designs of Harvey Ellis are much more than lines and shapes; they are expressions of ideals, explanations of harmony and balance. They are a distilled vision of the workings of nature, using the colors and textures of natural materials.

When Gustav Stickley introduced Craftsman furniture, he was quite adamant in his arguments against the use of applied ornament. While the furniture was plain and unadorned, there were ornamental features in the exposed joinery and in the use of hardware. With the introduction of the inlaid furniture he needed to soften his stance a bit, for here were elements whose sole purpose was visual decoration. But the addition of the Ellis-designed furniture, with and without inlays, is not the sudden surprising turn that some suggest.

Articles in *The Craftsman* in 1902 and 1903 often featured Art Nouveau decoration in other media and some examples of inlaid furniture by other makers. In letters to and from one of his readers, Stickley left open the possibility of new, more decorative designs. In the text accompanying the photos of the inlaid furniture in *The Craftsman* in January 1904, Stickley continues his argument of natural development of these designs:

These pieces, in every case, boldly assert the purpose for which they are designed. The chair does not reach out after the attributes of the table; nor yet does the round table purloin the characteristics of the square object of its own kind. Each specimen preserves a structural distinction as marked as that which separates, one from the other, the species and varieties of the animal and vegetable kingdoms. The principles upon which they are based follow nature, and must, therefore, be sound and true. [22]

As has been mentioned before, the furniture designs were successful without the addition of inlay. The inlays work so well with the overall designs that they do appear to be a natural addition and adornment to the furniture. Comparing the two versions is like comparing a dogwood or apple tree in bloom, to the same trees in midsummer. Both are attractive, and fit in naturally with their environment, yet the one has a special enhancement.

The inlaid designs produced by Albert Stickley's company in Grand Rapids, Stickley Brothers, preceded Gustav Stickley's inlaid furniture by several years, first appearing in 1900 as part of Albert's "English Designed" line of furniture. While these inlays were attractively designed, and skillfully produced, they do not approach the level of excellence of the Ellis pieces. Albert imported T. A. Conti to do this design work, and it is typical of other inlay work produced in England and in France at the time.

Many pieces of English Arts & Crafts furniture included similar inlays, a blending of Art Nouveau elements with simple Arts and Crafts furniture designs. The Stickley Brothers inlaid furniture was well crafted, but represented more typical examples of the genre than innovation in design. Albert Stickley and his younger brother Leopold were astute businessmen, and both knew the furniture trade well. A large part of their success was due to their ability to recognize and follow trends in design and public taste. While they were eventually more successful financially than Gustav Stickley, it should be remembered that they were followers rather than leaders.

INLAY MATERIALS & TECHNIQUES

The art of inlay, or marquetry, is one of the fine and delicate areas of woodworking. It is still woodworking, and most general principles apply, but the scale is much finer and the materials more precious. The presence of metal in some of these designs throws in an entirely different material, increasing the degree of difficulty and requiring an understanding that metal does not behave the same way as wood. Since the original publication of *Shop Drawings for Craftsman Inlays & Hardware*, a number of craftsmen have started offering assembled versions of some of these designs, made with laser or CNC machines. If you want the look, but would rather buy than make, these sources are worth consideration.

The current L. & J. G. Stickley Company has also introduced several pieces that include these designs and mention Harvey Ellis' name. Modern manufacturing has made it possible to include these inlays without the costs of the handwork in the originals, and many of these pieces are not reproductions of period pieces but new designs.

The designs presented in this book were the work of master craftsmen who had served long apprenticeships and who were specialists in this art. Good quality reproductions will require skill, practice and patience on the part of the maker. What follows are general techniques and some specific suggestions based on the uniqueness of these designs, but I highly recommend that the beginner research the art of inlay and marquetry, take some classes, and practice, practice, practice.

Technically the designs in this book are marquetry; all of the individual pieces are assembled in to a single piece, which is then applied to a substrate. A true inlay is a piece of contrasting material let into a routed recess in the background material. Because the term "inlay" is used so much in reference to these designs, I have chosen to perpetuate this technical error in the interests of continuity, and because the distinction between the two terms is disappearing from common use.

An incredible variety of wood species and cuts are available as veneers, much more so than with solid material. There are logs that contain truly unique color and figure, and it makes sense to make the best use of this rare material by using thin veneers to cover otherwise plain surfaces. In designs that are entirely of wood, it makes sense to use commercially sliced veneers. The difficulty that arises in the designs in this book that contain metal elements is that of thickness.

Commercial veneers are cut as thin as is possible, and will likely be thinner than available sheet metal. All of the elements need to be the same finished thickness. The easiest way to accomplish this is to do what George Jones, the original manufacturer, did: cut the veneer to the thickness of the available metal.

A decent quality band saw with a good fence and some practice in technique can be utilized to produce your own veneer. Many band saws will drift or produce a cut at a slight angle, especially when resawing. Determining the angle of drift and setting the fence to that angle will help to produce uniform slices of veneer. Small thicknessing sanders are the best choice for bringing the resawn veneer to final thickness. Temporarily attaching the veneer to a piece of MDF with double-sided tape will help to prevent the veneer from being damaged during sanding. Without a thicknessing sander, a cabinet scraper or a plane can be used to remove the saw marks from the veneer, but it can be difficult to achieve a precise and uniform thickness by hand.

For cutting the pieces of veneer to the shapes in the patterns, one of two tools is generally used: a knife, or a saw. An X-Acto knife, or a small surgical scalpel, is commonly used. The main difficulties associated with using a knife are the ability to make tight smooth curves, and the tendency of the knife blade to make a V-shaped cut. Cutting from the back instead of the front will give a better fit, but the knife is best suited to cutting straight lines where the material can be scored by making several passes on the same line.

Sawing of patterns may be done either by hand, or with a power scroll saw. Blades for coping saws are too thick to produce cuts of the quality needed, so the appropriate tool is a fret saw, or a jewelers saw, equipped with a thinner blade. Blade selection will be a compromise between making a fine cut, and too-easy breaking of the blades. These blades are quite thin and prone to break; only experimentation will determine how often is too often.

In use, a flat piece of wood with a V-shaped notch in the front, called a "bird's mouth," is used to support the veneer being cut. The saw is held near the apex of the opening, and moved up and down while held steady at a consistent angle. The material is guided by the other hand and moved into the saw blade. The skill to be mastered in sawing by hand is keeping the saw moving at the proper angle and speed with one hand, while guiding the work with the other hand.

Powered scroll saws will allow the worker to concentrate mainly on guiding the work, and will be faster and more consistent than sawing by hand. An appropriate saw should have variable speed, adjustable blade tension, and the ability to mount very thin blades.

When working with veneer only, the best way to ensure a good fit is to cut two adjoining pieces at the same time. This is quite difficult to do with a knife, especially on curves, but is relatively easy when sawing, either by hand or with a powered scroll saw. The key to getting a perfect fit is to saw at a slight angle. Ideally, the blade angle should compensate for the distance taken up by the kerf of the cut. This angle will be in the neighborhood of 12° to 13° degrees, but will vary depending on both the thickness of the material, and the thickness of the saw blade.

Sometimes the entire pattern can be cut at once, stacking the various veneers in layers, but for most of these designs it will be more practical to cut some pieces together, and then to use these as patterns for the next cut. In many of the designs veneer pieces of the same species are adjacent to each other, and the effect is achieved by variances in grain direction. As the pieces are cut, they can be placed together on top of a reference pattern. Plan your work so that the largest pieces are cut first. It is often helpful to cut a large, background piece in half, fit the interior pieces to each half, and then reassemble the two halves. For perfect circles, the veneer background may be held down to a wood scrap with double-sided tape, and then drilled with a Forstner bit.

Metal elements should be cut first: they are usually the largest elements in the piece and are more difficult to adjust than the adjacent veneer pieces. Care must be taken to not scratch the metals. Veneers should be sanded on their face before assembly, so that adjacent metal is not damaged. As the pieces are cut and fit into place, and sections of the pattern are completed, they can be held together with tape. Assembly can be done face up or face down but I prefer working face up so that the finished appearance can be seen. The advantage of face down assembly is that the back side can be sanded if all of the parts are not of uniform thickness.

This is a good way to work when the pattern is composed of all veneers, but sanding wood and metal at the same time is not a good idea because the metal is liable to heat and expand. Then it will either distort, or force the joints apart, and if run through a thicknessing sander, bits of metal will wind up in the abrasive material, only to be forced into the next piece of wood to be run through the machine.

As an alternative to sawing, the use of a CNC router or laser should be considered. I'm not recommending that the hobbyist woodworker run out and spend several thousands of dollars on a machine for one or two projects, but the professional trying to make a living ought to consider either purchasing a small machine, or contracting out the cutting of marquetry parts. Many relatively small professional shops have CNC machinery for such work, and the accuracy and speed of these machines could make this a reasonable choice.

When all of the pieces have been fit and taped together, they need to be applied to the substrate. Generally, the substrate is part of the finished piece of furniture, although in some instances a backing veneer might be used. Some of the smaller patterns might be inlaid into a larger solid-wood piece, but most should include a background piece of veneer large enough to cover the entire furniture part. The opposite side of the board should also be veneered, with a single piece of the same species as the background veneer surrounding the marquetry pattern. These pieces should be pressed in a veneer press, by clamping between thick pieces of particleboard or MDF, or with a vacuum bag system. Glues used should be plastic resin, urea formaldehyde, or reactive polyurethane. Water-based glues, such as the familiar white or yellow woodworking glues, should not be used because the moisture can cause either the veneers to buckle, or the substrate to warp, or both.

NOTES ON THE INLAY DRAWINGS

The drawings in this book were prepared by scanning photographs of the original inlays, and importing the digital images into AutoCAD. The outlines of the various forms within the designs were then drawn over the image. This gives an extremely accurate reproduction, but in some cases 100% accuracy is not possible. The angle of the point of view of the camera must be considered, and the drawing adjusted accordingly. This adjustment was a judgment call on my part, based on as many photographs as I could observe, and on my recollection of original pieces I have seen. They are as close to the originals as I could make them, but there will be some minor variations, many due to the quality and point of view of the original images I had to work with.

For most of the designs, I had photographs that were good enough to allow me to view the image at a resolution several times larger than the actual size of the inlay. At this scale, manufacturing imperfections were evident that would not normally be seen. It was interesting to discover places where one too many strokes had been taken with a saw or file, or where a small gap had been filled. In preparing these drawings, I have not included these minor imperfections. I do point them out, however, so today's craftsman can realize excellent work is never perfect and the things that can go wrong when making a reproduction often went wrong when the originals were produced.

My hope was to present all of the designs at full size, but the constraints of the printed format of this book make that impossible. Where the original designs are too large to be presented at full scale on a single page, they are shown in two versions—a scale image of the entire design, plus full-size details. Break marks on the drawings indicate where the details fit in the complete design. The original inlays were often used on more than one piece of furniture, usually with variations in size. In making a reproduction of any of these designs, it may be necessary to adjust the size of the drawings slightly. The easiest way to do this is with a copy machine, setting the zoom control to get a larger or smaller image.

Employees of copying services are often reluctant to make copies of copyrighted material such as this book.

My intention in presenting these designs is to allow the use of these patterns by the modern craftsman wishing to reproduce them. You may have to show this paragraph to the copy shop employee to demonstrate to them that such photocopying is fair use of this material. All other aspects of copyright law apply to the balance of this work.

There was also variation in the materials used in the originals. Some examples that contained metal elements were also produced in veneer only, and with different combinations of materials. In the drawings, different materials are represented by the way different areas of the drawing are filled in, or to use the AutoCAD term, "hatched." I have indicated the various woods only as light and dark, and in some cases as burls, rather than indicating particular species of veneers. Remember the original designs were mainly prototypes. Some of the drawings will contain a notation that the "colors and materials are speculative." This means the source image was not detailed enough to make an accurate determination of the actual materials.

I don't believe the existing references on materials are reliably accurate, so I will leave it to the individual maker to decide what wood species to use. The maker should choose a combination that is pleasing to the eye, and suited to the finished piece of furniture of which it will be part. The areas of the drawings that are not obviously wood grain were metal in the originals, usually copper or pewter. Copper sheet is relatively easy to obtain in appropriate sizes, but to the best of my knowledge, pewter is not. Any silver-colored metal could be substituted, such as aluminum, nickel silver, or sterling silver. Where two metals occur in the same design, there will be an indication as to which pattern represents copper, and which represents pewter. In a few instances, the only photos available were in black and white, and the exact metal used is not known. My best guess is that these were pewter, but other metals could be used with equal effect.

There are many ways to transfer the patterns of the designs to the materials to be cut. A photocopy should be made to start with, rather than marking and cutting from the pages of the book. Some older copy machines will produce an image slightly larger or smaller than the original image. Carbon paper, which is becoming a rare commodity, also can be used, or the back of the image can be rubbed with a soft lead pencil and the image then traced. The copy itself can be attached to the material with rubber cement, thus eliminating the step of tracing each line individually.

Digital versions of the inlay patterns are available in DXF file format from the author's website, readwatchdo.com.

Chapter 6
Hardware

As Gustav Stickley's company grew, he brought in-house the working of leather and textiles for upholstery, and metal work for the production of furniture hardware as well as for decorative and architectural items such as light fixtures and fireplace hoods. Much of this work was available in wrought iron and brass, but hammered copper was the dominant metal used. Just as quartersawn white oak became the typical wood for Craftsman furniture, hand-hammered copper became the preferred metal for hardware.

The manufactured, mass-produced hardware of the day was too delicate and fussy to fit with Stickley's furniture. He felt the need to complete the furniture with these rugged, elemental designs. The hammered texture and gradual oxidation of the copper was a harmonious addition to the Craftsman aesthetic. Like most areas of Stickley's work, the designs evolved over time and experiments and variations took place from year to year. Original Craftsman hardware was, like the furniture, relatively simple in design but fabricated in a way that displayed a high degree of craftsmanship and attention to detail.

Stickley made his hardware available for purchase by those who built their own furniture and his metal shop performed custom architectural work as well. *The Craftsman* magazine featured articles on working metal as a hobby; usually the designing and making of decorative copper items. Hinges and pulls were occasionally mentioned, usually accompanying an article on furniture construction, with very brief instructions. This was possibly because the construction of the hardware was relatively simple compared to the other projects presented.

The construction of the hardware is relatively simple, but a good deal of practice will be needed to achieve results of decent quality. Most of the pulls consist of a textured back plate, a bail, and two posts that hold the bail. The most common form seen on Craftsman furniture was the V-shaped pull, as seen in the drawing on page 315, but the construction process is much the same for all the designs.

In an article in *The Craftsman*,[23] the following list of tools and equipment was recommended:

The models for metal work shown this month are all simple, but, without exception, interesting. While not requiring any great amount of skill, they will give the amateur metal worker plenty to do if they are to be finished in a workmanlike way.

In the first place, before beginning even the simplest piece of metal work, the student requires the following list of tools:

1 bench anvil about 2" by 6" face.
1 vise—3½" jaws.
*1 hand drill press 18" high
    (drills generally come with small presses).*
1 piece of lead about 6" square and 1" thick.
1 ¾ lb. ball-peen hammer.
1 1½ lb. ball-peen hammer.
1 hacksaw, frame and blades.
1 pair tin snips, about 10" or 12" long.
*1 Bunsen burner and hose. (Nail sets can be
    annealed and hammered into a small chisel
    or punches as desired.)*
1 center punch.
1 cold chisel ¼" wide.
1 cold chisel ½" wide.
*1 ball iron to clamp in vise for hammering
    concave pieces.*
1 piece of iron ¾" sq. and 10" long, (for riveting).
*1 piece of iron ¾" diameter, round, 10" long,
    (for use in riveting).*
1 steel square.
1 2-foot rule.
1 pair of long flat-nose pliers.
*1 pair of end-cutting nippers
    (cutting off tacks, etc.).*
1 small screwdriver.
1 medium-size screwdriver.
1 pair steel dividers.
1 8" flat bastard file.
1 6" half-round bastard file.
1 6" round bastard file.
1 8" half-round smooth file.
Emery cloth of different surfaces.
Powdered pumice stone.

Most items will be needed to fabricate reproductions of Craftsman hardware, although there are a few only required for forming round items. A propane torch would be equivalent of the Bunsen burner suggested in the list.

Finding materials locally may be tough. One online source is www.onlinemetals.com. They do not offer a printed catalog, but their website is comprehensive and easy to navigate. The back plates for the hardware are just over one-sixteenth of an inch thick, and this equates to 14-gauge copper sheet (.086"). Cut with a good pair of tin snips, or a metal cutting blade in a jeweler's saw. Bails can be wrought from bar stock or cast.

Copper is an easy metal to work with due to its relative softness, and unlike iron, it is worked cold. It is not necessary to heat copper in order to change its shape or texture by hammering. Copper will become harder as it is being worked, so it needs to be annealed—heated to a bright red color and then rinsed in water and dried with a clean cloth, before and during working it.

Cutting the copper sheet will likely distort it, so it must be flattened before working and the rough edges must be filed smooth. Pieces can be flattened by placing them on a hard, flat surface, covering them with a block of hard wood, and hammering on the wood. This will keep the workpiece from being dented, and from becoming work hardened. Clean up rough edges with a file, which will leave a small burr. Remove the burr by pushing it along the edge of the metal with a piece of steel, such as a burnisher.

For hammering in the texture, place the copper on a flat surface that will absorb some of the force from the hammer. Use the lead block, a piece of wood covered with a few layers of wet burlap, or a stack of wet newspaper. Hammer marks should not show on the back of the piece; finding the right combination of work surface and applied force can take practice. Use the flat end of the ball peen hammer and be certain it is smooth. Remove sharp corners with a file or sandpaper, and polish the head.

Starting at one corner, make hammer marks evenly across the piece. Work in a steady rhythm, crisscrossing the piece until the area has been hammered evenly. If one area receives more hammer blows than another, the metal distorts and buckles due to the metal stretching in that area. Correct the problem by hammering around the perimeter of the stretched area. The final step is to hammer evenly around the edges, striking at a slight angle around the perimeter. It will likely be necessary to anneal the piece during the hammering process. If the copper becomes too brittle, it is possible to crack or pierce it.

After satisfactorily hammering the back plate, drill holes for the mounting screws and the bail holders. Forge the bail from either bar or rod worked cold on a small anvil, and anneal as often as is needed. The ends of the bail that fit in the holes of the bail holders should be filed round and roughly one-thirty-second of an inch smaller in diameter than the holes in which they fit. The fit should be slightly loose, but not sloppy.

Forging the bails is the most time consuming and difficult part of the process, and if more than a few are needed it would be more efficient to cast them in sand. This was the method used for the original factory produced pulls, and it will yield more consistent results, particularly with the difficult-to-forge V-shaped pulls.

The bail holders are bar stock cut to size with the top edges rounded by a bench grinder and files. Before shaping, drill holes for the bail ends and holes in the bottom for a small piece of rod that passes through the base plate and is then peened over as a rivet. After forming the parts, place the ends of the bails in the holes in the bail holders and the bail holders in position on the back plate, and insert the small pieces of rod through the holes in the base plate and into the holes in the bottom of the bail holders. With everything in place and working from the back, solder the bail holders to the back plate. Clean and flux the joints and use just enough solder to hold the joint together and hammer the rods extending through the back plate flat to secure.

Clean the hardware with a damp cloth and pumice, followed by clear water. Do not leave fingerprints on the piece because they will show later on. An aged patina—the color of an old penny—is appropriate. *The Craftsman* recommended heating the work over an open flame until reaching the desired color. If the color goes too dark, repeat the cleaning with pumice to lighten up the piece and to highlight the high spots. An aged, oxidized look is desired, so do not coat the hardware—allow it to mellow with time.

Chemical solutions are available for cleaning the metal and achieving the desired color. These are generally available at jeweler's supply or craft supply stores. Experiment first on scrap metal.

The hardware drawings beginning on page 312 are at full size, although there is and should be some small variation from piece to piece, as in the original examples and in reproductions. The numbers reflect Stickley's numbers used in Craftsman hardware catalogs. Pieces shown with keyhole cutouts were also made with a plain back plate. If using these with a lock, the lock should be obtained so the escutcheon will be the correct size. Drill a hole to start the cuts, then finish with a jeweler's saw and files.

Chapter 7
Shop Drawings

Image courtesy University of Wisconsin Digital Collections

A Craftsman living room showing a recessed window seat. (The Craftsman, October 1905.)

Drawings are the language of building, and are far better at communicating the subtle relationships between the parts of a piece of furniture than words. The pieces on the following pages are all excellent examples of designs that seem simple at first glance, but are complex compositions of line, proportion, and form. Drawings simplify three-dimensional objects by making us consider things in only two dimensions at a time. This leads to a deeper understanding of the underlying principles that set these pieces apart and give them lasting value. Time spent with the drawings will be repaid with confidence during construction.

Craftsman Dining Room Furnishings

Image courtesy University of Wisconsin Digital Collections

A Craftsman dining room, with built-in sideboard and recessed window. (The Craftsman, November 1905.)

Next to the living room, the most important division of the lower floor of a house is the dining room. The living room is the gathering place of the household, the place for work as well as for pleasure and rest, but the dining room is the center of hospitality and good cheer, and should hold a special welcome for guests and home folk alike. Instead of being planned to fulfill manifold functions like the living room, it has one definite use and purpose, and no disturbing element should be allowed to creep in.

Gustav Stickley
The Craftsman, November 1905

Preparing a good meal is remarkably similar to making a piece of furniture—there is a process of planning, preparing, and arranging numerous bits and pieces into a single creative effort. To be successful, everything needs to come together in the correct sequence, with all the parts in harmony. The biggest difference is that a meal is intended to be a singular event, leaving only a satisfying memory, while good furniture is intended to last. Craftsman designs for dining furniture can be considered as a recipe for creating an environment that makes every meal a special event. The ingredients are simple and natural, and they are combined in the right proportions to ensure satisfaction for all of the senses.

Can the environment improve the experience of eating a simple meal? Think of fresh seafood consumed within the sight and salt air of the ocean, or a Dutch oven-prepared stew on a camping trip and the answer is obvious. One of the noteworthy features of the pieces on the following pages is the way their designs place them in a supporting role. Even though some of them have a commanding presence, the food and the shared experience are the focus of attention, not the furniture. This doesn't diminish the value of these pieces—in fact, it enhances it. The

goal isn't to show off the furniture, the furniture serves to promote "hospitality and good cheer."

In January 1902, Stickley suggested to readers of *The Craftsman* that they should examine furniture in the same way they would examine prospective friends, to look for moral and agreeable qualities in both. That may seem like an odd way to look at furniture, but walk into any furniture store and liars and frauds—pieces that look nice at first but soon reveal their lack of substance, quality, and good taste—are common. What will become of us if we eat meals and entertain friends in such poor company?

A few lines later he writes of the good feelings that "possesses us whenever some one of our belongings affords us a moment of comfort or of aesthetic pleasure, which we have neither demanded or expected." The effort to make a table and a set of chairs, or a sideboard or china cabinet requires a personal investment—of time, attention to detail, and dedication to the results. The resulting objects are far more than a seat and a surface for your dinner plate, they become a reminder of the value of building well and building to last. The best companions are those friends who can remind us of the best qualities within us. Craftsman furniture is that kind of companion.

GUSTAV STICKLEY
NO. 386 ARM CHAIR

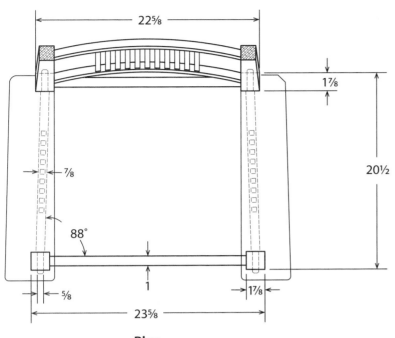

Plan

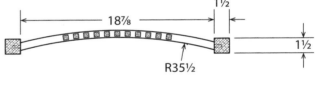

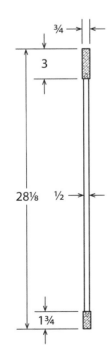

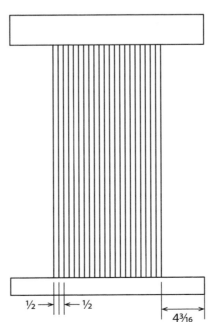

True Views of Back

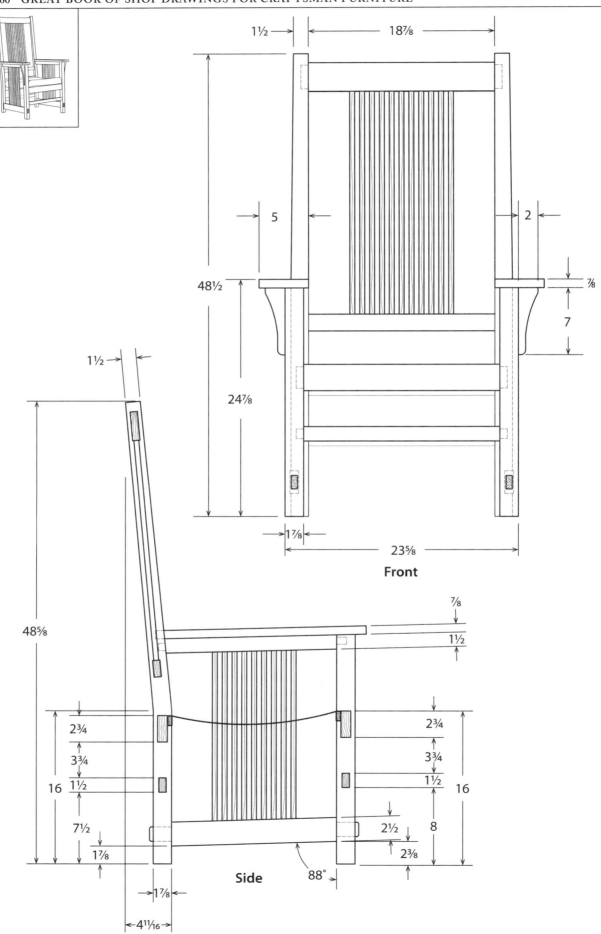

Front

Side

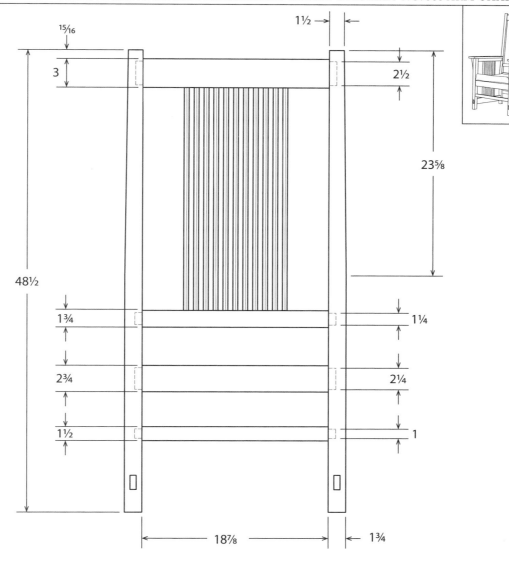

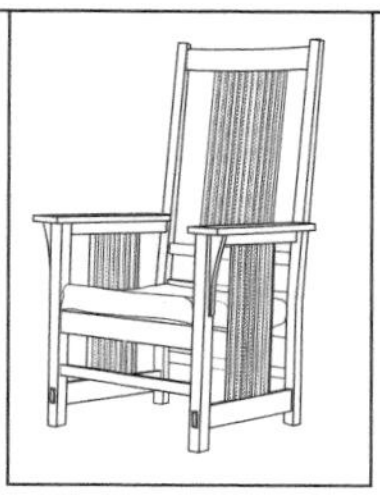

Front Section at Back of Chair

Gustav Stickley No. 386 Arm Chair

Qty	Part	Size	Notes
2	Front Legs	1⅞ x 1⅞ x 24	
2	Back Legs	1¾ x 4¹¹⁄₁₆ x 48⅝	do full-size layout
1	Back Bottom Stretcher	¾ x 1½ x 20⅜	18⅞ between tenons
1	Back Stretcher @ Seat	1 x 2¾ x 20⅜	18⅞ between tenons
1	Curved Back Top Stretcher	¾ x 3 x 22	make long for bending— 35½ inside radius, 18⅞ between tenons
1	Curved Back Bot. Stretcher	¾ x 1¾ x 22	
11	Back Spindles	½ x ½ x 24⅜	23⅜ between tenons
1	Front Bottom Stretcher	¾ x 1½ x 21⅞	19⅞ between tenons
1	Front Stretcher @ Seat	1 x 2¾ x 21⅞	19⅞ between tenons
2	Lower Side Stretchers	⅞ x 2½ x 21½	16¾ between angled tenons—do full-size layout to determine exact size and angle
2	Upper Side Stretchers	⅞ x 1½ x 19½	17⅝ between angled tenons—do full-size layout
18	Side Spindles	½ x ½ x 18⁹⁄₁₆	17⁹⁄₁₆ between angled tenons—do full-size layout
2	Arms	⅞ x 5 x 22½	notch corner @ back leg
2	Canvas Cleats	½ x 1 x 18½	

GUSTAV STICKLEY NO. 384 SIDE CHAIR

The seat cushions rest on a canvas or leather sling attached to the front and back rails with a narrow wooden cleat. Not much wood, but lots of mortises. Make full-size templates of the legs to be sure of the locations of the rails and stretchers.

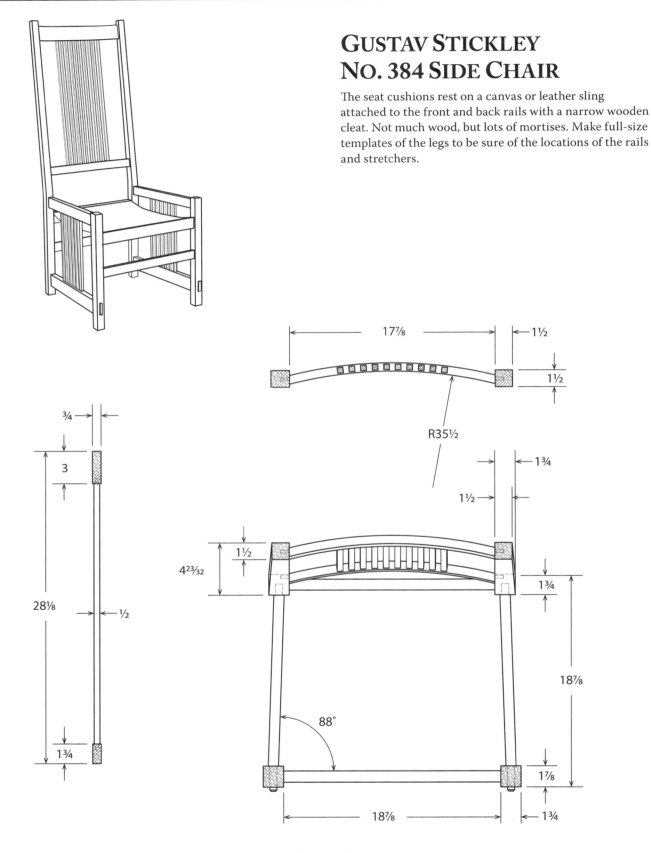

Seat and Back Plan

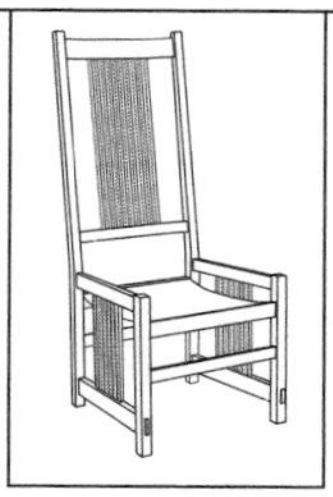

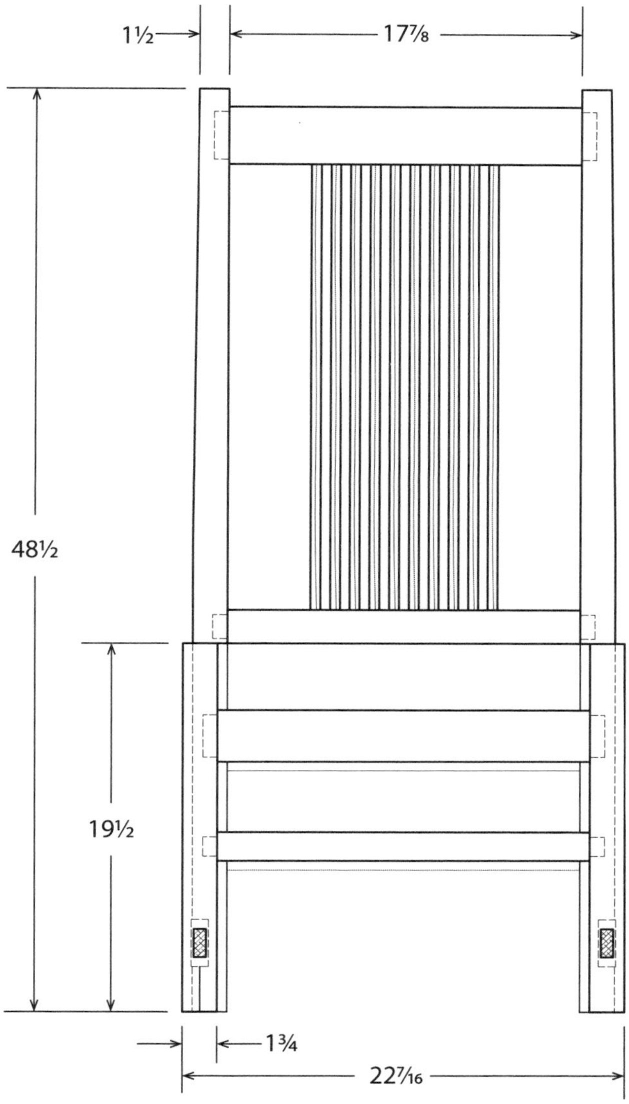
1½
17⅞
48½
19½
1¾
22 7⁄16

Front

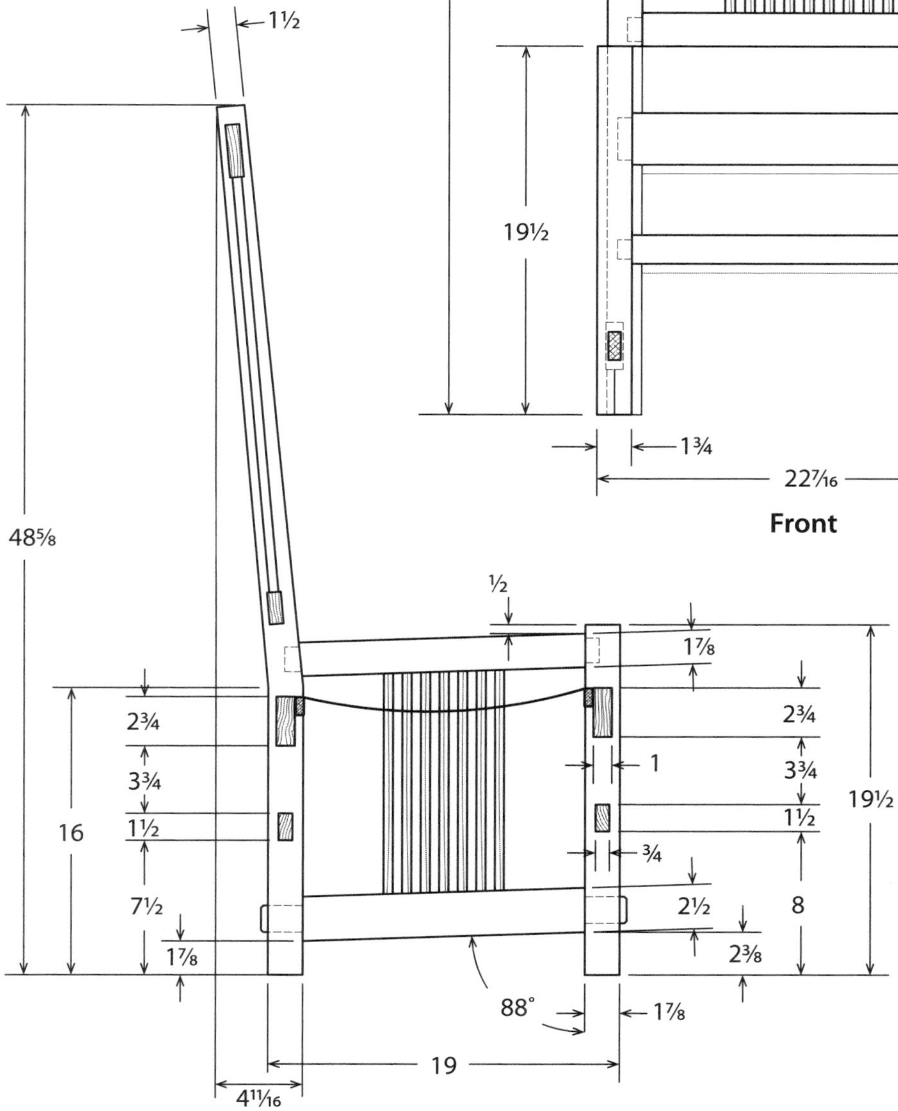
1½
48⅝
½
1⅞
2¾
2¾
3¾
1
3¾
1½
1½
16
¾
7½
2½
8
19½
1⅞
2⅜
88°
1⅞
19
4 11⁄16

Side

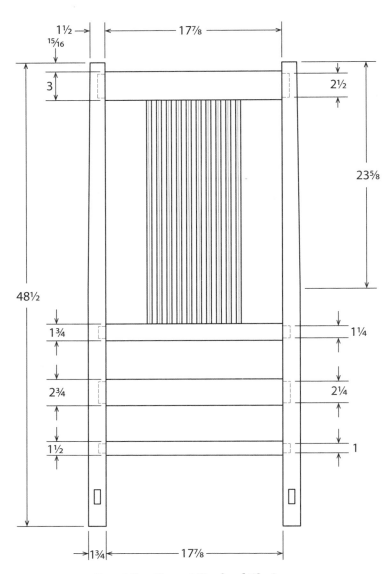

Front Section at Back of Chair

Gustav Stickley No. 384 Side Chair

Qty	Part	Size	Notes
2	Front Legs	1¾ x 1¾ x 19½	
2	Back Legs	1¾ x 4¹¹⁄₁₆ x 48⅝	do full-size layout
1	Back Bottom Stretcher	¾ x 1½ x 19⅜	17⅞ between tenons
1	Back Stretcher @ Seat	1 x 2½ x 19⅜	17⅞ between tenons
1	Curved Back Top Stretcher	¾ x 3 x 20½	make long for bending—35½ inside radius, 17⅞ between tenons
1	Curved Back Bot Stretcher	¾ x 1¾ x 20½	
10	Back Spindles	½ x ½ x 24⅜	23⅜ between tenons
1	Front Bottom Stretcher	¾ x 1½ x 20⅜	17⅞ between tenons
1	Front Stretcher @ Seat	1 x 2¾ x 20⅜	17⅞ between tenons
2	Lower Side Stretchers	⅞ x 2½ x 20½	15¼ between angled tenons—do full-size layout to determine exact size and angle
2	Upper Side Stretchers	⅞ x 1⅞ x 17¾	15⅝ between angled tenons—do full-size layout
14	Side Spindles	½ x ½ x 13¼	12¼ between angled tenons—do full-size layout
2	Canvas Cleats	½ x 1 x 17	

GUSTAV STICKLEY NO. 353 SIDE CHAIR NO. 353A ARM CHAIR

The seat cushion is a slip seat—either a hardwood frame, or a piece of plywood covered with padding and then wrapped with fabric. After the chair is finished, the completed seat is attached with screws through the corner blocks from underneath.

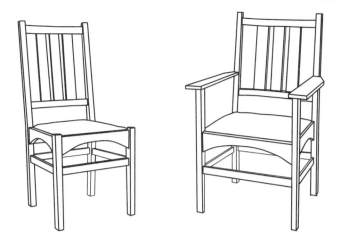

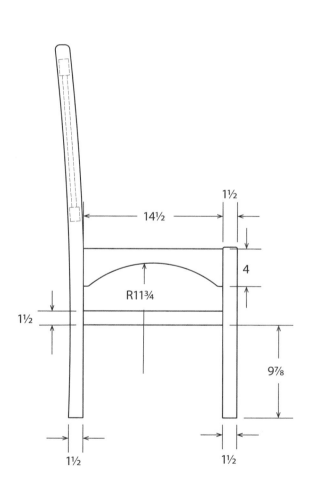

Side Elevation

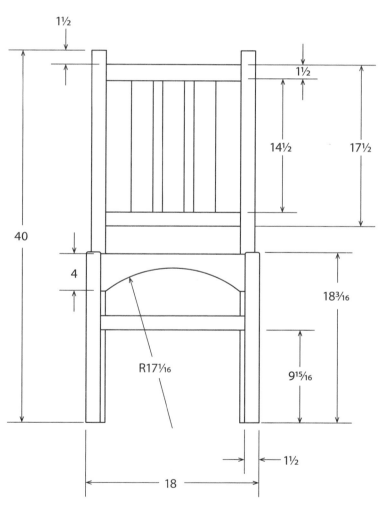

Front Elevation

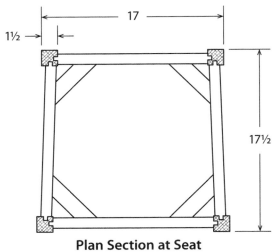

Plan Section at Seat

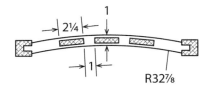

Plan Section Through Back

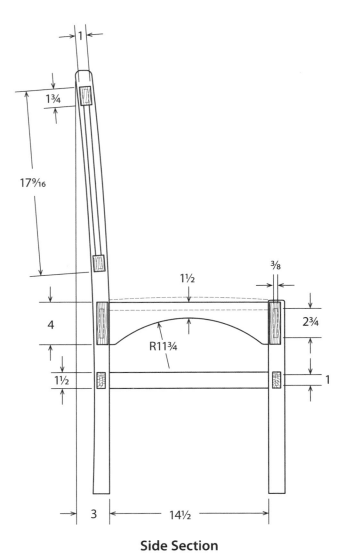

Side Section

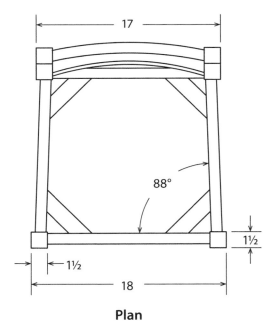

Plan

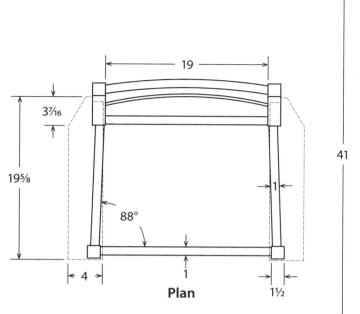

Plan

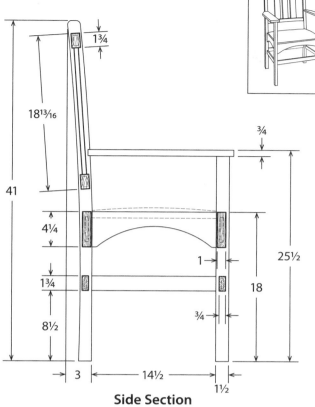

Side Section

Gustav Stickley No. 353 Side Chair

Qty	Part	Size	Notes
2	Front Legs	1½ x 1½ x 18³⁄₁₆	
2	Back Legs	1½ x 3 x 40	
1	Lower Front Rail	¾ x 1½ x 16	15 between tenons
1	Arched Front Rail	1 x 4 x 16	15 between tenons
1	Lower Back Rail	¾ x 1½ x 15	14 between tenons
1	Arched Back Rail	1 x 4 x 15	14 between tenons
2	Lower Side Rails	¾ x 1½ x 15½	14½ between tenons
2	Arched Side Rails	1 x 4 x 15½	14½ between tenons
1	Top Curved Back Rail	1 x 1¾ x 15	14 between tenons make longer for bending
1	Bottom Curved Back Rail	1 x 1½ x 15	14 between tenons make longer for bending
3	Back Slats	½ x 2¼ x 15⁵⁄₁₆	14⁵⁄₁₆ between tenons

Gustav Stickley No. 353A Arm Chair

Qty	Part	Size	Notes
2	Front Legs	1½ x 1½ x 25⅞	25½ below arm
2	Back Legs	1½ x 3 x 41	
1	Lower Front Rail	¾ x 1¾ x 21	20 between tenons
1	Arched Front Rail	1 x 4¼ x 21	20 between tenons
1	Lower Back Rail	¾ x 1¾ x 20	19 between tenons
1	Arched Back Rail	1 x 4¼ x 20	19 between tenons
2	Lower Side Rails	¾ x 1¾ x 15½	14½ between tenons
2	Arched Side Rails	1 x 4½ x 15½	14½ between tenons
2	Curved Back Rails	1 x 1¾ x 20½	19 between tenons—make longer for bending
3	Back Slats	½ x 2¾ x 16⁵⁄₁₆	15⁵⁄₁₆ between tenons
2	Arms	¾ x 4 x 19⅝	

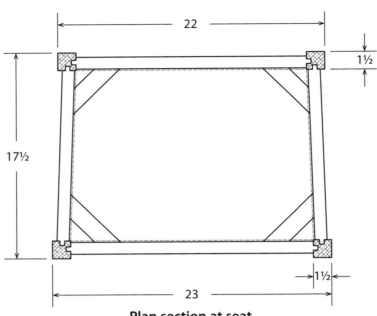

22

1½

17½

1½

23

Plan section at seat

2¾   1   1½

R60¼

1

Plan Section Through Back

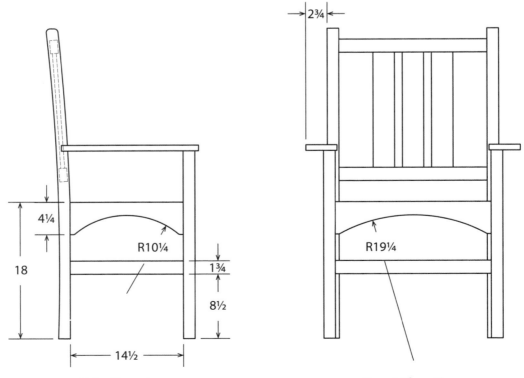

2¾

4¼

R10¼

18

1¾

8½

14½

R19¼

Side Elevation

Front Elevation

GUSTAV STICKLEY
NO. 800 SIDEBOARD

39" high x 54" wide x 21" deep

Originally produced in 1903, this Harvey Ellis design
is much lighter in feel than many Stickley pieces, while
providing a good deal of storage in a relatively small space.

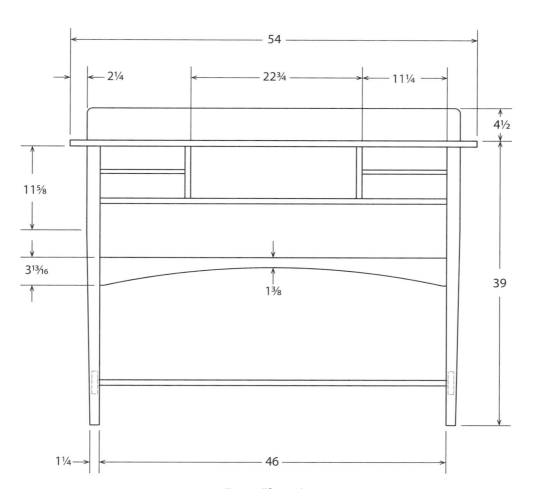

Front Elevation

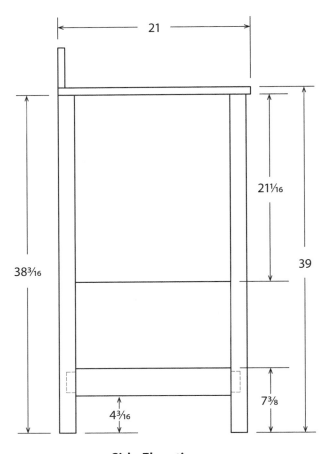

Side Elevation

Gustav Stickley No. 800 Sideboard

Qty	Part	Size	Notes
4	Legs	1¾ x 1¾ x 38³⁄₁₆	
1	Top	1³⁄₁₆ x 21 x 54	
1	Backsplash	¾ x 4½ x 49½	
2	Side Stretchers	¾ x 3⅛ x 19	17 between tenons
1	Shelf	¾ x 15⅞ x 47¼	46½ between tenons
2	Side Panels	¾ x 17¾ x 21¹⁄₁₆	17 exposed
1	Back Panel	¾ x 16½ x 46¾	46 exposed
1	Shelf Below Drawers	¾ x 19½ x 46¾	
1	Arched Front Apron	¾ x 31³⁄₁₆ x 47	46 between tenons
1	Front Rail	¾ x 2 x 46½	46 between tenons
2	Drawer Rails	⅝ x 2 x 11¾	11¼ between tenons
2	Drawer Dividers	¾ x 2 x 7³⁄₁₆	
1	Bottom Drawer Front	¾ x 7⅜ x 46	opening
1	Center Drawer Front	¾ x 7³⁄₁₆ x 22	opening
2	Drawer Fronts	¾ x 3⅜ x 11¼	opening
2	Drawer Fronts	¾ x 3⅛ x 11¼	opening

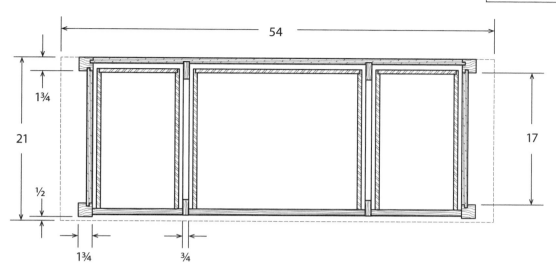

Plan Section

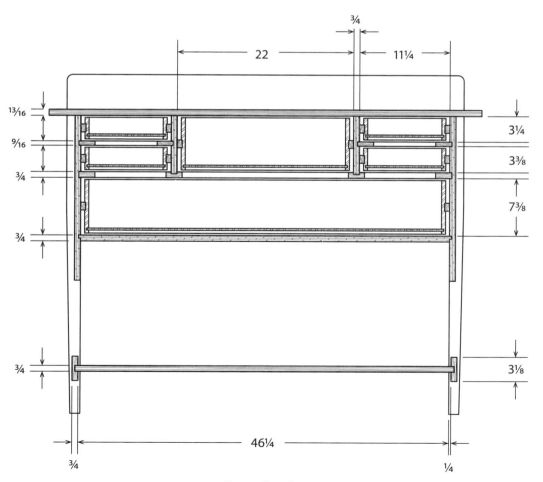

Front Section

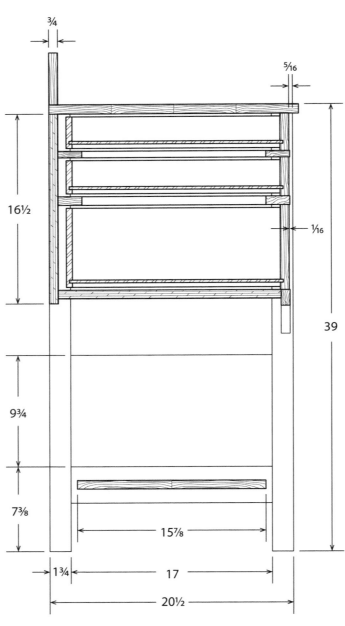

Side Section

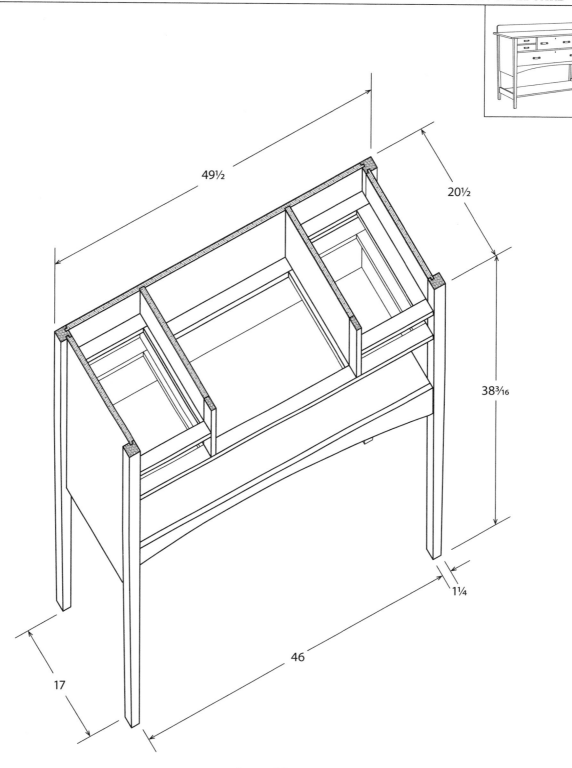

Assembly

GUSTAV STICKLEY
NO. 802 SIDEBOARD

36" high x 42" wide x 18" deep

This is one of the few pieces that has a rail above the drawers. The back rail under the top has no arch.

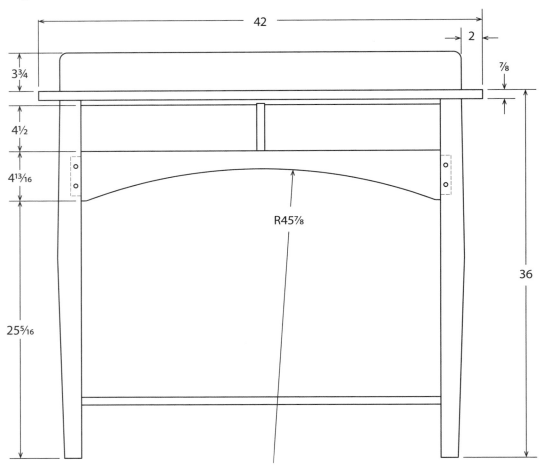

42

2

3¾

⅞

4½

4¹³⁄₁₆

R45⅞

36

25⁵⁄₁₆

Front

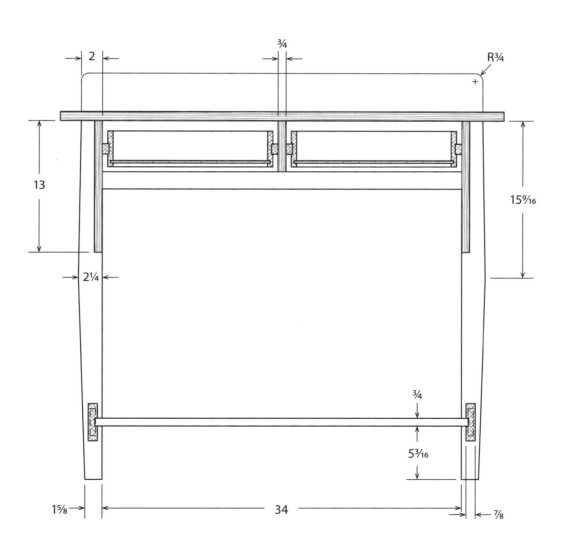

Front Section

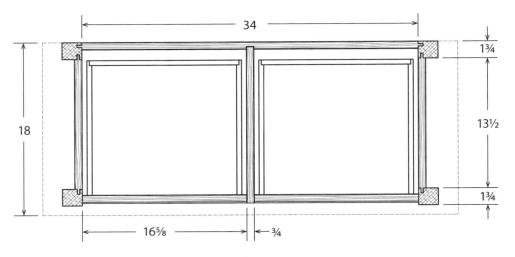

Plan

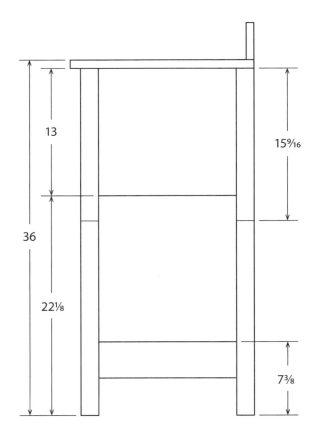

Side

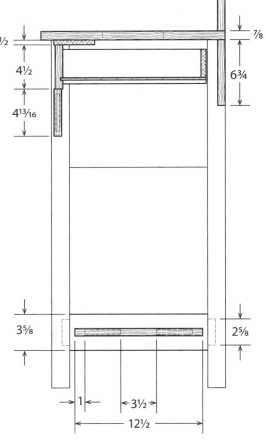

Side Section

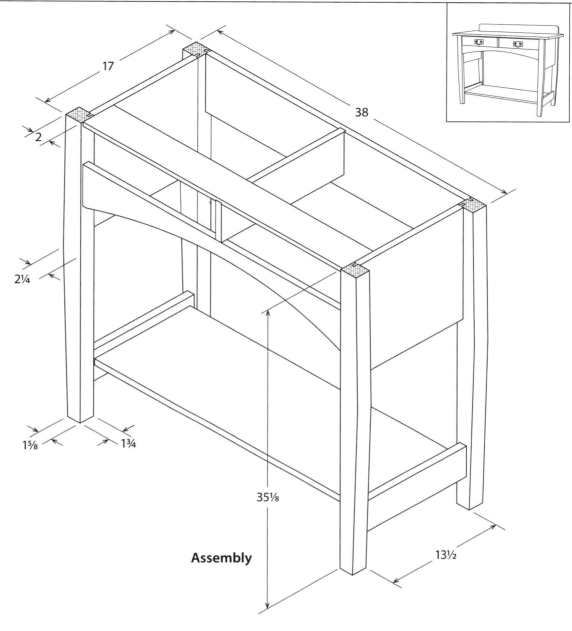

17

38

2

2¼

1⅝   1¾

35⅛

13½

Assembly

Gustav Stickley No. 802 Sideboard

QTY	PART	SIZE	NOTES
1	Top	⅞ x 18 x 42	
4	Legs	1¾ x 2¼ x 35⅛	tapered
2	Side Panels	¾ x 15 x 13	
1	Back Rail	¾ x 6¾ x 35½	34 between tongues
1	Middle Divider	¾ x 5 x 16¼	
1	Top Front Rail	½ x 4 x 34	pocket screw or biscuit to leg & panel, or add for tenons
1	Stretcher below Drawers	¾ x 4¹³⁄₁₆ x 36	34 between tenons
2	Drawer Fronts	¾ x 4½ x 16⅝	opening size—less gaps around drawers
1	Backsplash	¾ x 3⅝ x 38	
2	Bottom Stretchers	⅞ x 3⅝ x 15	13½ tenon to tenon
1	Bottom Shelf	¾ x 12½ x 35½	35 exposed

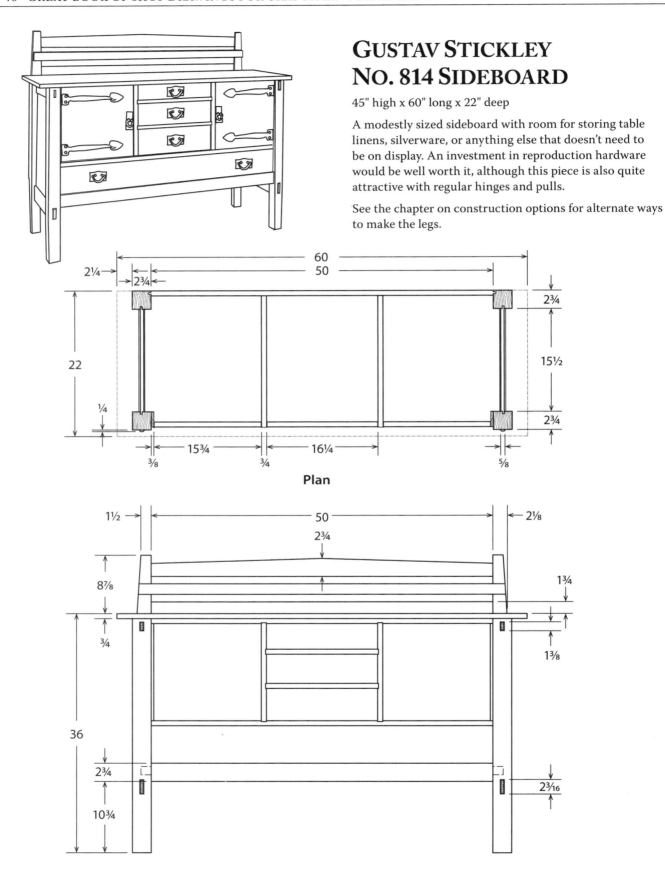

GUSTAV STICKLEY
NO. 814 SIDEBOARD

45" high x 60" long x 22" deep

A modestly sized sideboard with room for storing table linens, silverware, or anything else that doesn't need to be on display. An investment in reproduction hardware would be well worth it, although this piece is also quite attractive with regular hinges and pulls.

See the chapter on construction options for alternate ways to make the legs.

Plan

Front

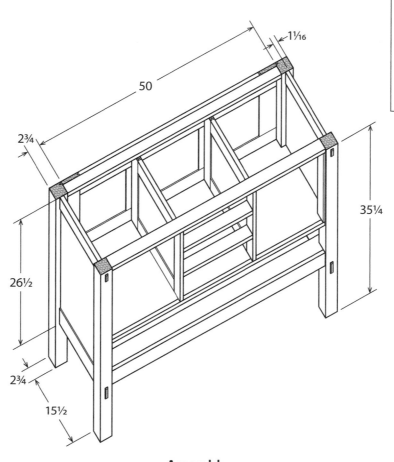

Assembly

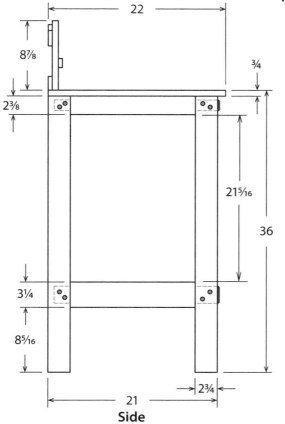

Side

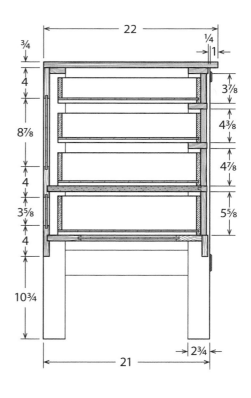

Side Section

Gustav Stickley No. 814 Sideboard

Qty	Part	Size	Notes
1	Top	¾ x 22 x 60	
4	Legs	2¾ x 2¾ x 35¼	
2	Top, Side Rail	¾ x 2⅜ x 20½	15½ between tenon shoulders
2	Bottom, Side Rail	¾ x 3¼ x 20½	15½ between tenon shoulders
2	Side Panels	½ x 16¼ x 22 1/16	15½ x 21 5/16 exposed
1	Bottom-Frame & Panel	¾ x 19½ x 52¾	parts detailed below—19¼ x 52 exposed—notch @ legs
1	Bottom Back Rail	¾ x 4¼ x 47½	46¾ between tenon shoulders
1	Bottom Front Rail	¾ x 3¼ x 47½	46¾ between tenon shoulders
2	Bottom End Stile	¾ x 3 x 19¼	
1	Bottom Mid Stile	¾ x 3 x 12½	11¾ between tenon shoulders
2	Bottom Panels	¼ x 12½ x 22⅝	11¾ x 21⅞ exposed
1	Back-frame & Panel	¾ x 24½ x 50¾	parts detailed below—24½ x 50 exposed
2	Outer Stiles	¾ x 4⅜ x 24½	4 exposed
2	Inner Stiles	¾ x 4 x 9⅝	8⅞ between tenon shoulders
3	Top, Mid, & Bottom Rail	¾ x 4 x 42¾	42 between tenon shoulders
3	Upper Back Panels	¼ x 9⅝ x 12 1/16	8⅞ x 11 5/16 exposed
1	Lower Back Panel	¼ x 4⅜ x 42¾	3⅝ x 42 exposed
1	Shelf	¾ x 19⅜ x 52¾	plywood—19⅛ x 52 exposed—notch @ legs
1	Shelf Edge	¾ x 1⅛ x 50	¼ x ⅜ tongue into groove in plywood
2	Divider Panels	¾ x 20½ x 15⅝	parts detailed below—20¼ x 15⅜ exposed—notch for top rail
4	Stiles	¾ x 3 x 15⅝	
4	Rails	¾ x 3 x 15¼	14½ between tenon shoulders
2	Panels	¼ x 15¼ x 10⅜	9⅝ x 14½ exposed
1	Front Apron	¾ x 2¾ x 53	50 between tenon shoulders
1	Front Top Rail	¾ x 2½ x 50	biscuit or pocket screw to legs, or add tenons
1	Back Top Rail	¾ x 2 x 50	biscuit or pocket screw to legs, or add tenons
2	Hinge Strips	⅜ x 2½ x 14⅝	
2	Doors	¾ x 15¾ x 14⅝	opening size—trim for desired gaps
1	Drawer Front	¾ x 4⅞ x 16¼	opening size—trim for desired gaps
1	Drawer Front	¾ x 4⅜ x 16¼	opening size—trim for desired gaps
1	Drawer Front	¾ x 3⅞ x 16¼	opening size—trim for desired gaps
1	Drawer Front	¾ x 5⅝ x 50	opening size—trim for desired gaps
2	Plate Rack Uprights	¾ x 2⅛ x 8⅞	taper to 1½
1	Plate Rack Top Rail	½ x 2¾ x 54¼	taper to 2 @ ends, trim flush to outer edge of uprights
2	Plate Rack Middle, Bottom Rail	½ x 1¾ x 54¼	trim flush to outer edge of uprights

GUSTAV STICKLEY
NO. 962 SERVER

36" high x 59¼" wide x 17" deep

This design appeared in 1902, and could be considered the granddaddy of Gustav Stickley's servers. In later years many variations on this theme were produced, usually in smaller versions, without the exposed joinery this piece features.

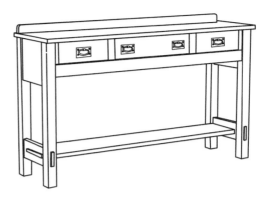

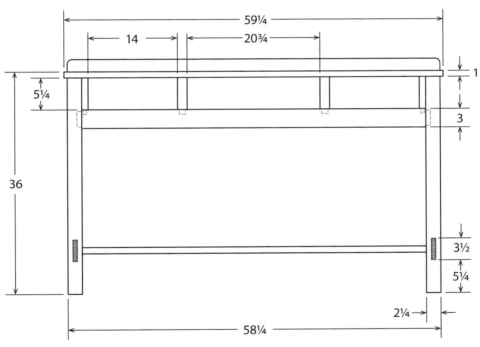

Front Elevation

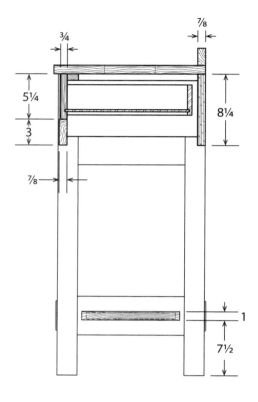

Side Section

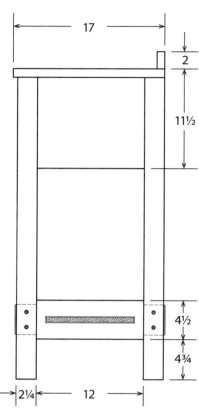

Side Elevation

Gustav Stickley No. 962 Server

Qty	Part	Size	Notes
4	Legs	2¼ x 2¼ x 35	
2	Rails	1¼ x 4½ x 17	12 between tenons
1	Lower Shelf	1 x 11 x 57½	55 between tenons
2	End Panels	¾ x 10½ x 13½	12 between tenons
1	Back Panel	¾ x 8¼ x 54½	53¾ between tenons
2	Dividers Between Drawers	¾ x 6½ x 14¾	
1	Front Rail	⅞ x 3 x 55¾	53¾ between tenons
1	Rail Above Drawers	¾ x 1½ x 54¾	53¾ between tenons
2	Vertical @ Drawers	¾ x 1 x 6	5¼ exposed
2	Vertical Between Drawers	¾ x 1½ x 6	5¼ exposed
2	Drawer Fronts	¾ x 5¼ x 14	opening
1	Drawer Front	¾ x 5¼ x 20¾	opening
1	Top	1 x 17 x 59¼	
1	Backsplash	⅞ x 2 x 58¼	

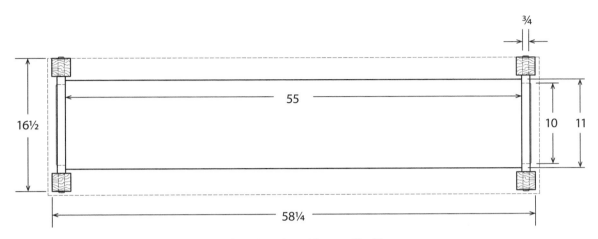

Plan Section Above Shelf

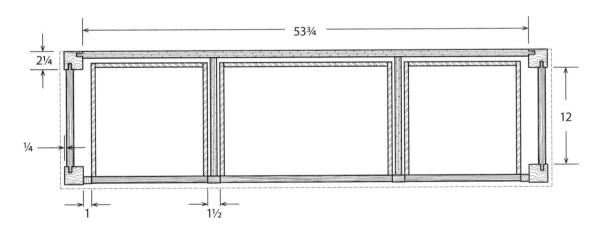

Plan Section Through Drawers

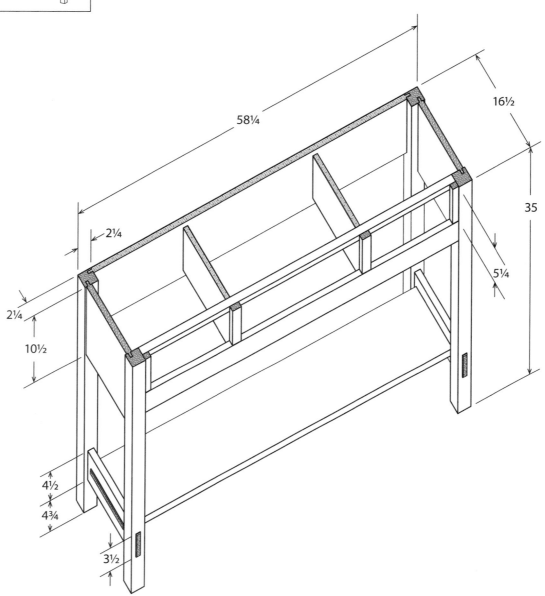

Assembly

L. & J. G. STICKLEY
NO. 552 GATELEG TABLE

42" x 42" x 30" high open, 14" x 42" closed

A marvelous little table. With the leaves down, it can be used behind a sofa or as an entry table. With the leaves up, it can seat four for breakfast or lunch. Great to use on the holidays for extra seating.

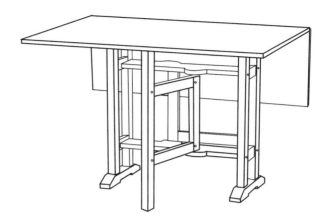

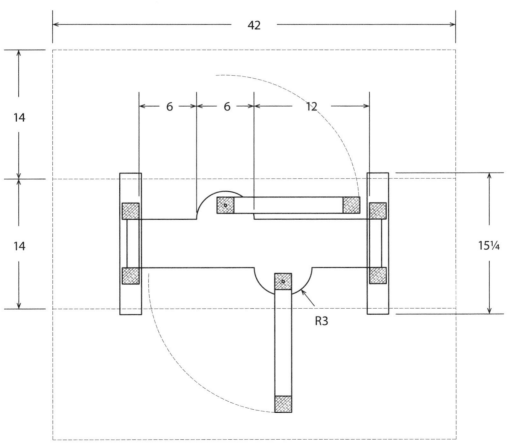

Plan

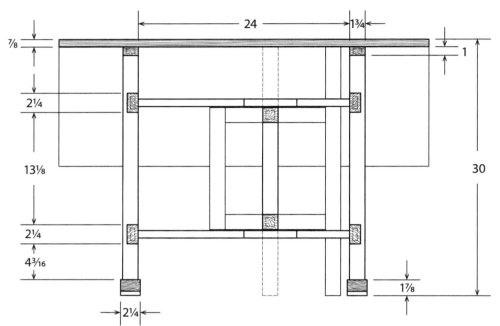

Front Section

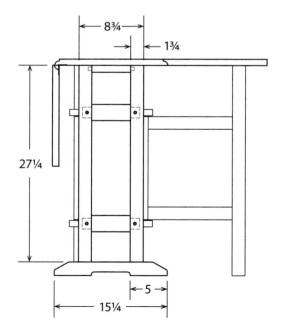

Side Elevation

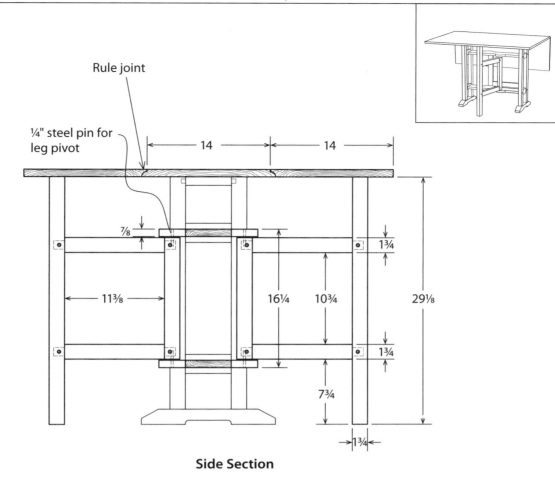

Rule joint

¼" steel pin for
leg pivot

14

14

⅞

1¾

11⅜

16¼

10¾

29⅛

1¾

7¾

1¾

Side Section

L. & J. G. Stickley No. 552 Gateleg Table

Qty	Part	Size	Notes
1	Top	⅞ x 15½ x 42	14 exposed between rule joints
2	Leaves	⅞ x 14 x 42	
4	Fixed Legs	1¾ x 1¾ x 27¼	
2	Feet	1⅞ x 2¼ x 15¼	
4	Leg Stretchers	1¼ x 2¼ x 7¾	5¼ between tenons
2	Top Leg Rails	⅞ x 1¾ x 6¼	5¼ between tenons
2	Shelves	⅞ x 11¼ x 25	24 between tenons
2	Pivoting Legs	1¾ x 1¾ x 29⅛	
2	Pivot Uprights	1¾ x 1¾ x 14¼	
4	Pivot Rails	1¾ x 1¾ x 13⅞	11⅜ between tenons

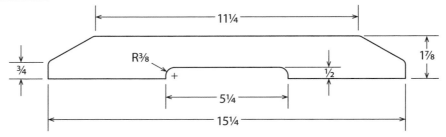

Foot Detail

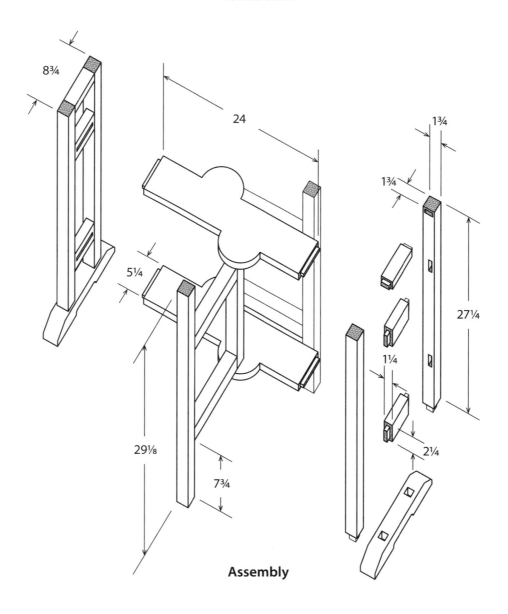

Assembly

L. & J. G. STICKLEY NO. 599 TRESTLE TABLE

29" high x 42" x 84"

A massive Arts & Crafts style table. The construction is obvious, so no section views are really needed. Large screws through oversized holes in the top rails attach the top.

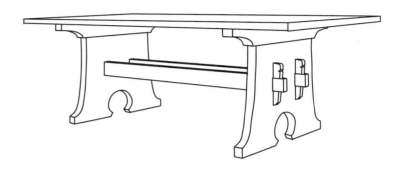

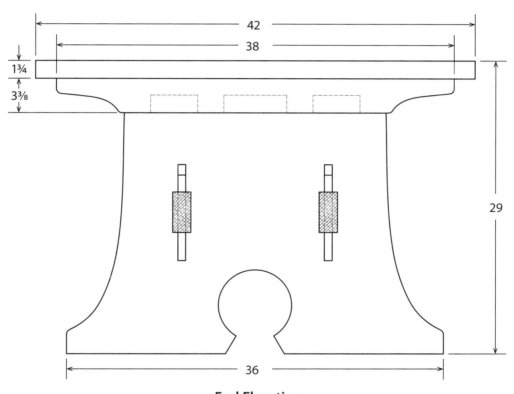

End Elevation

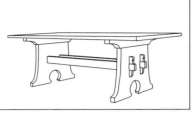

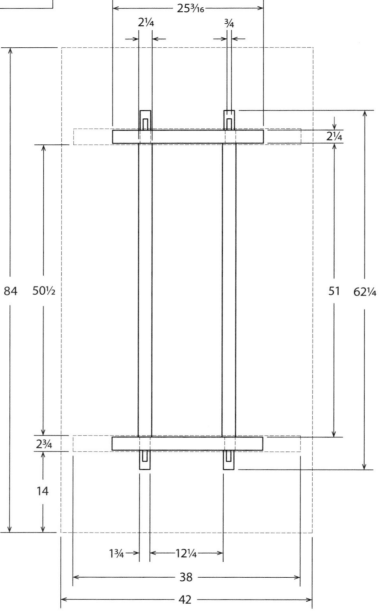

Plan

L. & J. G. Stickley No. 599 Trestle Table

Qty	Part	Size	Notes
1	Top	1¾ x 42 x 84	
2	Ends	2¼ x 36 x 25¾	23⅞ exposed
2	End Rails	2¾ x 3⅜ x 38	
2	Stretchers	2¼ x 4 x 62¼	51 between tenons
4	Keys	¾ x 1⅞ x 9½	

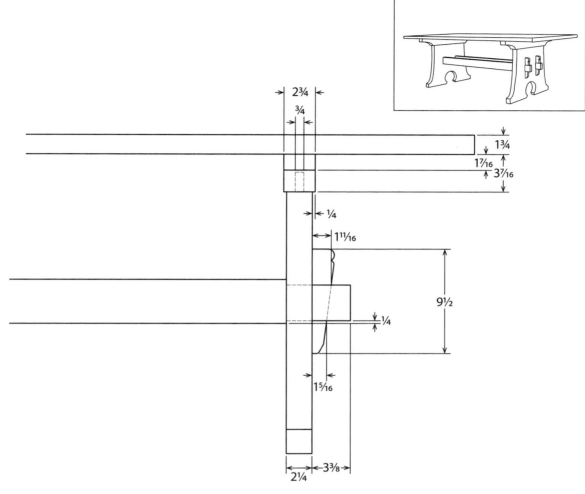

Joint Detail

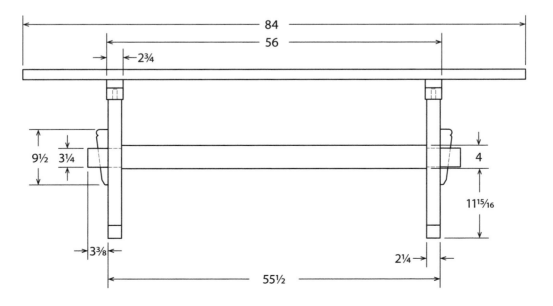

Front Elevation

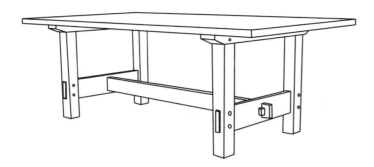

GUSTAV STICKLEY
NO. 622 TRESTLE TABLE

42" x 84" x 30"

A very substantial table, yet much lighter in appearance than the L. & J. G. Stickley No. 599 table. Fasten the top with large screws in elongated holes through the top stretcher. This table can be made to knock down for moving if you don't glue the joints at the keyed tenons.

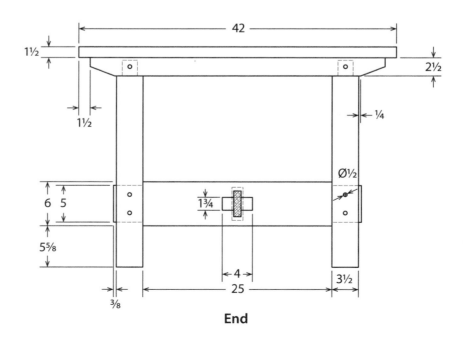

End

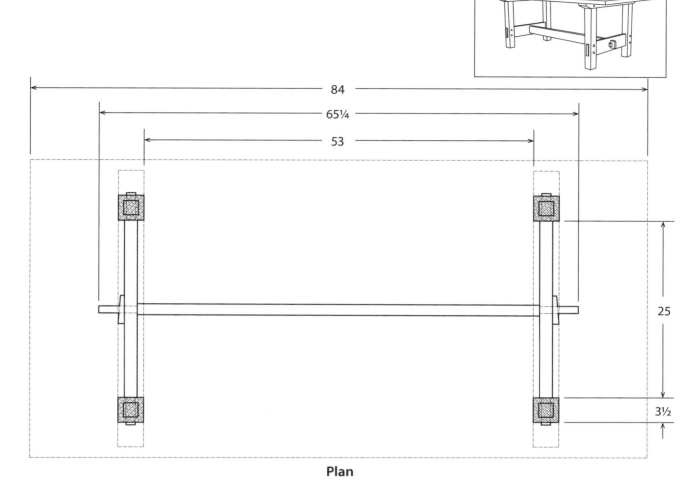

Plan

Front

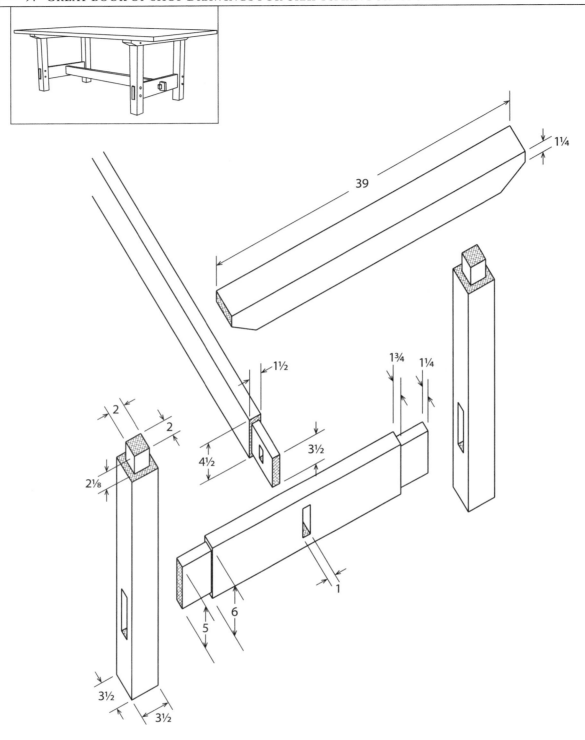

Gustav Stickley No. 622 Trestle Table

Qty	Part	Size	Notes
1	Top	1½ x 42 x 84	
4	Legs	3½ x 3½ x 28	26 floor to tenon shoulder
2	Top Stretchers	2½ x 3½ x 39	
2	Bottom Stretchers	1¾ x 6 x 32¾	25 between tenon shoulders
1	Stretcher	1½ x 4½ x 65¼	54¾ between tenon shoulders
2	Keys	¾ x 2¾ x 4	

GUSTAV STICKLEY
NO. 624 HEXAGONAL TABLE

48" x 29" high

This was listed as a library table, and often seen with a leather top. The design was simplified in later years, the keyed tenons disappeared, and the stretchers were unstacked. Do a full-size layout of the central joint of the stretchers to determine the locations of the lap joints, which are pinned.

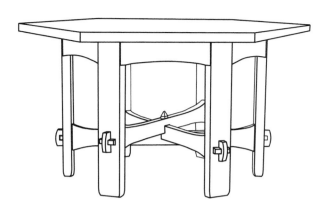

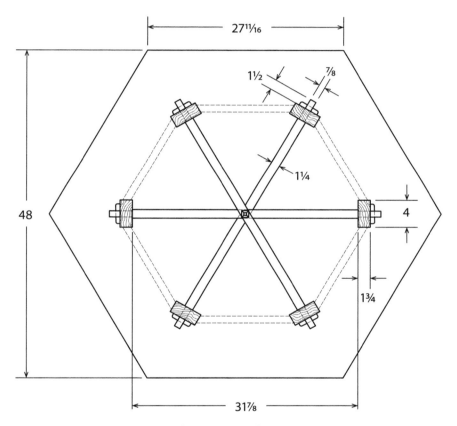

Plan at Stretchers

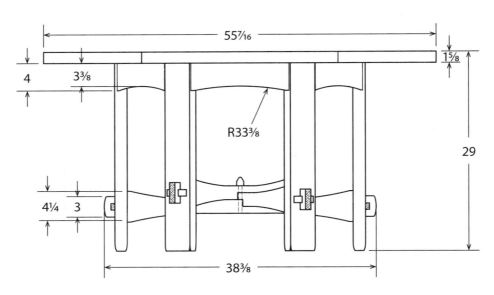

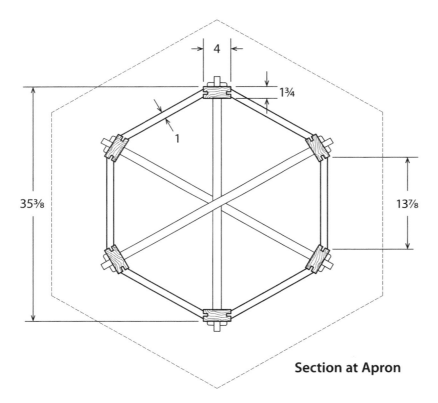

Section at Apron

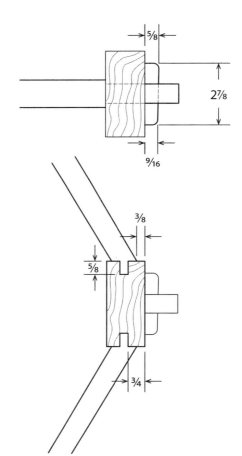

Gustav Stickley No. 624 Hexagonal Table

Qty	Part	Size	Notes
1	Top	1⅝ x 48 x 55⁷⁄₁₆	
6	Legs	1¾ x 4 x 27⅜	
3	Stretchers	1¼ x 4½ x 38½	31⅞ between tenons
6	Aprons	1 x 4 x 13⅞	exposed—add for tenons
6	Keys	⅝ x ¹⁵⁄₁₆ x 2⅞	
1	Pin	1 x 1 x 5¼	½ diameter turned end

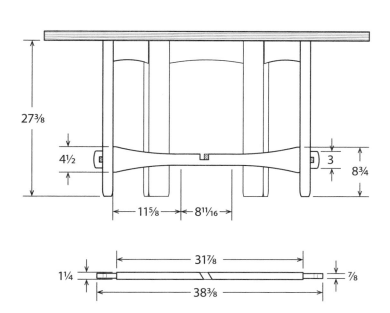

27³⁄₈

4¹⁄₂

3

8³⁄₄

11⁵⁄₈

8¹¹⁄₁₆

31⁷⁄₈

1¹⁄₄

⁷⁄₈

38³⁄₈

Section at Bottom Stretcher

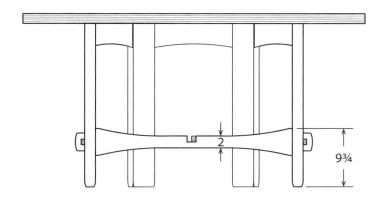

2

9³⁄₄

Section at Middle Stretcher

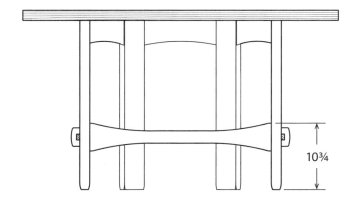

10³⁄₄

Section at Top Stretcher

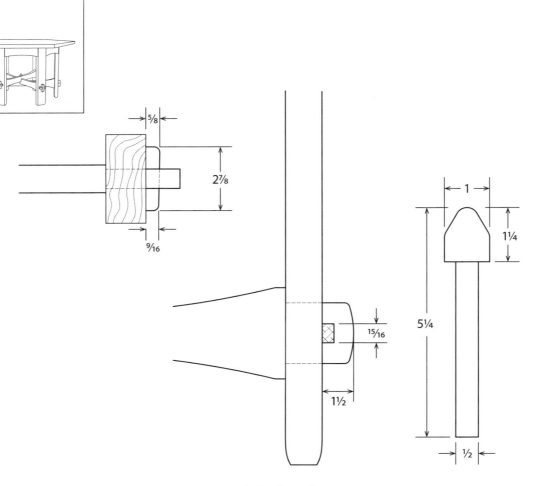

Joint Details

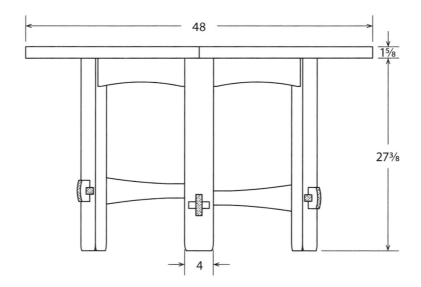

Front Elevation

GUSTAV STICKLEY NO. 634 ROUND EXTENSION TABLE

54" x 29" high

This design has been attributed to LaMont Warner, Stickley's chief draftsman from 1900–1906. It is designed to extend, but can be made as a fixed table.

If made as an extension table, a wooden extension mechanism is bolted to a plate fixed to the tops of the two halves of the pedestal. Two rows of dowels align the pedestal as it comes together.

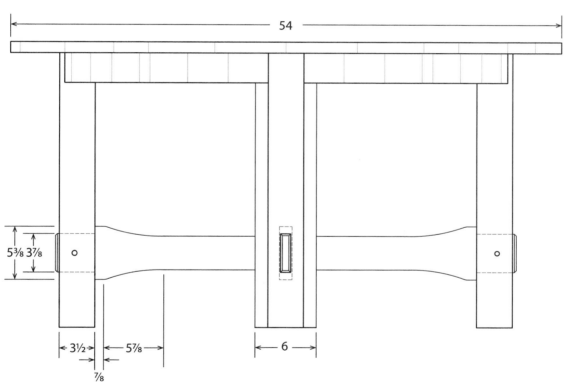

Front

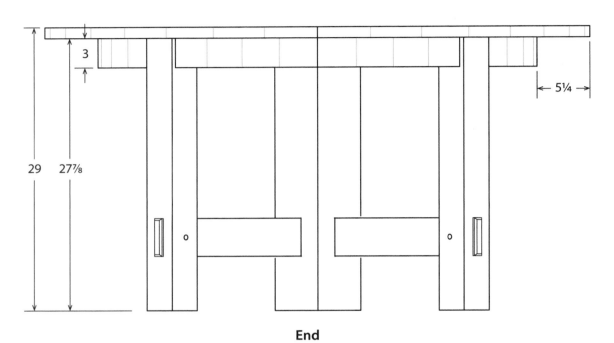

End

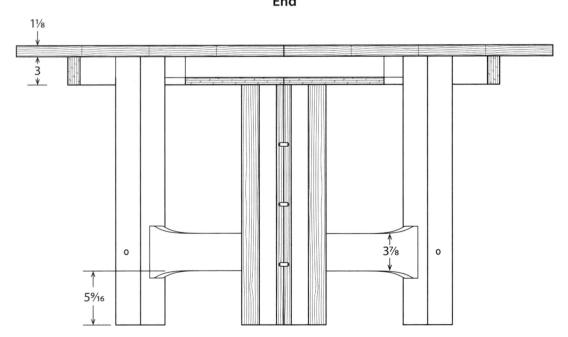

End Section

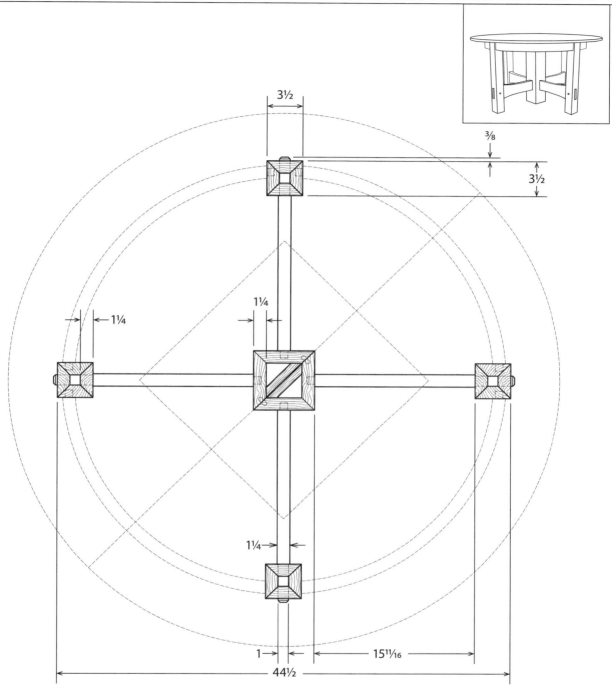

Plan Section Through Legs

Gustav Stickley No. 634 Round Extension Table

Qty	Part	Size	Notes
1	Top	1⅛ x 54 diameter	
16	Leg Sides	1¼ x 3½ x 27⅞	
4	Middle Leg Sides	1¼ x 6 x 24⅞	if building as extension table, double-check height required for slide mechanism
2	Middle Leg Brace	¾ x 4¹⁵⁄₁₆ x 24⅞	
1	Plate for Slides	¾ x 20 x 20	plywood—adjust size to fit slide mechanism
4	Stretchers	1¼ x 5⅜ x 20¹⁵⁄₁₆	15¹¹⁄₁₆ between tenons—tenon extends ⅜ beyond leg
4	Curved Aprons	1¼ x 3 x 36	rough length for bending—inside radius = 20½ finished arc length = 30 ²¹⁄₃₂ between tenon shoulders

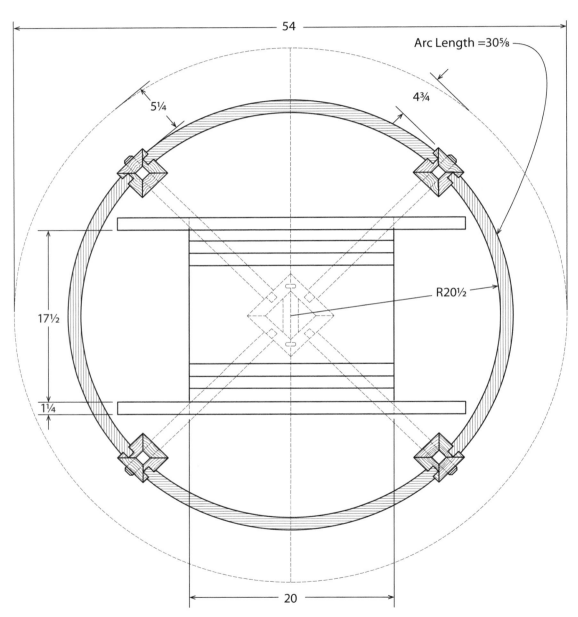

Plan Section Through Apron

CHARLES LIMBERT OCTAGONAL TABLE

48" x 48" x 29½" high

The corbels below the top are fake-screwed into the uprights. Make the upright pieces by ripping the stock, cutting out the openings, and gluing the pieces back together. Use dowels to keep everything aligned during the glue-up.

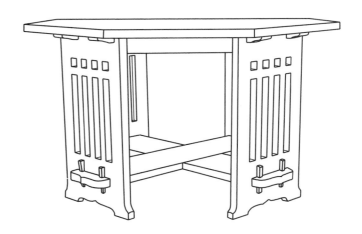

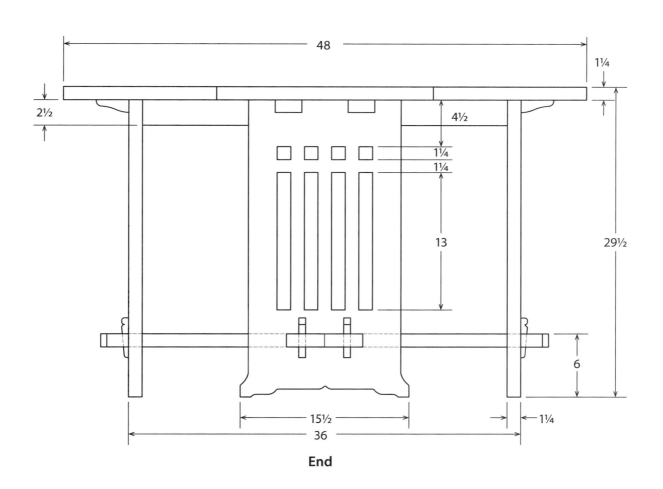

End

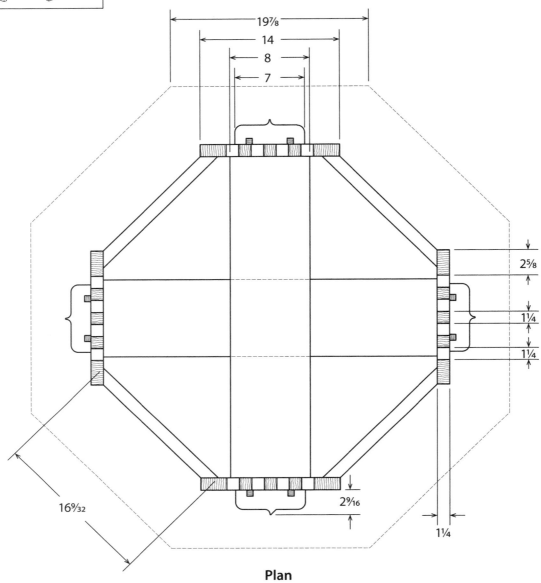

Plan

Limbert Octagonal Table

QTY	PART	SIZE	NOTES
1	Top	1¼ x 48 x 48	
4	Legs	1¼ x 15½ x 28¼	finished width—add 1½" for saw kerfs and planing
4	Top Stretchers	1¼ x 2½ x 16⁹⁄₃₂	
2	Bottom Stretchers	1¼ x 8 x 41⅛	33½ between tenons—half lap together in middle
8	Keys	⅝ x ⅝ x 3¾	
8	Top Corbels	1¼ x 2½ x 3	

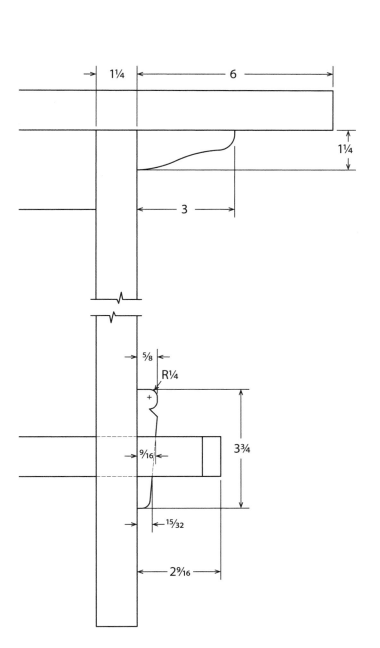

Corbel and Wedge Detail

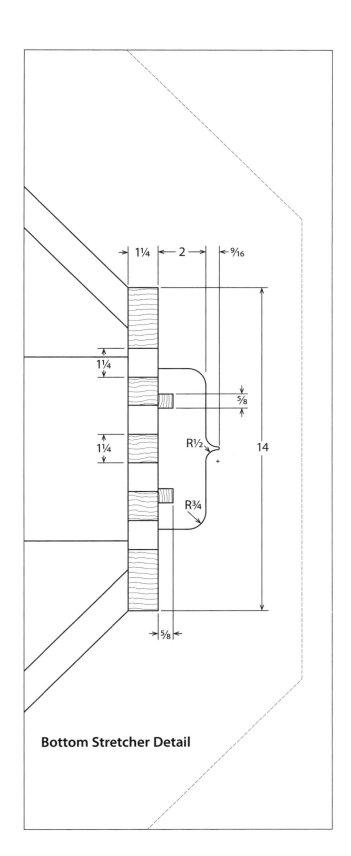

Bottom Stretcher Detail

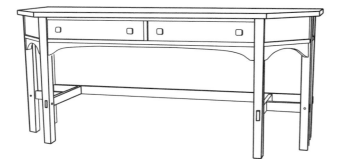

LIMBERT CONSOLE TABLE

66" wide x 21" deep x 29" high

The ¾" wide strip below the drawers is applied,
⅛" thick, attached with small brads.

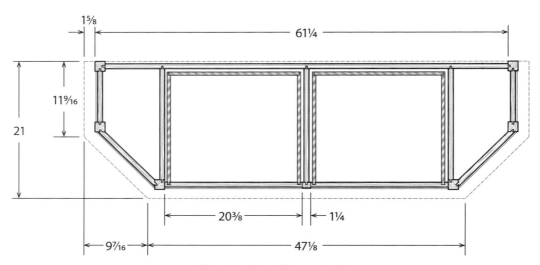

Plan Section Through Drawers

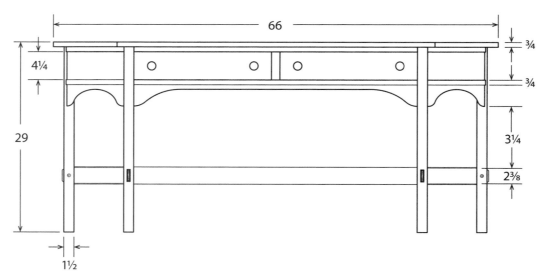

Front Elevation

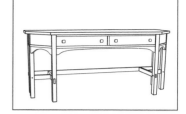

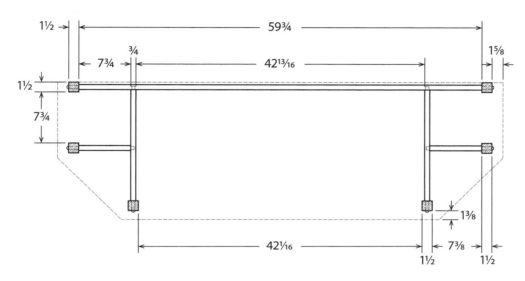

Plan Section Above Stretchers

Limbert Console Table

Qty	Part	Size	Notes
1	Top	¾ x 21 x 66	
6	Legs	1½ x 1½ x 28¼	
1	Long Stretcher	¾ x 2⅝ x 63¼	59¾ between tenons
2	Stretchers	¾ x 2⅜ x 17¾	17 between tenons
2	Stretchers	¾ x 2⅜ x 10¼	7¾ between tenons
1	Front Apron	¾ x 3¼ x 42 1/16	add for tenons
2	Angled Panels	¾ x 9 x 12	
2	Side Panels	¾ x 9 x 8½	7¾ between tenons
1	Back Panel	¾ x 9 x 60½	59¾ between tenons
2	Dividers	¾ x 4¼ x 17¾	17 between tenons
1	Dividers	¾ x 4¼ x 18⅛	17⅜ between tenons
1	Drawer Front Divider	¾ x 1¼ x 4¼	
2	Drawer Fronts	¾ x 4¼ x 20⅜	opening
1	Rail Above Drawers	¾ x 1⅜ x 42 1/16	add for tenons
4	Side Trim	⅛ x ¾ x 7 13/16	
4	Angled Trim	⅛ x ¾ x 12 13/16	
2	Front Trim	⅛ x ¾ x 42 1/16	

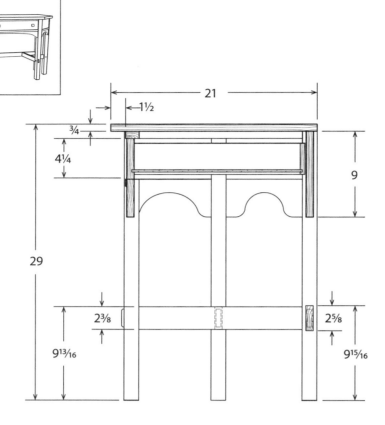

Side Section

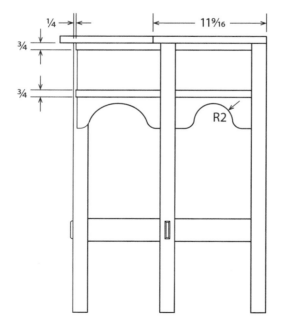

Side Elevation

L. & J. G. STICKLEY
NO. 719 CORNER CHINA CABINET

65" high x 48" wide x 26" deep

The shiplap back panels are rabbetted top and bottom to fit within the frame as shown in the three dimensional view. The top attaches to this frame with table irons. Use substantial hinges on the door, since it will be heavy and wide.

Note that the side sections are taken on two different cutting planes.

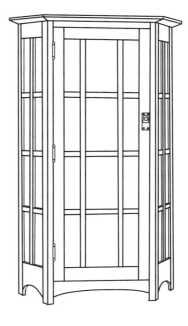

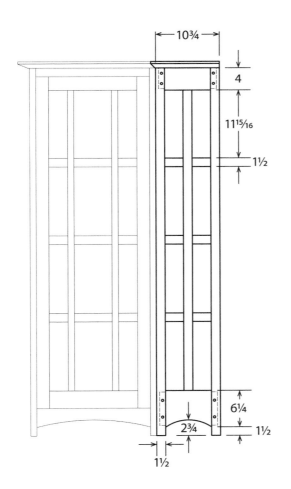

Side Elevation

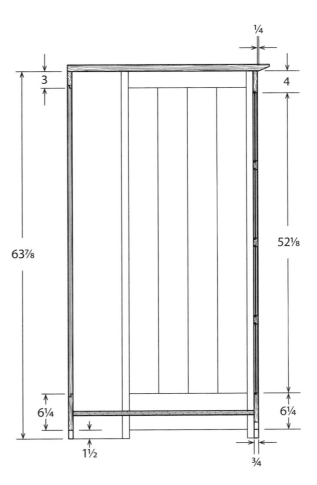

Side Section

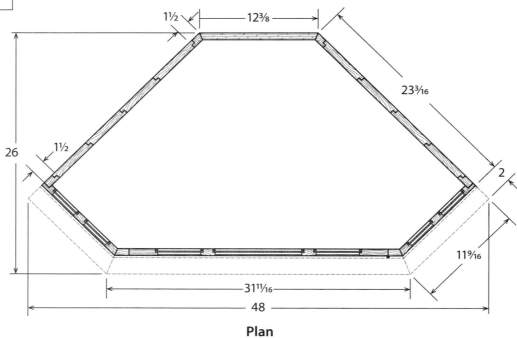

Plan

L. & J. G. Stickley No. 719 Corner China Cabinet

Qty	Part	Size	Notes
2	Glass Panels	¾ x 10¾ x 63⅞	assembled—parts detailed below
4	Stiles	¾ x 1½ x 63⅞	
2	Bottom Rails	¾ x 6¼ x 9¾	7¾ between tenons
2	Top Rails	¾ x 4 x 9¾	7¾ between tenons
2	Mullions	¾ x 1½ x 53⅛	52⅛ between tenons
12	Muntin	¾ x 1½ x 4⅛	3⅛ between tenons
1	Door	¾ x 27 x 57⅝	opening size—parts detailed below
2	Stiles	¾ x 3 x 57⅝	
1	Bottom Muntins	¾ x 3 x 23	21 between tenons
1	Top Rail	¾ x 2½ x 23	21 between tenons
2	Mullions	¾ x 1½ x 53⅛	52⅛ between tenons
3	Center Muntins	¾ x 1½ x 10	9 between tenons
6	Side Muntins	¾ x 1½ x 5½	4½ between tenons
6	Cabinet Stiles	¾ x 1½ x 63⅞	
2	Back Bottom Rails	¾ x 6¼ x 20⁹⁄₁₆	
2	Back Top Rails	¾ x 3 x 20⁹⁄₁₆	
1	Front Bottom Rail	¾ x 3¼ x 29	27 between tenons
1	Front Top Rail	¾ x 1½ x 29	27 between tenons
1	Back	¾ x 12⅜ x 63⅞	
8	Back Planks	¾ x 5⁵⁄₁₆ x 53⅞	
1	Bottom	¾ x 22½ x 43¹⁄₁₆	
3	Shelves	¾ x 22¼ x 43¹⁄₁₆	opening
1	Top	1⅛ x 26 x 48	

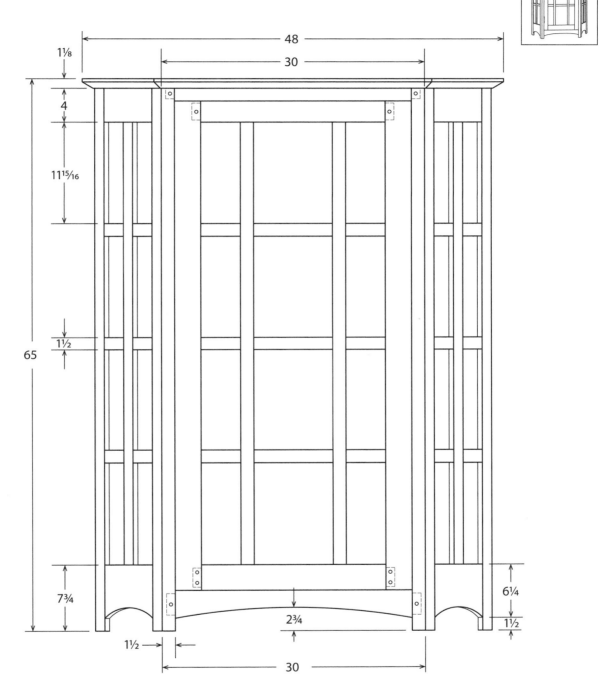

Front Elevation

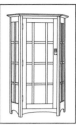

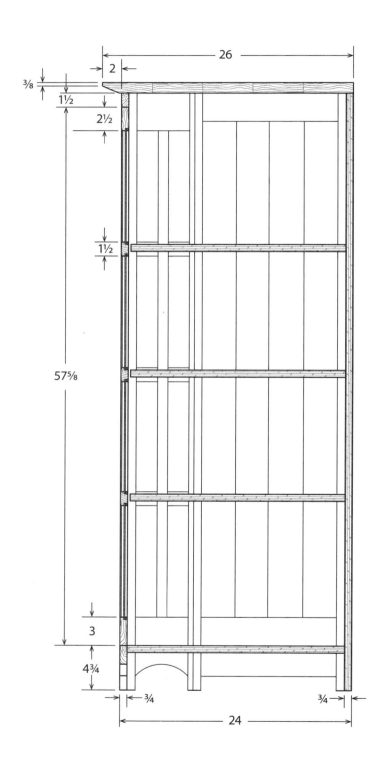

Section

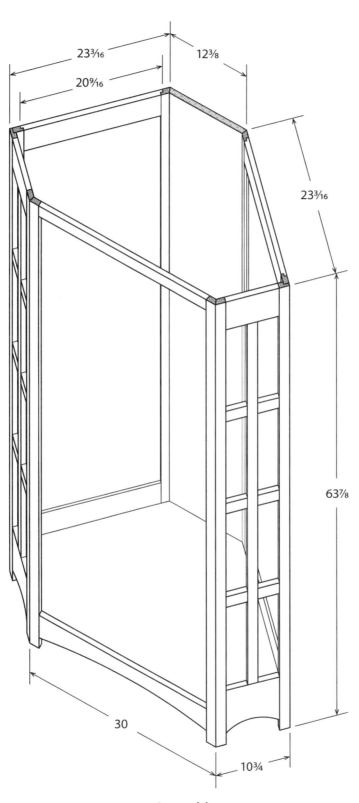

23³⁄₁₆

12³⁄₈

20⁹⁄₁₆

23³⁄₁₆

63⁷⁄₈

30

10¾

Assemble back as open frame, and attach ship-lap back after finishing. Shelves may be permanently fastened in line with the mullions, or allowed to sit on pegs in bored holes.

Assembly

L. & J. G. STICKLEY
NO. 729 CHINA CABINET

70" high x 50" wide x 17" deep

This very large cabinet could be put to a variety of contemporary uses. However, if it was to house electronic gear, it might need to be made a few inches deeper. You'll have to shop around to find suitable hardware, though reproduction specialists generally do carry large strap hinges such as the ones on the lower section.

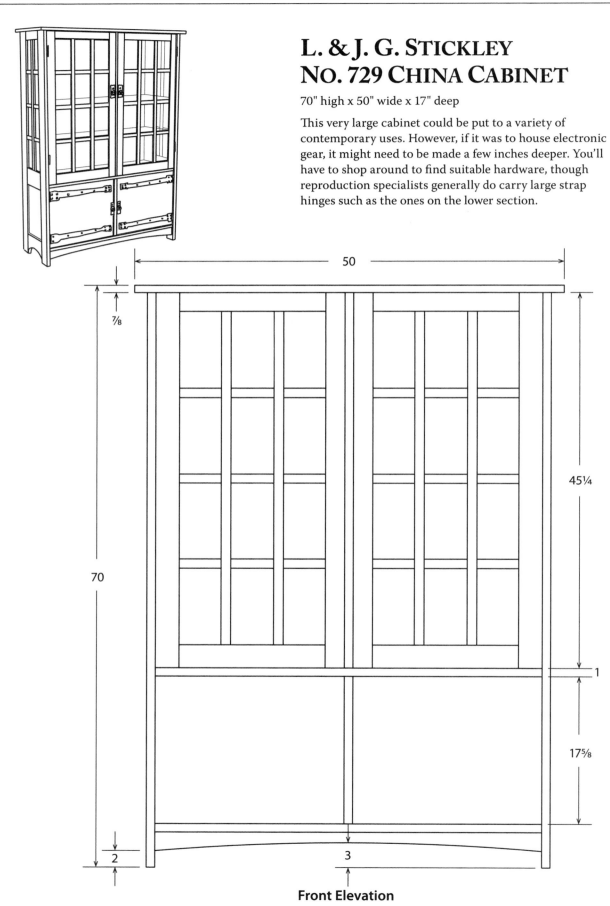

Front Elevation

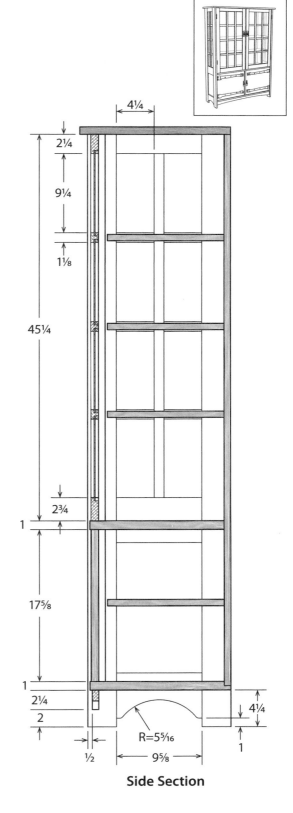

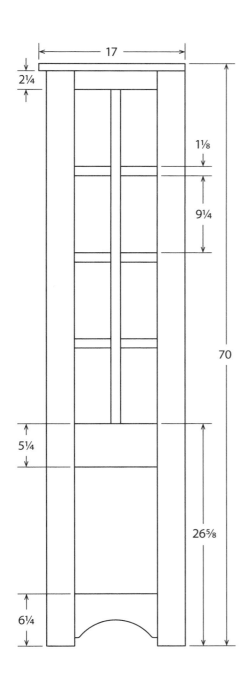

Side Elevation

Side Section

L. & J. G. Stickley No. 729 China Cabinet

Qty	Part	Size	Notes
2	Sides	1 x 16⅛ x 69⅛	assembled-parts detailed below
4	Stiles	1 x 3¼ x 69⅛	
4	Bottom & Middle Rails	1 x 5¼ x 11⅛	9⅝ between tenons
2	Top Rails	1 x 2¼ x 11⅛	9⅝ between tenons
2	Mullions	1 x 1⅛ x 41¼	40¼ between tenons
12	Muntins	1 x 1⅛ x 5¼	4¼ between tenons
2	Upper Doors	⅞ x 22 x 45¼	opening-parts detailed below
2	Hinge Stiles	⅞ x 2¾ x 45¼	
2	Latch Stiles	⅞ x 2¼ x 45¼	
2	Bottom Rails	⅞ x 2¾ x 18½	17 between tenons
2	Top Rails	⅞ x 2¼ x 18½	17 between tenons
4	Mullions	⅞ x 1⅛ x 41¾	40¼ between tenons
18	Muntins	⅞ x 1⅛ x 5¹¹⁄₁₆	4¹⁵⁄₁₆ between tenons
2	Lower Doors	⅞ x 22 x 17⅝	opening
1	Bottom	1 x 16 x 45¾	45 between tenons
1	Fixed Shelf	1 x 15¼ x 45¾	45 between tenons
1	Top	⅞ x 17 x 50	
1	Lower Vertical Divider	1 x 15¼ x 18⅜	17⅝ between tenons
2	Lower Doorstops	¾ x ¾ x 17⅝	
1	Upper Divider Stile	1 x 1¾ x 45¼	
2	Upper Door Stops	¾ x ¾ x 45¼	
3	Upper Shelves	¾ x 13⅜ x 45	
2	Lower Shelves	¾ x 13⅜ x 22	
1	Arched Apron	¾ x 2¼ x 45¾	45 between tenons
8	Back Planks	¾ x 5¾ x 64⅜	

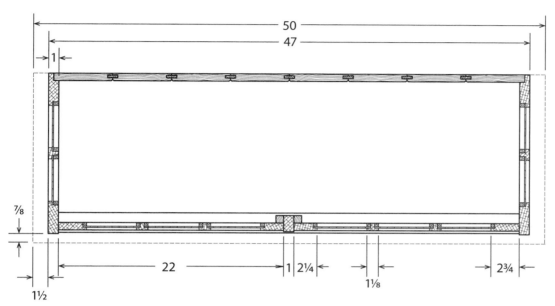

Plan Section Through Top

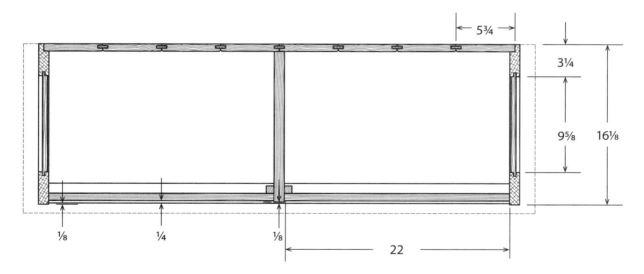

Plan Section Through Base

GUSTAV STICKLEY
NO. 803 CHINA CABINET

60" high x 36" wide x 15" deep

A classic example of the high points of Harvey Ellis' designs—a thin top with a wide overhang, arches at the top of the door and the bottom front rail, and subtly tapered legs.

The legs actually have a flat area between the two tapers—see the front section.

Make the door well, and use good hinges.

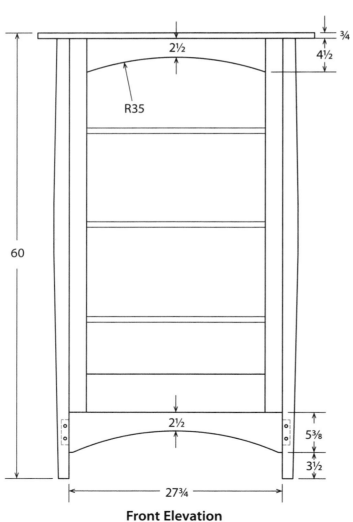

Front Elevation

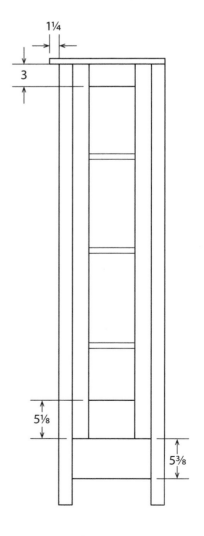

Side Elevation

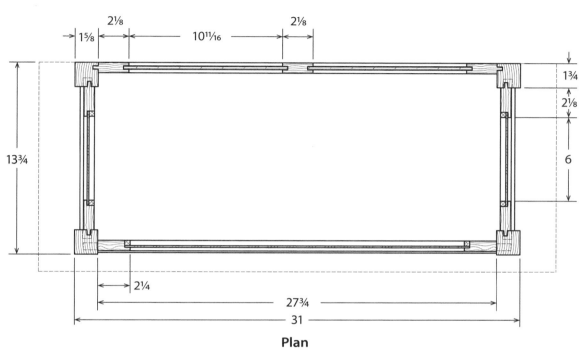

Plan

Gustav Stickley No. 803 China Cabinet

Qty	Part	Size	Notes
4	Legs	1¾ x 2 x 59¼	
1	Door	¾ x 27¾ x 50	opening—parts detailed below
2	Stiles	¾ x 2¼ x 50	
1	Top Rail	¾ x 4½ x 25¼	23¼ between tenons
1	Bottom Rail	¾ x 5½ x 25¼	23¼ between tenons
1	Arched Apron	⅞ x 5⅜ x 29½	27¾ between tenons
2	Side Panels	¾ x 10¼ x 50⅜	assembled—parts detailed below
4	Stiles	¾ x 2½ x 50⅜	2⅛ exposed
2	Bottom Rails	¾ x 5½ x 6¾	5⅛ x 6 between tenons
2	Top Rails	¾ x 3 x 6¾	6 between tenons
2	Lower Rails	⅞ x 5⅜ x 11½	10¼ between tenons
1	Back Panel	¾ x 28½ x 50⅜	assembled—27¾ x 50 exposed—parts detailed below
2	Outer Stiles	¾ x 2½ x 50⅜	2⅛ exposed
1	Mid Stile	¾ x 2⅛ x 43	42¼ between tenons
1	Bottom Rail	¾ x 5½ x 23½	22¾ between tenons
1	Top Rail	¾ x 3 x 23½	22¾ between tenons
2	Panels	¼ x 11⁷⁄₁₆ x 43	42¼ between tenons
1	Bottom Arched Apron	¾ x 4⅝ x 29½	27¾ between tenons
1	Bottom	¾ x 12¾ x 28¼	
3	Shelves	¾ x 11⅞ x 28¼	notch corners at legs
1	Top	¾ x 15 x 36	

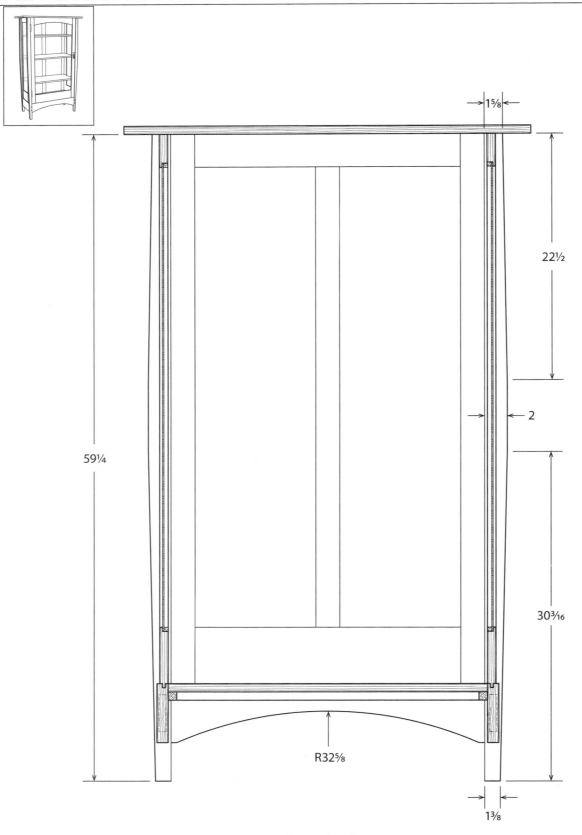

Front Section

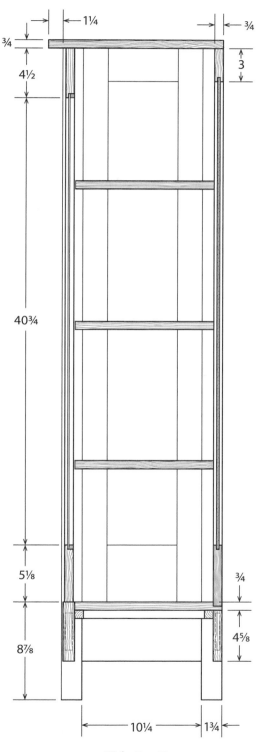

Side Section

GUSTAV STICKLEY
NO. 815 CHINA CABINET

42" wide x 15" deep x 66" high

The catalog describes this china cabinet as having "fixed shelves along the lines of the mullions." Don't attach the shelves until finishing is complete and the glass is in place. The shelves can be permanently attached by screwing through cleats recessed below, or by pegs in holes drilled in the stiles.

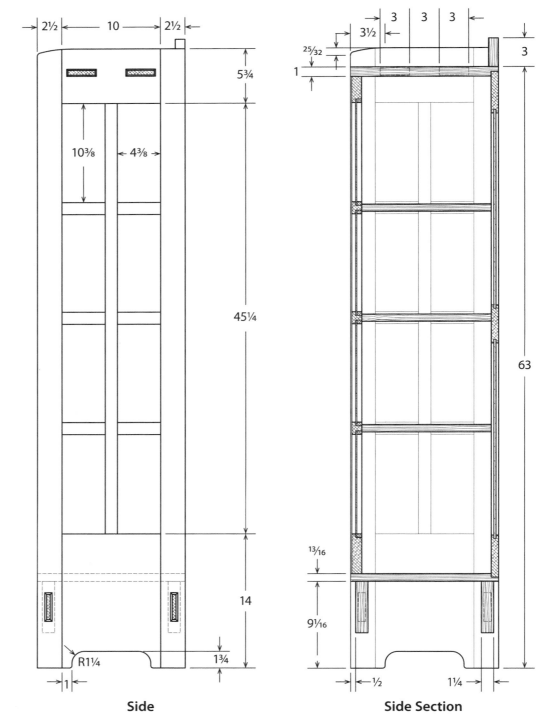

Side

Side Section

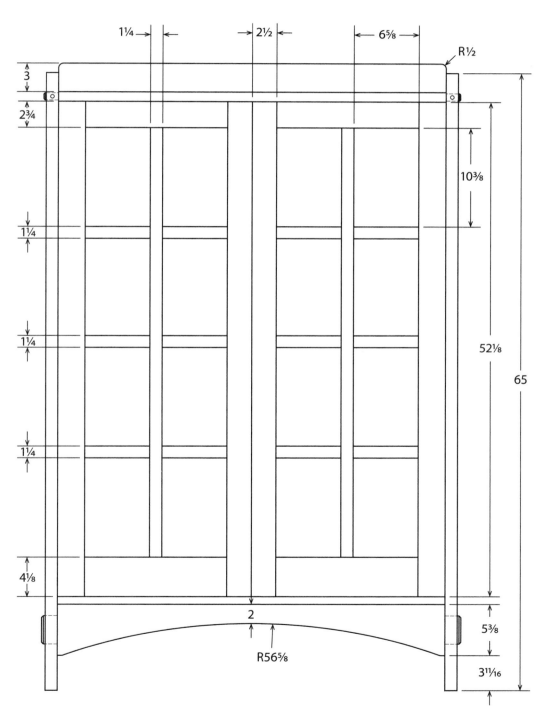

Front

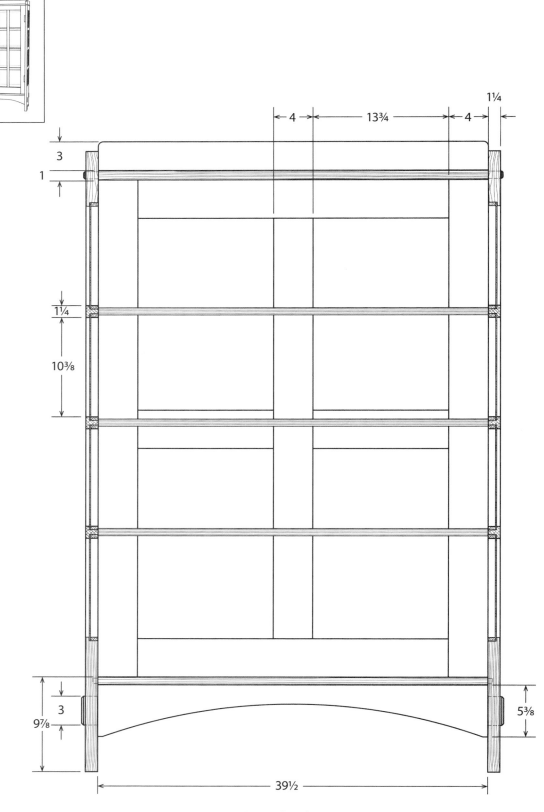

Front Section

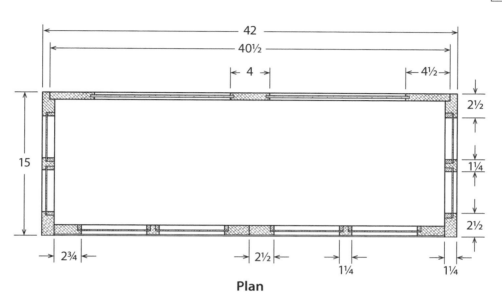

Plan

Gustav Stickley No. 815 China Cabinet

QTY	PART	SIZE	NOTES
2	Sides	1¼ x 15 x 65	parts detailed below
4	Side Stiles	1¼ x 2½ x 65	
2	Side Top Rails	1¼ x 5¾ x 12	10 between tenon shoulders
2	Side Bottom Rails	1¼ x 14 x 12	10 between tenon shoulders
2	Side Mullions	1¼ x 1¼ x 47¾	46¼ between tenon shoulders
12	Side Muntins	1¼ x 1¼ x 4⅞	4⅜ between tenon shoulders
1	Top	1 x 15 x 42¾	39½ between tenon shoulders
1	Bottom	¹³⁄₁₆ x 15 x 40½	39½ between tenon shoulders
2	Front & Back Aprons	1¼ x 5⅜ x 42¾	39½ between tenon shoulders
1	Backsplash	1 x 3 x 39½	
1	Paneled Back	¾ x 40½ x 53⅛	39½ x 52⅛ opening between rabbets —parts detailed below
2	Outer Back Stiles	¾ x 4½ x 53⅛	4 x 52⅛ exposed
2	Back-Top & Bottom Rails	¾ x 4½ x 32½	4 exposed width—31½ between tenon shoulders
1	Back- Middle Stile	¾ x 4 x 45⅛	44⅛ between tenon shoulders
2	Back-Middle Rails	¾ x 4 x 14¾	13¾ between tenon shoulders
4	Back Panels	¼ x 14¾ x 21¹⁄₁₆	13¾ x 20¹⁄₁₆ exposed
2	Doors	1 x 19¾ x 52⅛	opening size—trim for desired gaps—parts detailed below
2	Door Hinge Stiles	1 x 2¾ x 52⅛	
2	Door Inner Stiles	1 x 2½ x 52⅛	
2	Door Top Rails	1 x 2¾ x 15½	14½ between tenon shoulders
2	Door Bottom Rails	1 x 4⅛ x 15½	14½ between tenon shoulders
2	Door Mullions	1 x 1¼ x 46¼	45¼ between tenon shoulders
12	Door Muntins	1 x 1¼ x 7½	6⅝ between tenon shoulders
3	Shelves	¾ x 13⅛ x 39½	opening size—make smaller for adjustable shelves

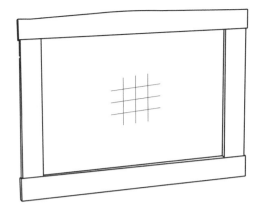

GUSTAV STICKLEY
NO. 66 WALL MIRROR

36" wide x 28" high

I was surprised to see the piece of plywood on the back of the original, but it makes sense—it stiffens and strengthens the frame. If you use ¼" thick mirror as drawn, it will be heavy. In some catalog illustrations, mirrors like this were shown with three or four coat hooks attached to the bottom rail.

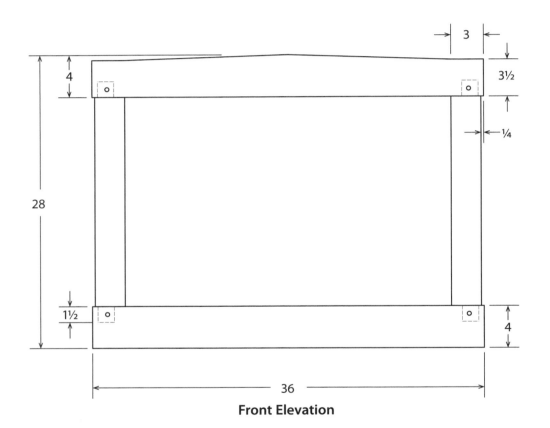

Front Elevation

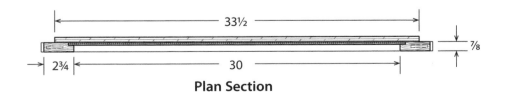

Plan Section

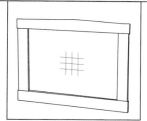

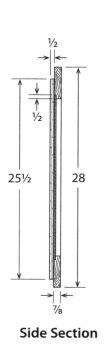

Side Section

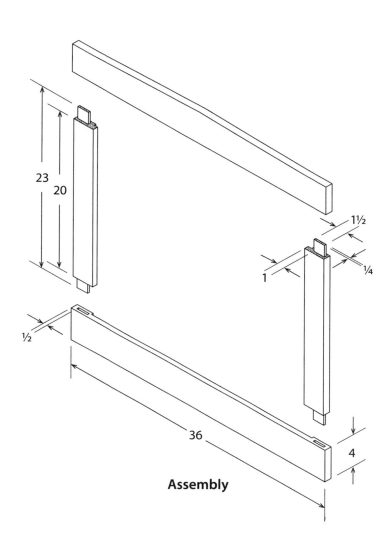

Assembly

Gustav Stickley No. 66 Wall Mirror

Qty	Part	Size	Notes
2	Stiles	⅞ x 3 x 23	20 between tenons
1	Bottom Rail	⅞ x 4 x 36	
1	Top Rail	⅞ x 4 x 36	tapers to 3½ at ends
1	Back	½ x 25½ x 33½	plywood

Craftsman Living Room Furnishings

Image courtesy University of Wisconsin Digital Collections

In the living room of a home, more than in almost any other place, is felt the influence of material things. It is a place where work is to be done, and it is also the haven of rest for the workers. It is the place where children grow and thrive, and gain their first impressions of life and of the world. It is the place to which a man comes home when his day's work is done, and where he wishes to find himself comfortable and at ease in surroundings that are in harmony with his daily life, thoughts and pursuits.

Gustav Stickley
The Craftsman, October 1905

A Craftsman living room where the fireplace is the central feature. (The Craftsman, October 1905.)

In our modern world, we can pretend where we sit doesn't matter, and that what we sit on only has an influence on our momentary comfort. In reality, the objects with which we choose to live affect us in more ways and at deeper levels than we consciously realize. It takes a serious commitment in time and materials to build a Craftsman chair or table, but when the furniture is completed, it is committed to you, and to everyone who comes in contact with it. If you surround yourself with excellent furniture, made by your own hands, you become part of a legacy that will outlive you, a legacy of quality and honesty that makes the world a better place.

If this sounds like lofty idealism, or some new-age nonsense, try it for yourself as proof. Build one of these pieces and live with it for a while. Be prepared for questions from family and friends, and take note of how you answer. Chances are good that you'll start with descriptions of white oak and through tenons, but quickly move on to a greater discussion of values and meaning. It's difficult for anyone to talk about Craftsman furniture without making that transition, and including an appreciation for the material provided by our natural world.

Quartersawn white oak isn't the easiest wood to work, but with experience and an understanding of its character, it is steady and predictable. In gaining that experience, you'll better understand your own character. The work becomes a partnership between man and material, each helping the other to become something more, something that fits any situation and meets challenges with dignity and grace. When finished and put in place, the furniture contains the memories of the process in the maker and speaks to any who sees it of the effort involved in making it right, and building it to last.

There are innumerable ways to spend our time, but very few that have the kind of lasting impact, or rewards that are found in hand crafting furniture. Many original pieces of Craftsman furniture survived because they were too sturdy to break and too nice to throw away. Your descendants may not share your taste and style, but they will have a difficult time disposing of the furniture you make. The physical qualities are obvious, but there are also qualities far beyond the physical. Instead of putting it on the curb, or in the yard sale with your golf clubs or fishing gear, something unspoken will lead them to keep it.

GUSTAV STICKLEY
NO. 323 ROCKER

40" high x 30" wide x 30" deep

The original of this chair had a drop-in spring seat cushion, covered
in leather. There was also a back cushion that tied to the top of
the back posts. A note about the drawing views—the plan, front
elevation, elevation of the back, and side section are all drawn with
the arms and side rails parallel to the plane of the floor. Technically
this is not correct, but it shows the important parts in their true
sizes and shapes. Sometimes being incorrect is the right thing to do.

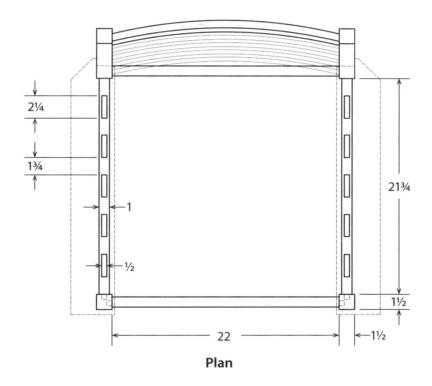

Plan

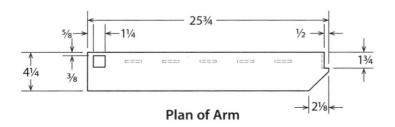

Plan of Arm

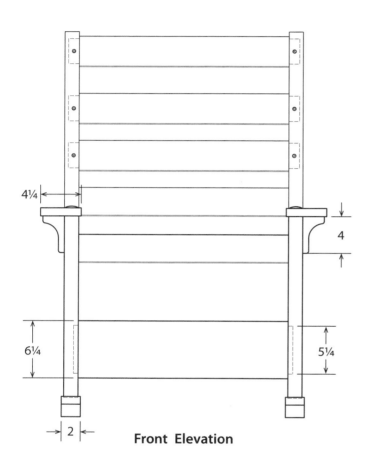

Front Elevation

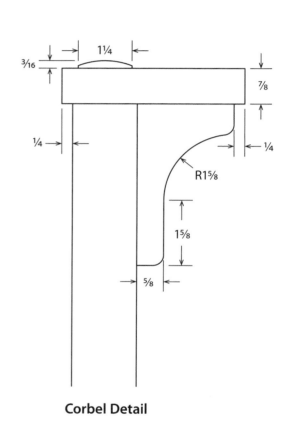

Corbel Detail

Gustav Stickley No. 323 Rocker

Qty	Part	Size	Notes
2	Front Legs	1½ x 1½ x 21¼	
2	Back Legs	1½ x 5⁷⁄₁₆ x 39	
2	Rockers	⅞ x 2 x 32¹¹⁄₁₆	arc length—make longer for bending
1	Front Rail	1 x 6¼ x 23	22 between tenons
1	Bottom Back Rail	1 x 6¼ x 23	22 between tenons
5	Curved Back Slats	¾ x 3 x 24¼	22 between tenons—make longer for bending
2	Arms	⅞ x 4¼ x 25¾	
10	Arm Slats	½ x 2¼ x 12	11¼ between tenons
2	Bottom Side Rails	1 x 6¼ x 23¼	21¾ between tenons
2	Corbels	¾ x 2¼ x 4	

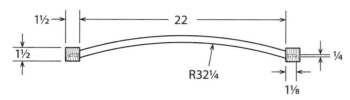

Plan of Curved Back Slat

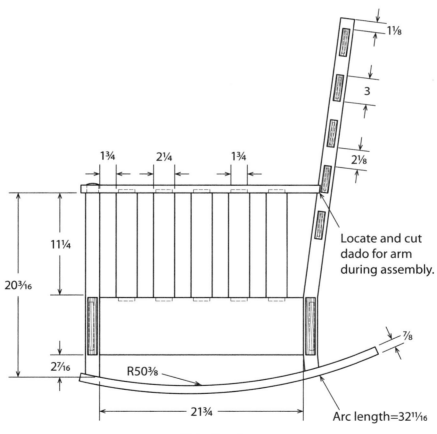

Side Section

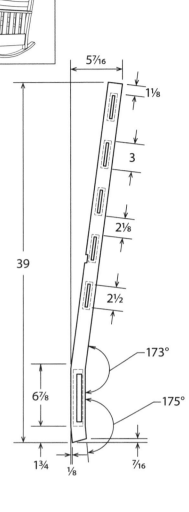

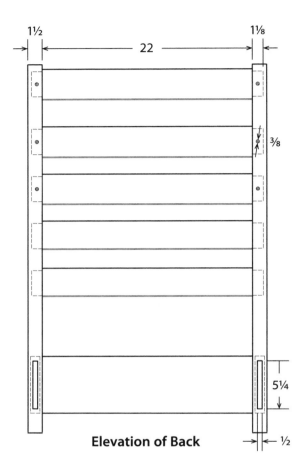

Elevation of Back

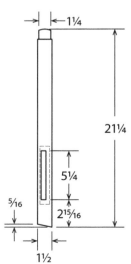

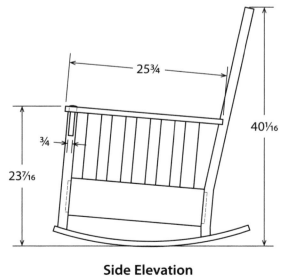

Side Elevation

GUSTAV STICKLEY
NO. 332 MORRIS CHAIR

A favorite among collectors, this chair is a challenging project. It is also a rewarding project, because once you are finished, you will have the perfect chair in which to relax.

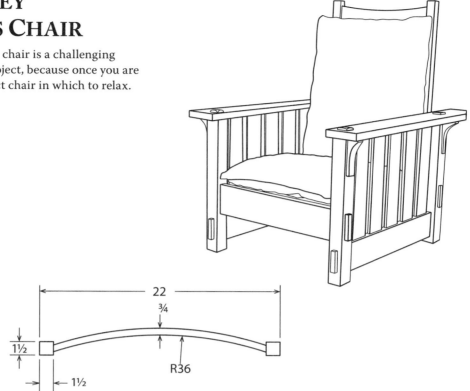

True Plan of Back

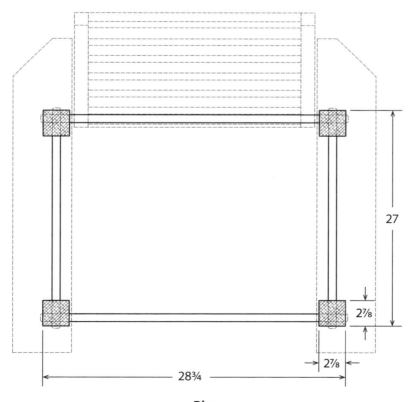

Plan

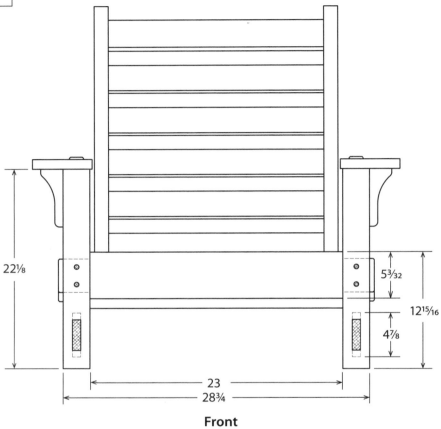

Front

Gustav Stickley No. 332 Morris Chair

QTY	PART	SIZE	NOTES
2	Front Legs	2⅞ x 2⅞ x 23½	22¹⁄₁₆ to bottom of arm @ front
2	Rear Legs	2⅞ x 2⅞ x 23⅛	21⁹⁄₁₆ to bottom of arm @ back. Shoulders at tops of legs are angled—do a full-size layout to determine exact location and angle of legs, arms, slats, and side rails
2	Bottom Side Rails	⅞ x 4⅞ x 27¾	18¼ tenon to tenon—tenons are at an angle—do full-size layout
10	Side Slats	⅝ x 3 x 18	longer than needed—do full-size layout
2	Arms	1⅛ x 6⅜ x 38	
1	Front Rail	⅞ x 5⅛ x 29¼	23 between tenon shoulders
1	Back Rail	⅞ x 5⅛ x 29¼	23 between tenons—angle on top edge
2	Back Uprights	1½ x 1½ x 31	
1	Back Top Slat—curved	¾ x 3¼ x 30	19 between tenons, bent to 36" inside radius—make long for bending
4	Back Middle Slats—curved	¾ x 3 x 30	19 between tenons, bent to 36 inside radius—make long for bending
1	Back Bottom Slat	¹⁵⁄₁₆ x 2¹³⁄₃₂ x 30	19 between tenons, bent to 36 inside radius—make long for bending
4	Pegs	1 x 1 x 4³⁄₁₆	turn post slightly less than ⅝ diameter x 2½ long
2	Washers	¼ thick x 1½ diameter	⅝ hole between back and rear legs

Leg Detail

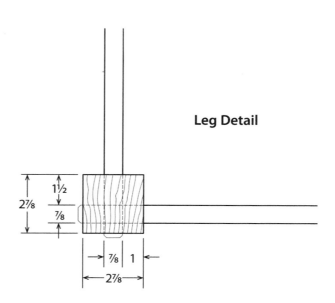

Corbel Detail

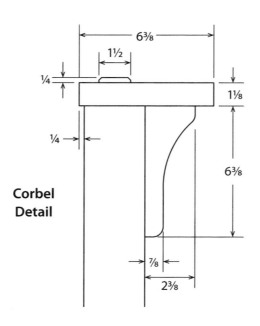

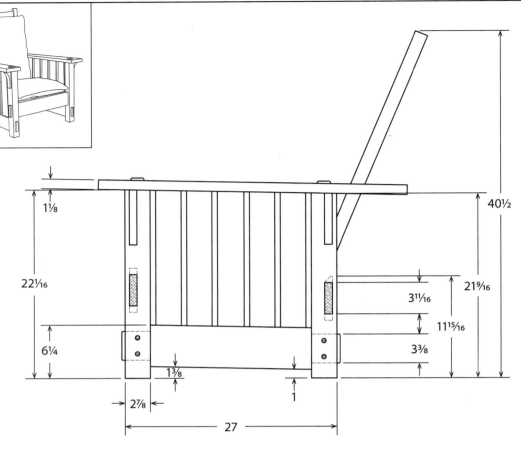

Side

Side Section:

The pegs shown in detail on page 137 go in these holes—one allows the back to pivot, and the other adjusts the angle

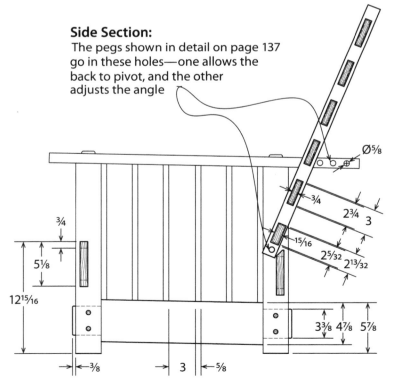

Ø⁵⁄₈

Side

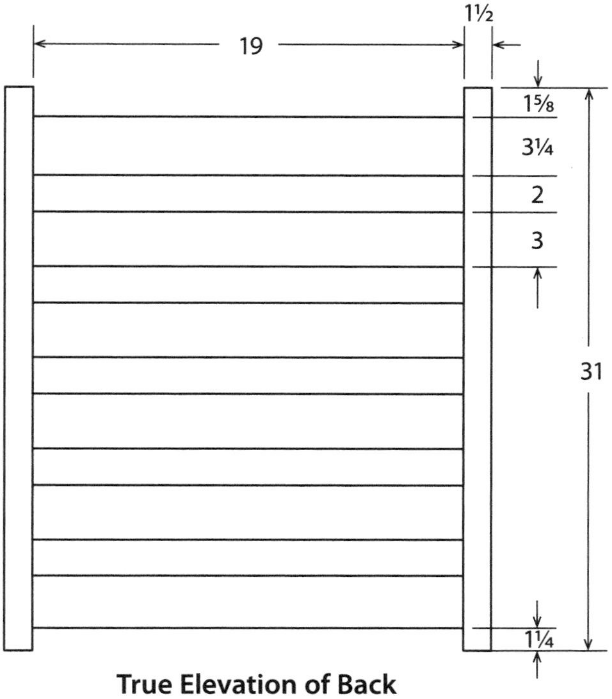

19

1½

1⅝

3¼

2

3

31

1¼

True Elevation of Back

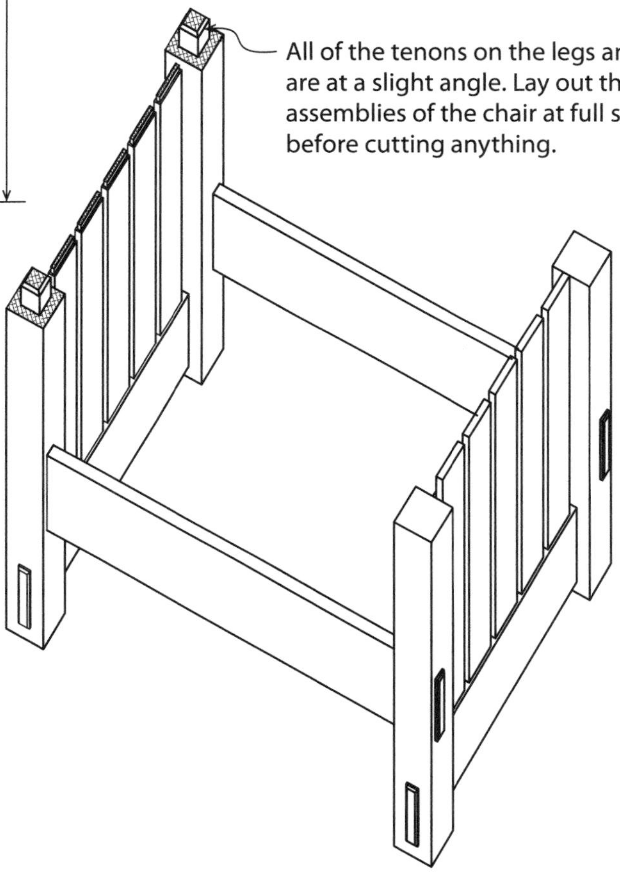

All of the tenons on the legs and slats are at a slight angle. Lay out the side assemblies of the chair at full size before cutting anything.

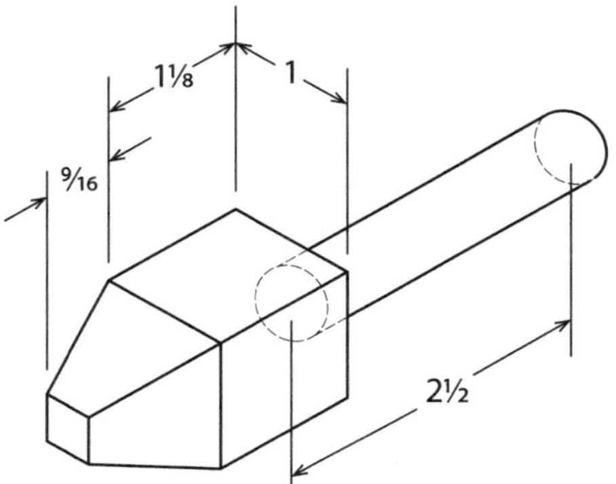

1⅛ 1

⁹⁄₁₆

2½

Peg Detail

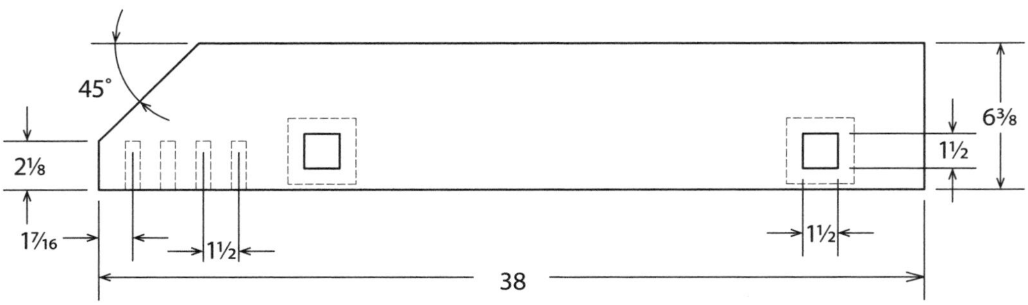

45°

2⅛

1⁷⁄₁₆

1½

1½

6⅜

1½

38

True Plan of Arm

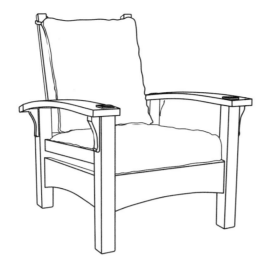

GUSTAV STICKLEY NO. 336 BOW ARM MORRIS CHAIR

31½" wide x 37" high x 37" deep

Although this looks as if it could be a Harvey Ellis design, this chair originally appeared, with slightly different legs, in 1901, two years before Ellis came to work for Stickley. The loose seat cushion was used until 1909, when it was replaced with a spring cushion. The steam-bent bowed arms, plus the angle of the cushion, make this one of the most comfortable of all the Morris chairs. Later versions of this chair had legs that were 2 inches longer, added to the bottom of the leg, as seen in the perspective view at left.

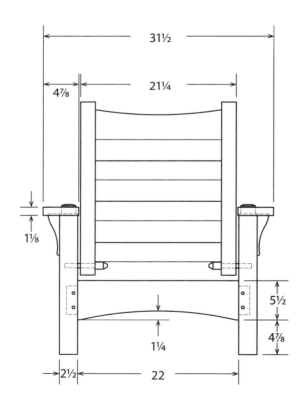

Front of Elevation

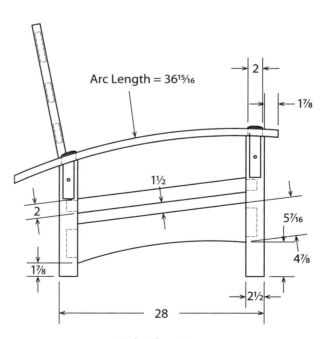

Arc Length = 36¹⁵⁄₁₆

Side Elevation

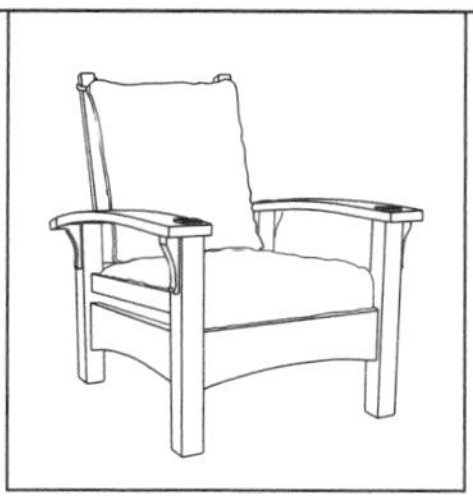

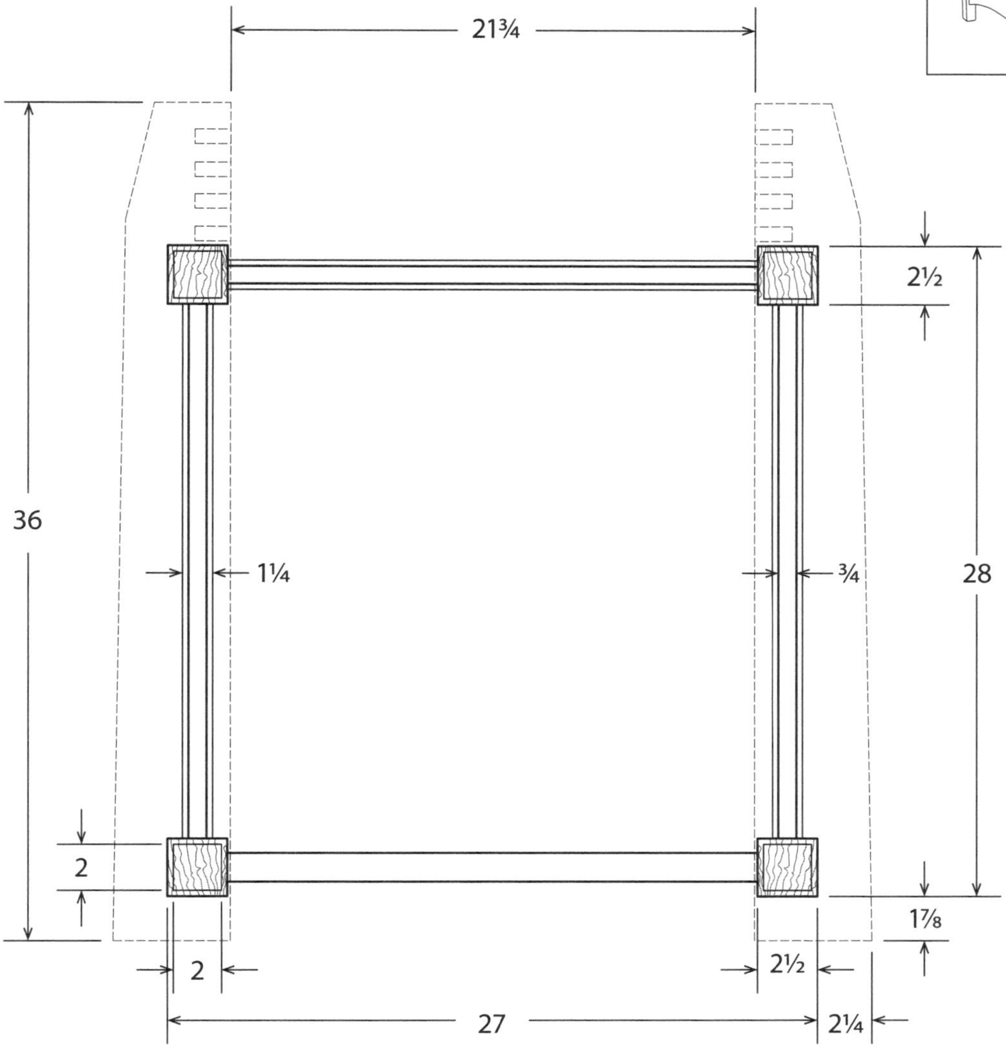

Plan

Gustav Stickley No. 336 Bow Arm Morris Chair

Qty	Part	Size	Notes
2	Front Legs	2½ x 2½ x 21¹⁄₁₆	19⅝ to high point below arm
2	Rear Legs	2½ x 2½ x 17⁹⁄₁₆	16⅜ to high point below arm
1	Front Rail	1¼ x 5½ x 25	22 between tenons
1	Lower Back Rail	1¼ x 5½ x 25	22 between tenons
1	Upper Back Rail	¾ x 2 x 25	22 between tenons
2	Lower Side Rails	1¼ x 5⁷⁄₁₆ x 26	23 between angled tenons
2	Upper Side Rails	¾ x 2 x 26	23 between angled tenons
2	Arms	1⅛ x 4⅞ x 36¹⁵⁄₁₆	finished arc length
4	Corbels	1½ x 1⁹⁄₁₆ x 5⅞	
2	Back Uprights	1⅛ x 2 x 24¾	
3	Curved Back Rails	¾ x 2¾ x 19¼	17¼ between tenons—bend longer stock then trim
1	Back Top Rail	¾ x 4¼ x 19¼	17¼ between tenons—bend longer stock then trim

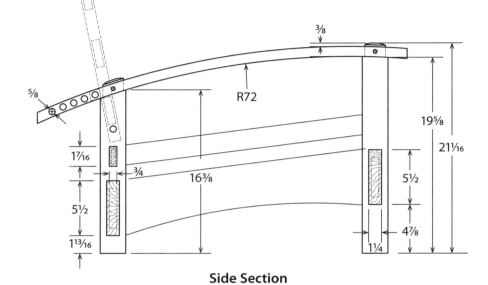

Side Section

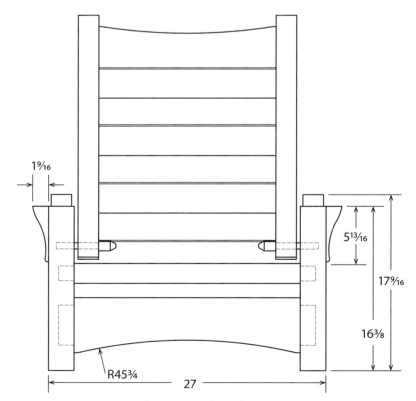

Front Elevation of Back Legs

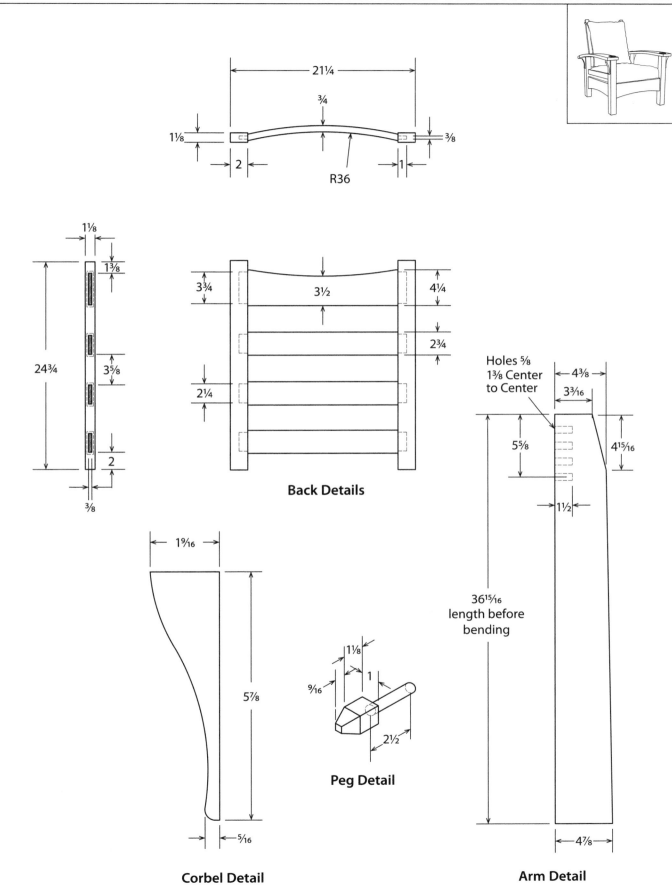

Back Details

Corbel Detail

Peg Detail

Arm Detail

GUSTAV STICKLEY
NO. 347 EASTWOOD CHAIR

37" high x 38½" wide x 32½" deep

Named after the suburb of Syracuse, New York, where Stickley's factory was located, this early chair was featured in *The Craftsman* Magazine in November 1901. A loose seat cushion was supported by a frame of woven cane supported inside the rails. I would run a ¾" x ¾" cleat inside the front and back seat rails, and support the cushion with thin wood slats. If you have the space for it, you won't find a more comfortable chair.

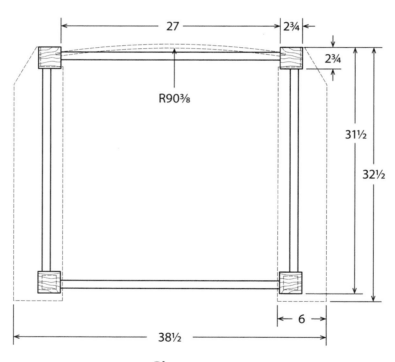

Plan

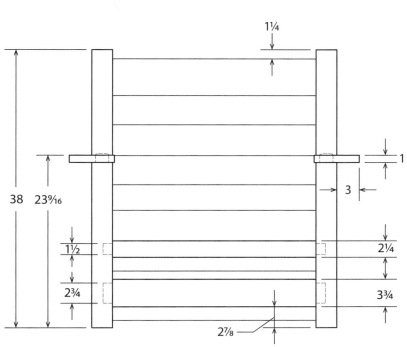

1¼

38   23⁹⁄₁₆

1

3

1½

2¼

2¾

3¾

2⅞

Front Elevation

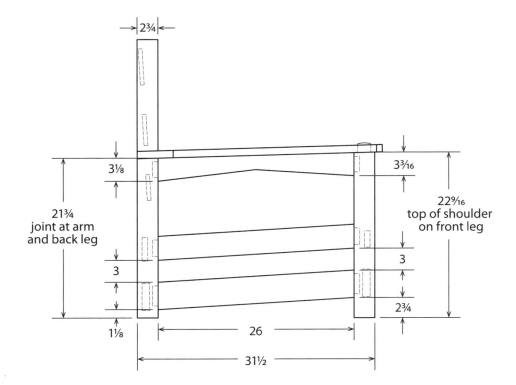

2¾

3⅛

3³⁄₁₆

21¾
joint at arm
and back leg

22⁹⁄₁₆
top of shoulder
on front leg

3

3

2¾

1⅛

26

31½

Side Elevation

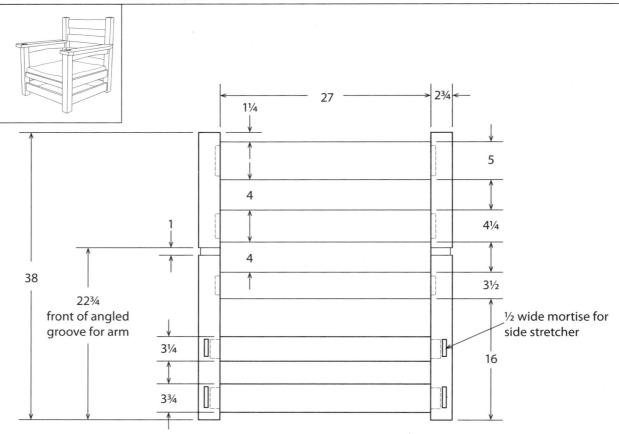

27

2¾

1¼

5

4

4¼

1

4

3½

38

22¾
front of angled
groove for arm

3¼

½ wide mortise for
side stretcher

16

3¾

Elevation of Assembled Back–Viewed from the Front

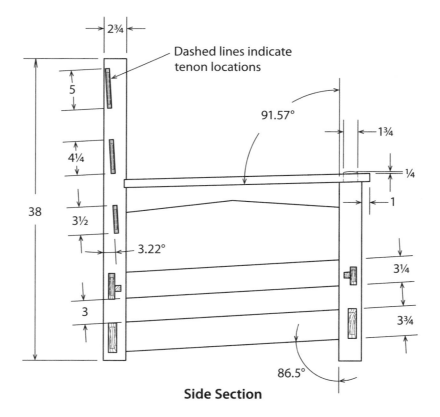

2¾

Dashed lines indicate
tenon locations

5

91.57°

1¾

4¼

¼

38

1

3½

3.22°

3¼

3

3¾

86.5°

Side Section

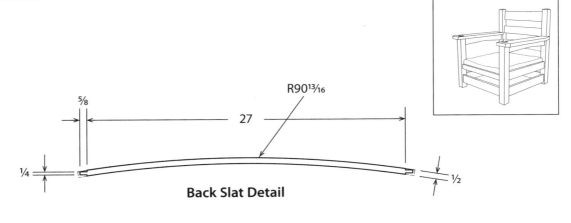

Back Slat Detail

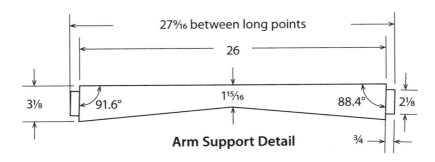

Arm Support Detail

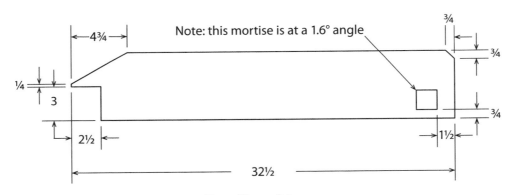

Note: this mortise is at a 1.6° angle

True Plan of Arm

Gustav Stickley No. 347 Eastwood Chair

Qty	Part	Size	Notes
2	Front Legs	2¾ x 2¾ x 23¹³⁄₁₆	22⁹⁄₁₆ to top of shoulders below arms
2	Back Legs	2¾ x 2¾ x 38	
2	Lower Front & Back Rails	1 x 3¾ x 30	27 between tenons
1	Upper Front Rail	¾ x 2¼ x 30	27 between tenons
1	Upper Back Rail	¾ x 3¼ x 30	27 between tenons
2	Lower Side Rails	1 x 3¾ x 27⁹⁄₁₆	26 between angled tenons
2	Upper Side Rails	1 x 3¼ x 27⁹⁄₁₆	26 between angled tenons
2	Rails Below Arms	¾ x 3³⁄₁₆ x 27⁹⁄₁₆	26 between angled tenons
1	Top Curved Back Rail	½ x 5 x 28¼	27 between tenons—make longer for bending
1	Middle Curved Back Rail	½ x 4¼ x 28¼	27 between tenons—make longer for bending
1	Bottom Curved Back Rail	½ x 3½ x 28¼	27 between tenons—make longer for bending
2	Arms	1 x 6 x 32½	

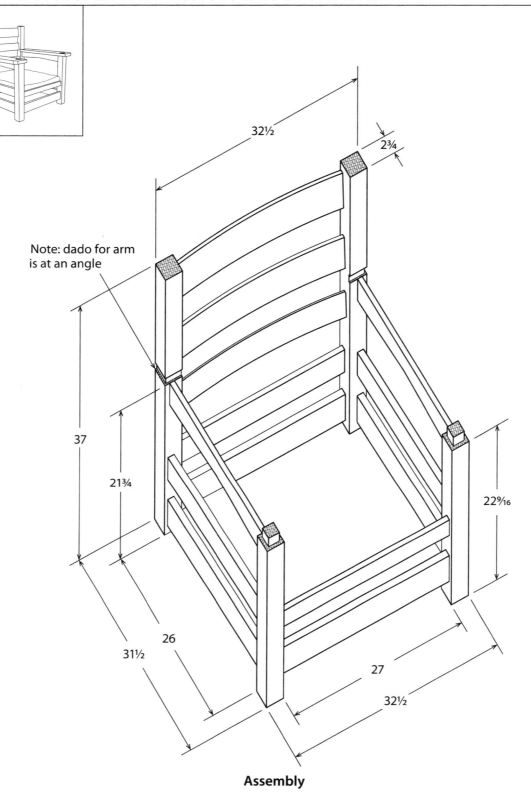

32½

2¾

Note: dado for arm
is at an angle

37

21¾

22⁹⁄₁₆

26

31½

27

32½

Assembly

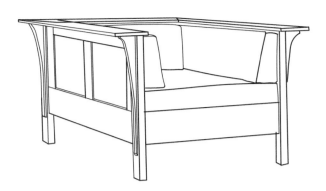

L. & J. G. Stickley
No. 416 Prairie Chair

The Prairie chair was designed to accompany the No. 220 Prairie sofa (page 150). These pieces owe as much to the designs of Frank Lloyd Wright as to the rest of the Stickley output.

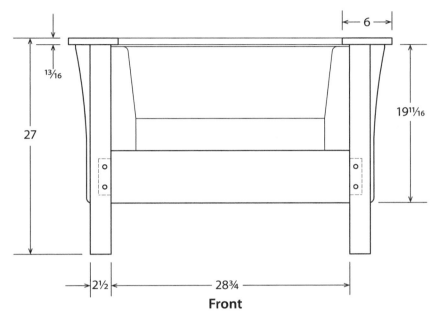

Front

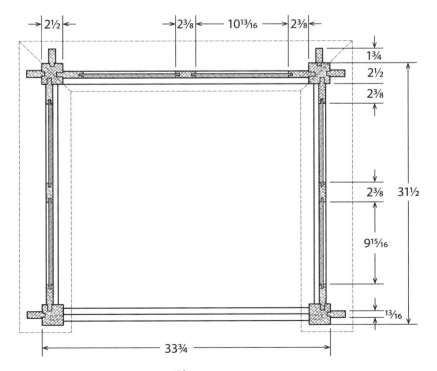

Plan

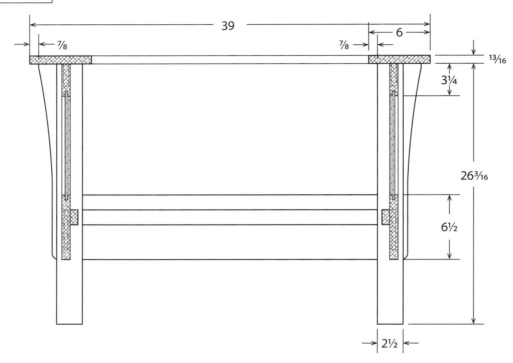

Front Section

L. & J.G. Stickley No. 416 Prairie Chair

Qty.	Part	Size	Notes
4	Legs	2½ x 2½ x 26³⁄₁₆	
2	Side Panels	1³⁄₁₆ x 28 x 19¹¹⁄₁₆	26½ x 19¹¹⁄₁₆ exposed—parts detailed below
4	Side Outer Stiles	1³⁄₁₆ x 3⅛ x 13¹¹⁄₁₆	2⅜ x 13³⁄₁₆ exposed
2	Side Middle Stiles	1³⁄₁₆ x 2⅜ x 10¹⁵⁄₁₆	9¹⁵⁄₁₆ between tongues
2	Side Top Rails	1³⁄₁₆ x 3¼ x 22¾	21¾ between tongues
2	Side Bottom Rails	1³⁄₁₆ x 6½ x 28	26½ between tenon shoulders
4	Side Panels	½ x 10¹⁵⁄₁₆ x 10¹⁵⁄₁₆	9¹⁵⁄₁₆ x 9¹⁵⁄₁₆ exposed
1	Back Panel	1³⁄₁₆ x 30¼ x 19¹¹⁄₁₆	28¾ x 19¹¹⁄₁₆ exposed—parts detailed below
1	Back Bottom Rail	1³⁄₁₆ x 6½ x 31¾	28¾ between tenon shoulders
1	Back Top Rail	1³⁄₁₆ x 3¼ x 25½	24 between tongues
2	Back Outer Stiles	1³⁄₁₆ x 3⅛ x 13¹¹⁄₁₆	2⅜ x 13³⁄₁₆ exposed
1	Back Middle Stiles	1³⁄₁₆ x 2⅜ x 10¹⁵⁄₁₆	9¹⁵⁄₁₆ tongue to tongue
2	Back Panels	½ x 11¹³⁄₁₆ x 10¹⁵⁄₁₆	10¹³⁄₁₆ x 9¹⁵⁄₁₆ exposed
1	Front Rail	1³⁄₁₆ x 6½ x 31¾	28¾ between tenon shoulders
2	Arms	1³⁄₁₆ x 6 x 35	
1	Top Cap @ Back	1³⁄₁₆ x 6 x 39	
6	Corbels	1³⁄₁₆ x 2¼ x 19¹¹⁄₁₆	1¾ exposed
2	Seat Supports	¾ x 1½ x 26½	
2	Seat Supports	¾ x 1½ x 28¾	

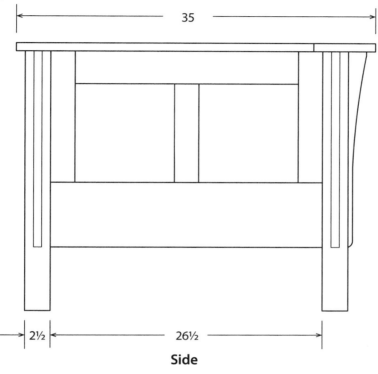

Side

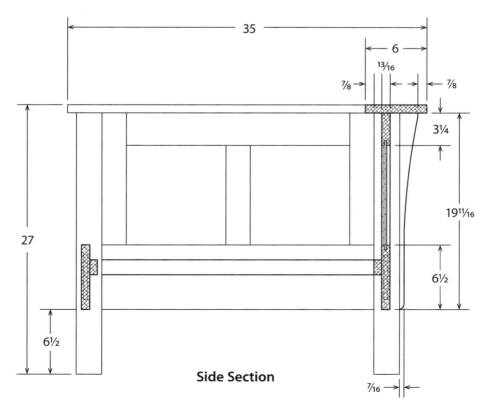

Side Section

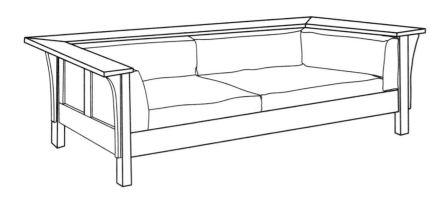

L. & J. G. STICKLEY
NO. 220 PRAIRIE SOFA

29" high x 84½" wide x 36¾" deep

The Prairie settle or sofa and chair (page 147) represent a truly distinct design from Leopold Stickley. Unlike anything ever created in Gustav's workshops, this suite is a classic example of excellent Arts & Crafts design.

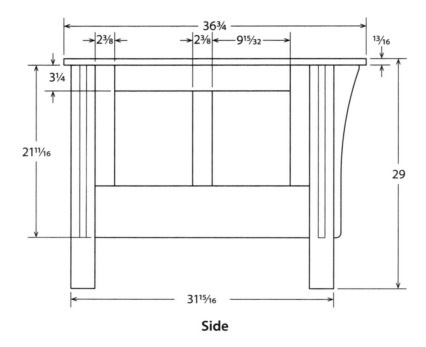

Side

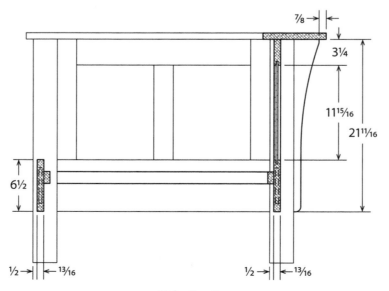

Side Section

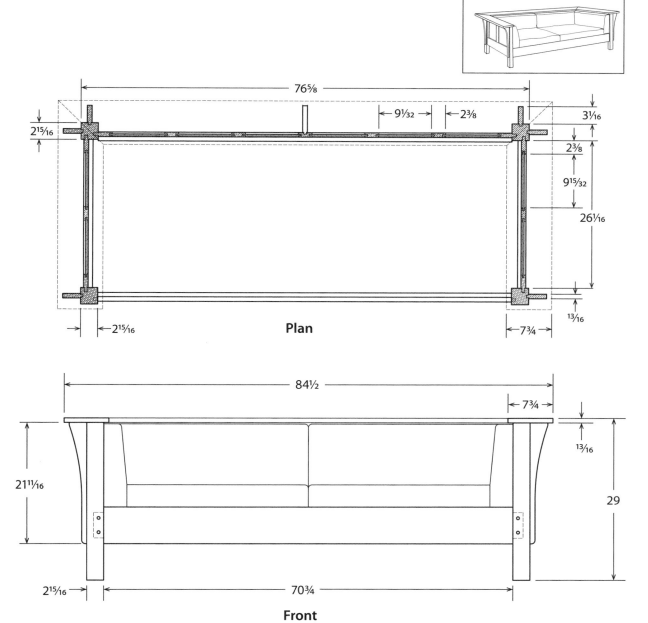

Plan

Front

Back

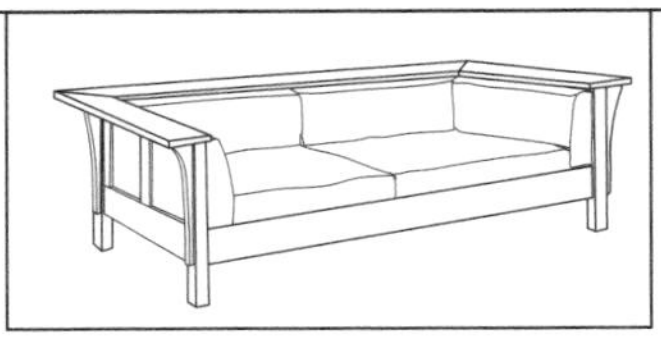

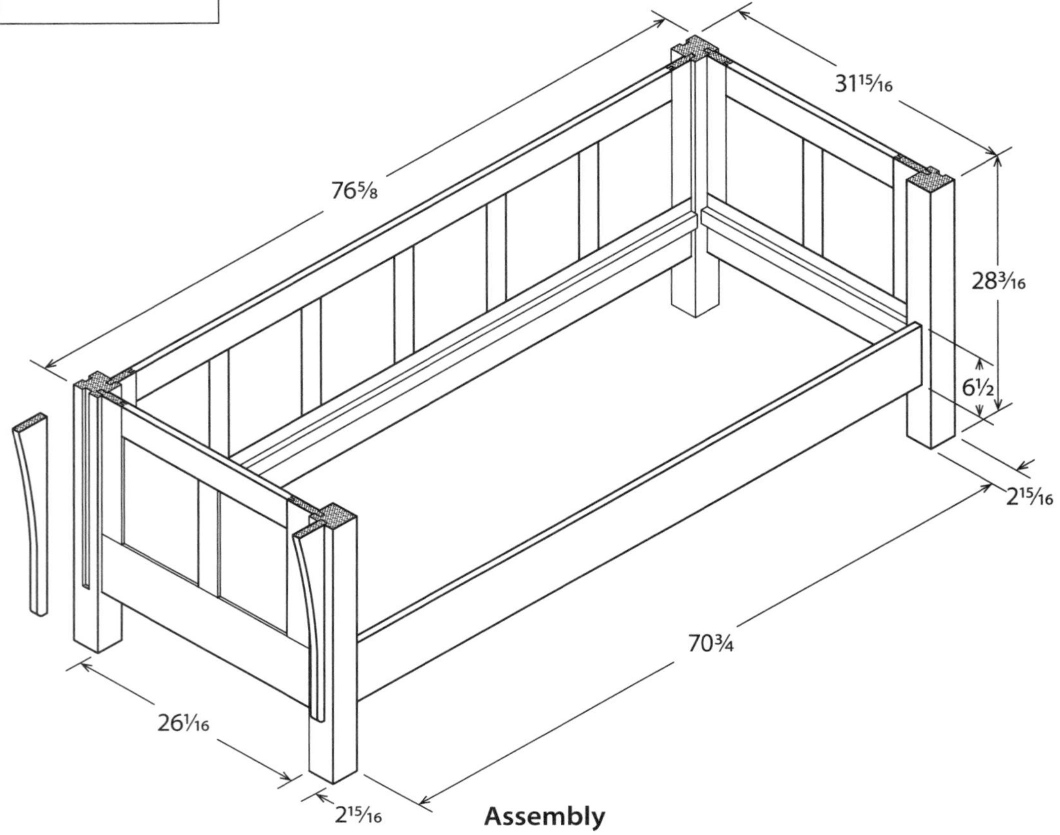

Assembly

L. & J.G. Stickley No. 220 Praire Sofa

Qty	Part	Size	Notes
4	Legs	2¹⁵⁄₁₆ x 2¹⁵⁄₁₆ x 28³⁄₁₆	
2	Side Panels	¹³⁄₁₆ x 27⁹⁄₁₆ x 21¹¹⁄₁₆	26¹⁄₁₆ x 21¹¹⁄₁₆ exposed—parts detailed below
4	Side Outer Stiles	¹³⁄₁₆ x 3⅛ x 15¹¹⁄₁₆	2⅜ x 15³⁄₁₆ exposed
2	Side Middle Stiles	¹³⁄₁₆ x 2⅜ x 12¹⁵⁄₁₆	11¹⁵⁄₁₆ between tongues
2	Side Top Rails	¹³⁄₁₆ x 3¼ x 22⁵⁄₁₆	21⁵⁄₁₆ between tongues
2	Side Bottom Rails	¹³⁄₁₆ x 6½ x 27⁹⁄₁₆	26¹⁄₁₆ between tenon shoulders
4	Side Panels	½ x 10½ x 12¹⁵⁄₁₆	9½ x 11¹⁵⁄₁₆ exposed
1	Back Panel	¹³⁄₁₆ x 72¼ x 21¹¹⁄₁₆	70¾ x 21¹¹⁄₁₆ exposed—parts detailed below
1	Back Bottom Rail	¹³⁄₁₆ x 6½ x 73¾	70¾ between tenons
1	Back Top Rail	¹³⁄₁₆ x 3¼ x 67	66 between tenons
2	Back Outer Stiles	¹³⁄₁₆ x 3⅛ x 15¹¹⁄₁₆	2⅜ x 15³⁄₁₆ exposed
5	Back Inner Stiles	¹³⁄₁₆ x 2¾ x 12¹⁵⁄₁₆	11¹⁵⁄₁₆ between tongues
6	Back Panels	½ x 10 x 12¹⁵⁄₁₆	9 x 11¹⁵⁄₁₆ exposed
1	Front Rail	¹³⁄₁₆ x 6½ x 73¾	70¾ between tenon shoulders
2	Arms	¹³⁄₁₆ x 7¾ x 36¾	
1	Top Cap @ Back	¹³⁄₁₆ x 7¾ x 84½	
6	Corbels	¹³⁄₁₆ x 3½ x 21¹¹⁄₁₆	3 exposed
1	Corbel	¹³⁄₁₆ x 5¹⁄₁₆ x 21¹¹⁄₁₆	4¹¹⁄₁₆ exposed
2	Seat Supports	¾ x 1½ x 70¾	
2	Seat Supports	¾ x 1½ x 26¹⁄₁₆	

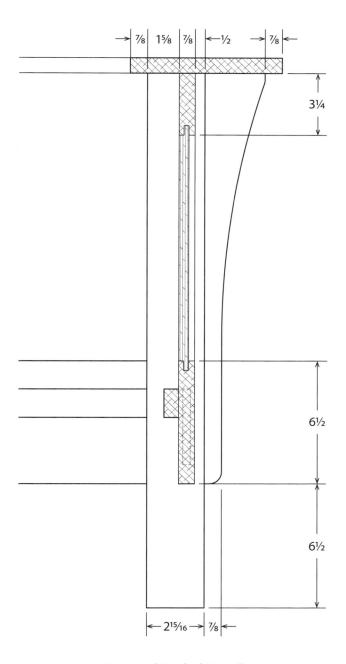

Leg and Corbel Detail

GUSTAV STICKLEY NO. 206 SETTLE

60" wide x 40" high x 28" deep

This love-seat size settle is unusual because of the rounded tops of the rails, and the angle of the back and sides. These features make it more comfortable than similar settles. The original seat cushion was supported by woven cane, and was available upholstered in "Craftsman Canvas" or leather.

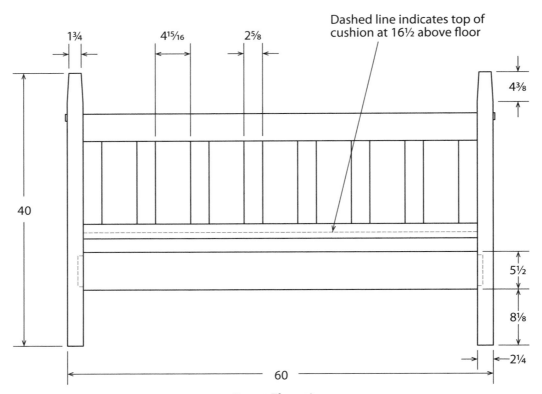

Dashed line indicates top of cushion at 16½ above floor

1¾   4¹⁵⁄₁₆   2⅝   4⅜   40   5½   8⅛   2¼   60

Front Elevation

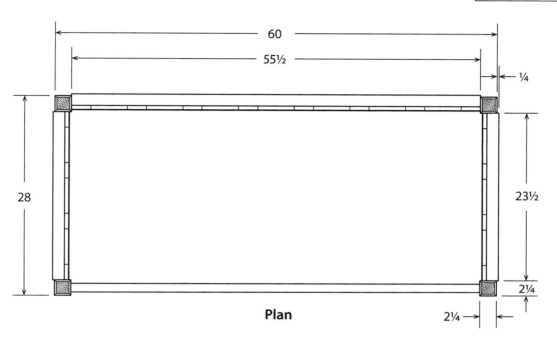

Plan

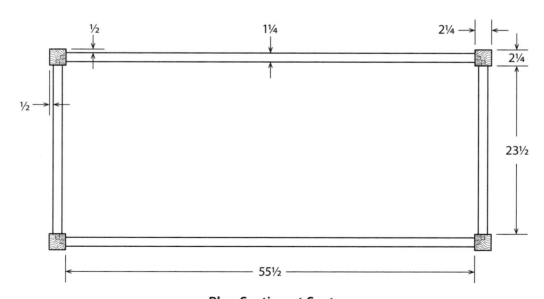

Plan Section at Seat

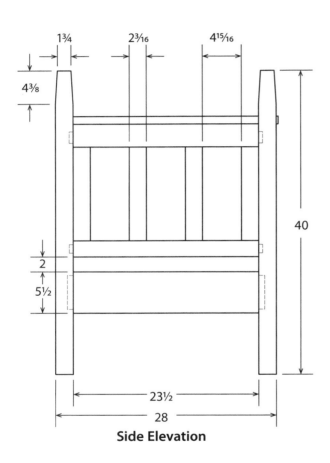

Side Elevation

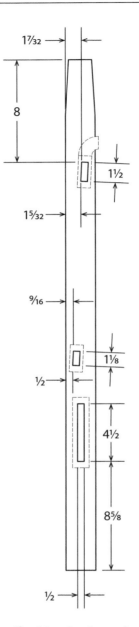

Detail—Mortise Locations on Leg

Gustav Stickley No. 206 Settle

Qty	Part	Size	Notes
4	Legs	2¼ x 2¼ x 40	
2	Lower Front & Back Rails	1¼ x 5½ x 57	55½ between tenons
2	Lower Side Rails	1¼ x 5½ x 25	23½ between tenons
2	Middle Side Rails	1 x 2⅛ x 24½	23½ between tenons
2	Top Side Rails	1 x 2½ x 24½	23½ between tenons
2	Side Rail Caps	1⅛ x 2⅛ x 23½	
1	Middle Back Rail	1 x 2⅛ x 56½	55½ between tenons
1	Top Back Rail	1 x 2½ x 56½	55½ between tenons
1	Back Rail Cap	1⅛ x 2⅛ x 55½	
6	Side Slats	⅝ x 4¹⁵⁄₁₆ x 13¼	12¼ between tenons
7	Back Slats	⅝ x 4¹⁵⁄₁₆ x 13¼	12¼ between tenons

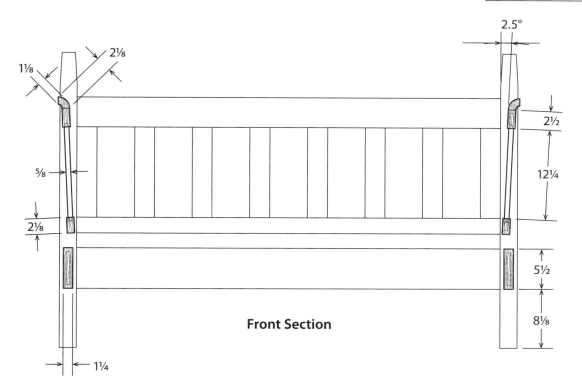

Front Section

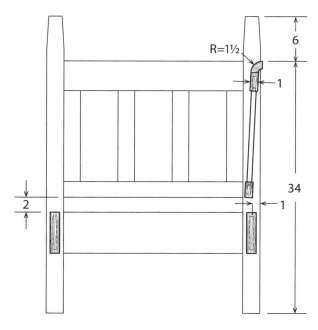

Side Section

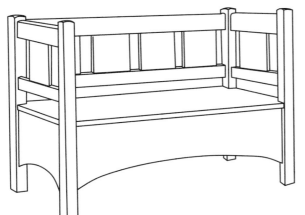

L. & J. G. STICKLEY NO. 207 SETTLE

32" high x 42" wide x 18" deep

Note that the tenons on the rails are offset. This allows them to be long enough to accept a peg through the joint. The seat is hinged at the back to allow access to the storage space beneath.

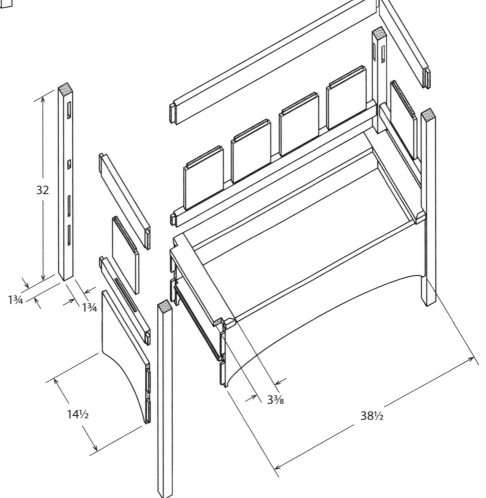

Assembly

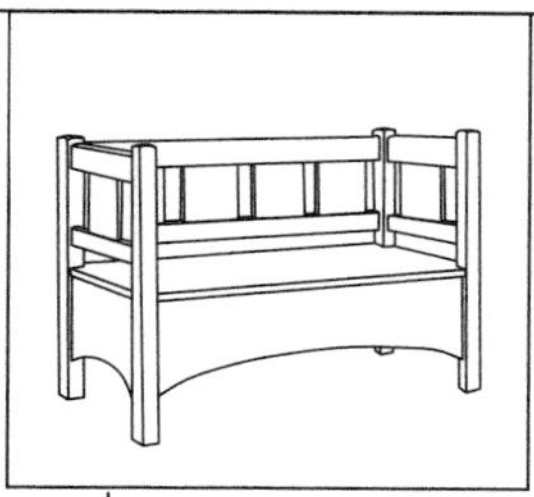

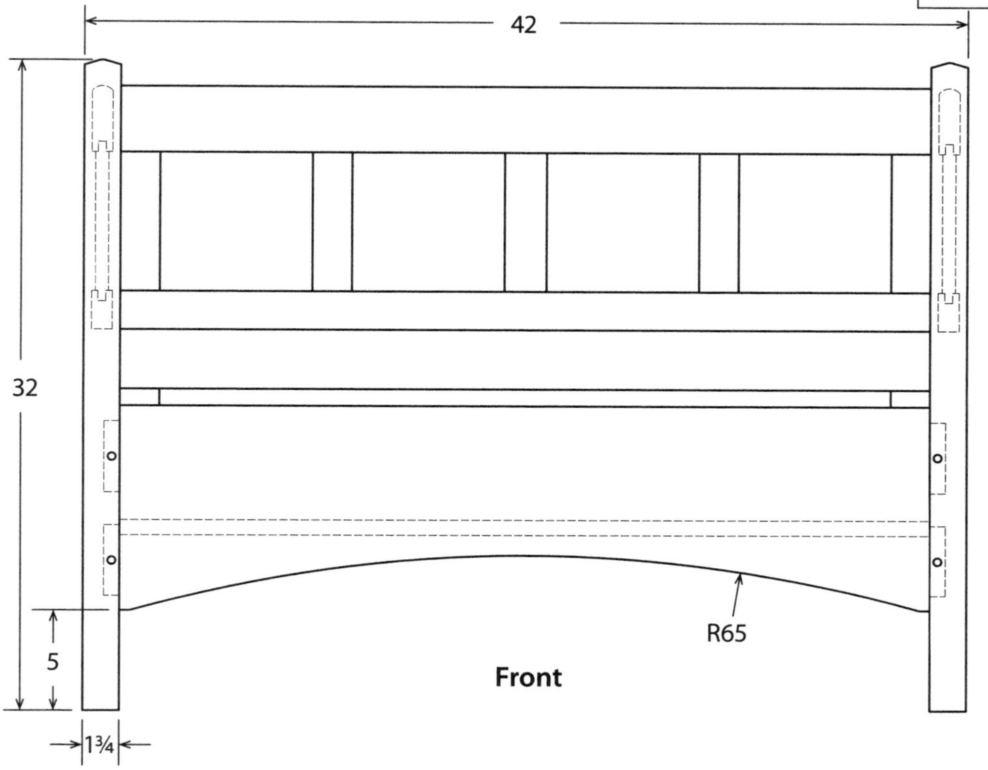

42

32

5

1¾

Front

R65

1

3¼

⁵⁄₈

1⁷⁄₈

¹³⁄₁₆

15⁷⁄₈

1¼

6¹³⁄₁₆

5⁵⁄₈

10⅛

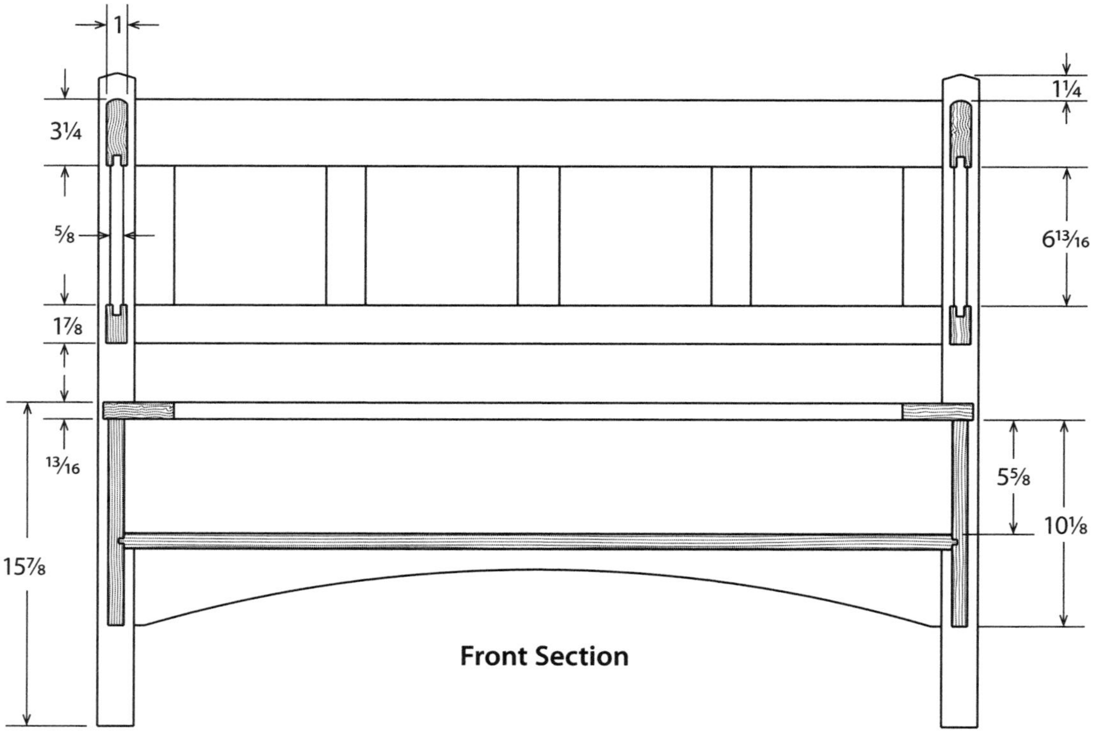

Front Section

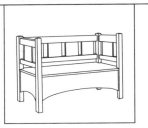

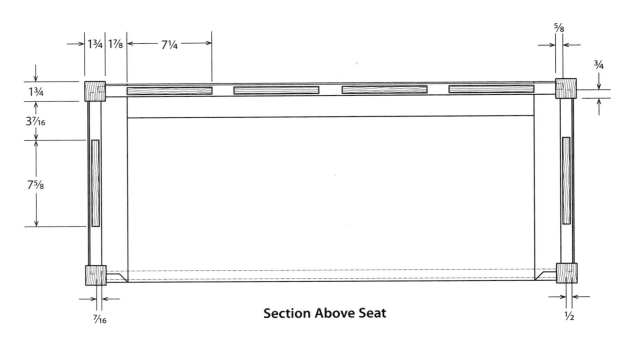

Section Above Seat

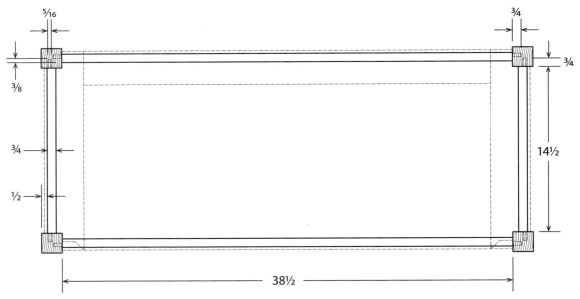

Section Below Seat

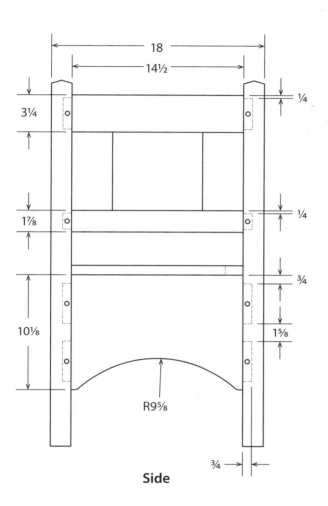

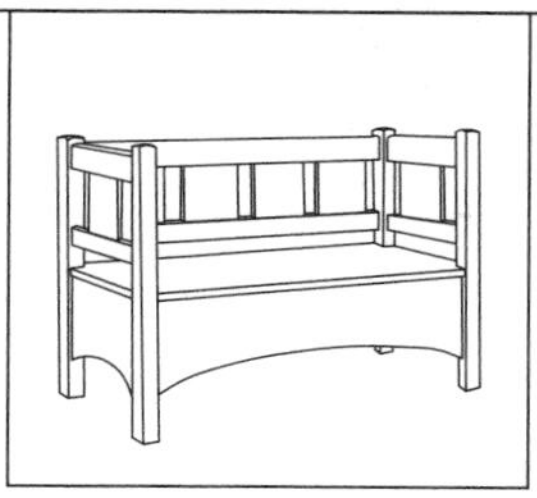

Side

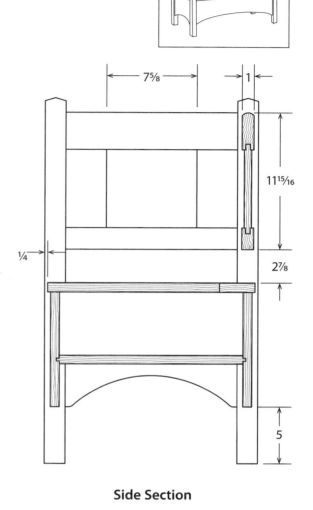

Side Section

L. & J.G. Stickley No. 207 Settle

Qty	Part	Size	Notes
4	Legs	1¾ x 1¾ x 32	
1	Top Back Rail	1 x 3¼ x 39¾	38½ between tenon shoulders
1	Bottom Back Rail	1 x 1⅞ x 39¾	38½ between tenon shoulders
4	Back Slats	⅝ x 7¼ x 7¹³⁄₁₆	6¹³⁄₁₆ between tenon shoulders
2	Top Side Rails	1 x 3¼ x 16	14½ between tenon shoulders
2	Bottom Side Rails	1 x 1⅞ x 16	14½ between tenon shoulders
2	Side Slats	⅝ x 7⅝ x 7¹³⁄₁₆	6¹³⁄₁₆ between tenon shoulders
2	Arched Sides Below Seat	¾ x 10⅛ x 16	14½ between tenon shoulders
2	Arched Front & Back Below Seat	¾ x 10⅛ x 40	38½ between tenon shoulders
2	Seat Stiles	¾ x 3⅜ x 17½	notch @ legs, mitered return @ front
1	Seat	¾ x 14½ x 34¾	opening size—trim for desired gaps
1	Bottom Below Seat	¾ x 16 x 40	15½ x 39½ exposed between tongues

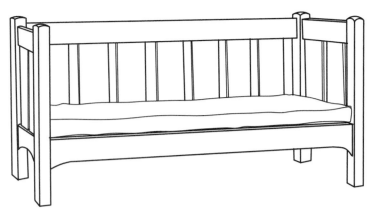

L. & J. G. STICKLEY NO. 216 SETTLE

72" wide x 26" deep x 36" high

The original had a spring support for the cushion. The modern, easy way out is to have a futon mattress made to the appropriate size, and support it with wooden slats running from front to back.

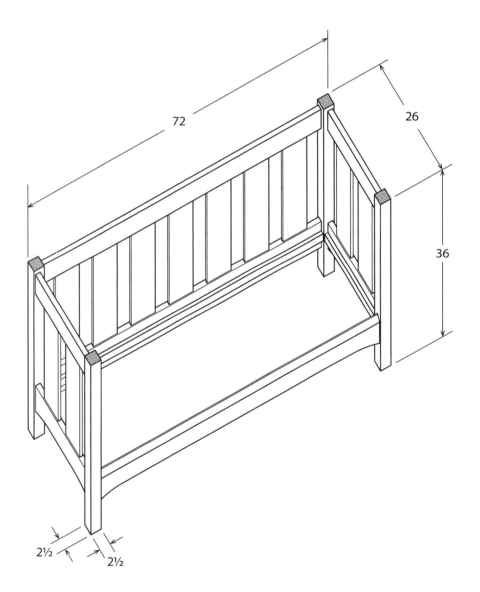

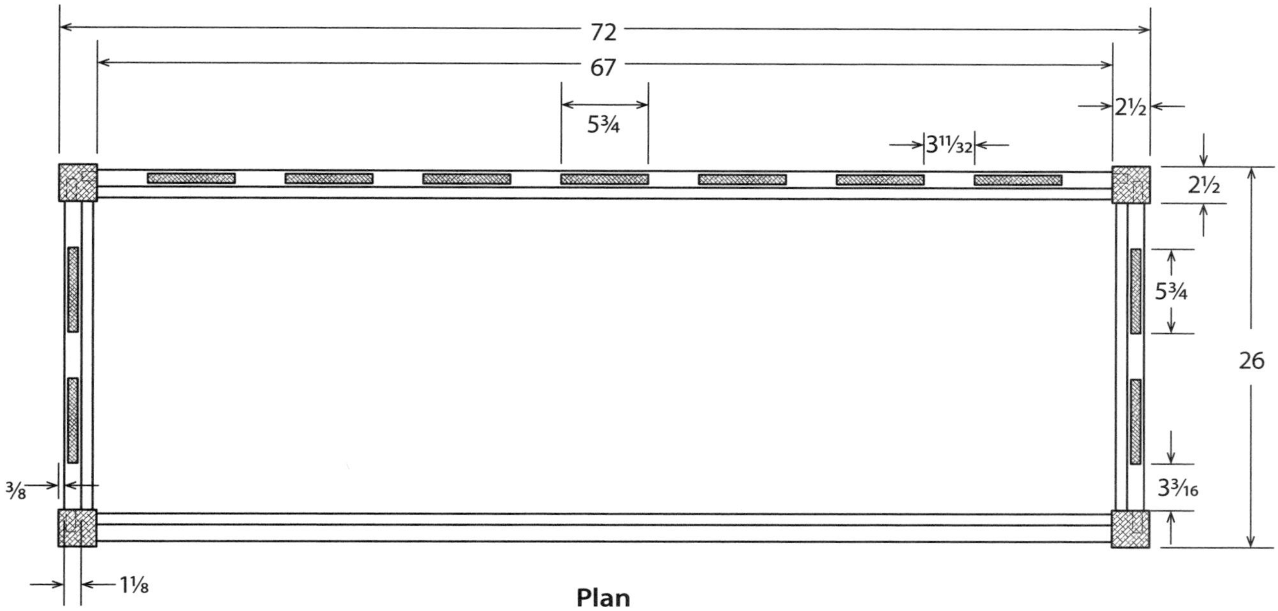

Plan

72

67

5¾

3¹¹⁄₃₂

2½

2½

5¾

26

3³⁄₁₆

³⁄₈

1⅛

Front

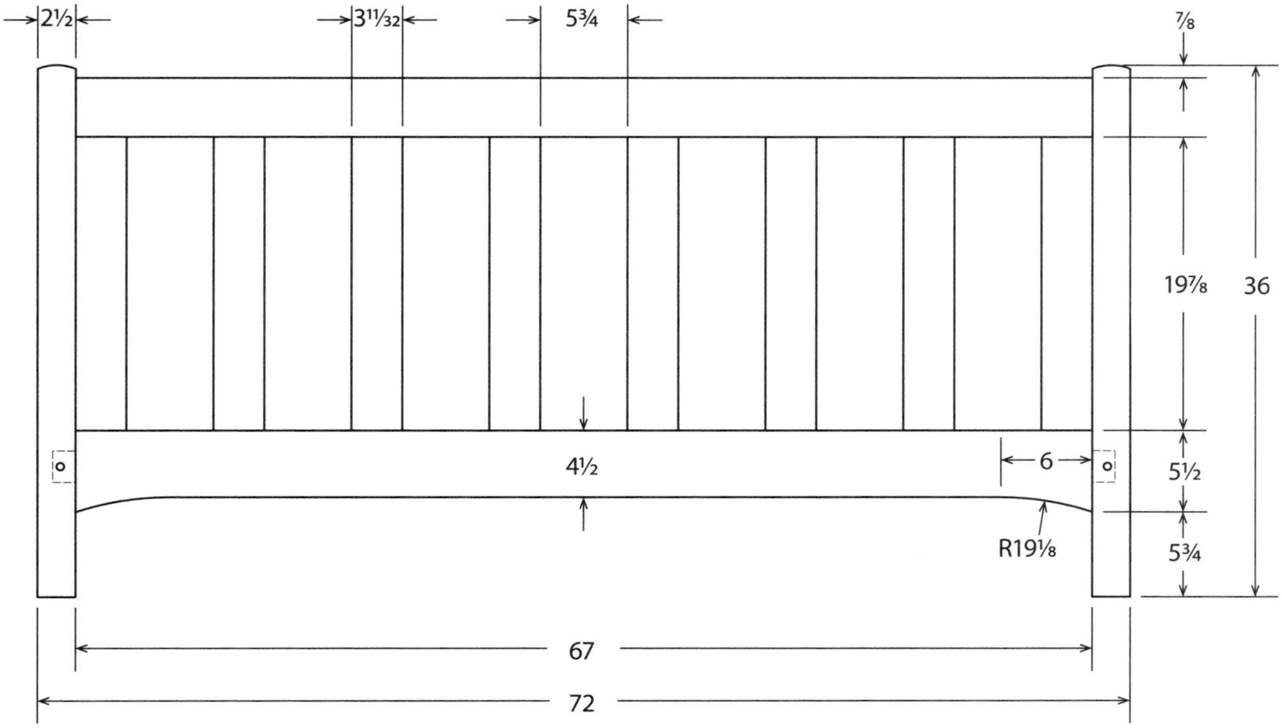

2½

3¹¹⁄₃₂

5¾

⁷⁄₈

19⅞

36

4½

6

5½

R19⅛

5¾

67

72

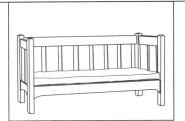

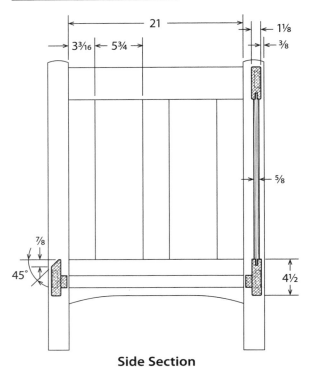

Side Section

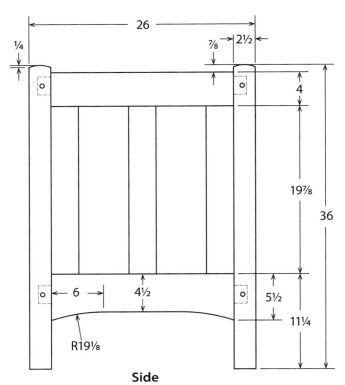

Side

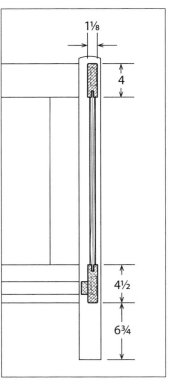

Front Section

L. & J.G. Stickley No. 216 Settle

Qty	Part	Size	Notes
4	Legs	2½ x 2½ x 36	
1	Top Back Rail	1⅛ x 4 x 69	67 between tenon shoulders
1	Bottom Back Rail	1⅛ x 4½ x 69	67 between tenon shoulders
7	Back Slats	⅝ x 5¾ x 20⅞	19⅞ between tenon shoulders
1	Front Rail	1⅛ x 5½ x 69	67 between tenon shoulders
2	Top Side Rails	1⅛ x 4 x 24	21 between tenon shoulders
2	Bottom Side Rails	1⅛ x 4½ x 24	21 between tenon shoulders
2	Side Slats	⅝ x 5¾ x 20⅞	19⅞ between tenon shoulders
2	Seat Supports	¾ x 1½ x 67	
2	Seat Supports	¾ x 1½ x 21	

L. & J. G. STICKLEY
NO. 225 SETTLE

47⅛" wide x 22¾" deep x 36½" high

The original catalog description speaks of this having a "spring seat cushion." There is enough space below the top rails for a frame with sinuous wire springs attached, or a simple cushion supported by slats could be used.

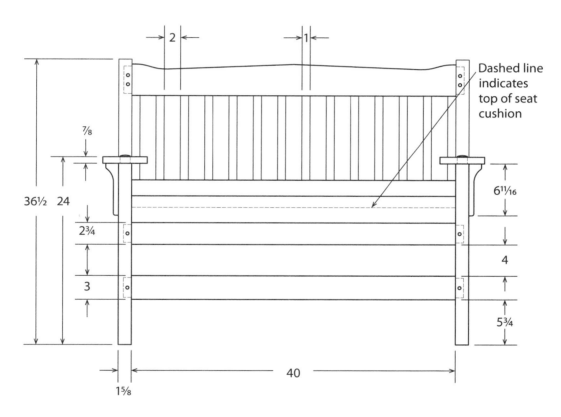

Dashed line indicates top of seat cushion

Front Elevation

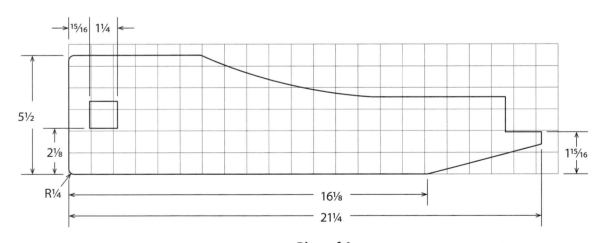

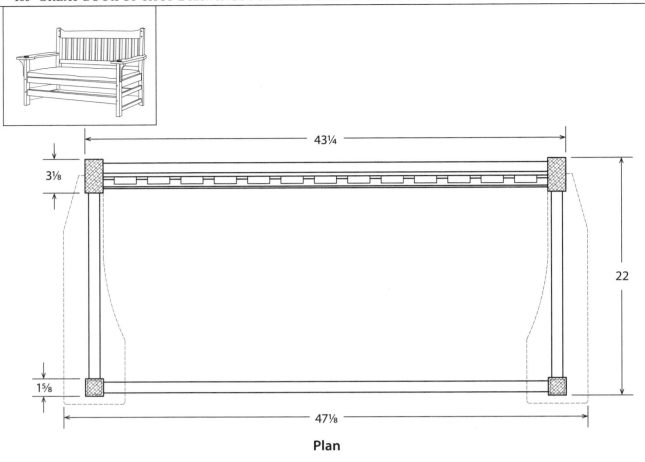

Plan

Plan of Arm
Grid = 1" squares

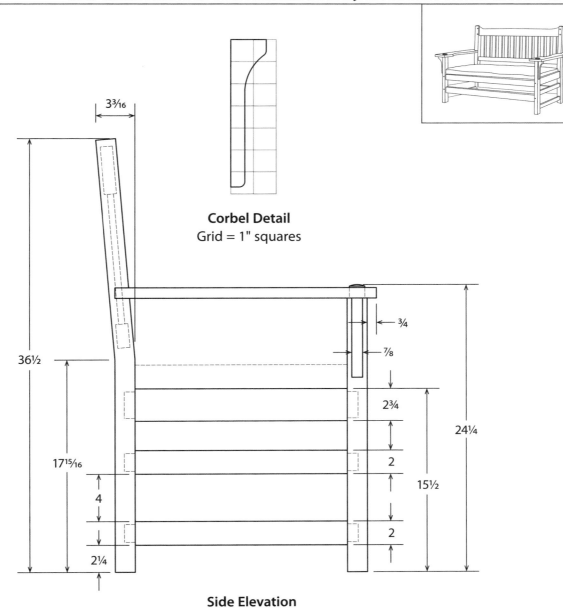

Corbel Detail
Grid = 1" squares

Side Elevation

L. & J. G. Stickley No. 225 Settle

Qty	Part	Size	Notes
2	Front Legs	1⅝ x 1⅝ x 24¼	23⅛ below shoulder under arm
2	Back Legs	1⅝ x 3³⁄₁₆ x 36½	
2	Lower Front & Back Rail	1 x 3 x 42	40 between tenons
2	Front & Back Seat Rail	1 x 2¾ x 42	40 between tenons
2	Lower Side Rails	1 x 2 x 19¼	17¼ between tenons
2	Side Seat Rails	1 x 2¾ x 19¼	17¼ between tenons
2	Arms	⅞ x 5½ x 21¼	
1	Lower Back Rail	1 x 2 x 42	40 between tenons
1	Upper Back Rail	1 x 4 x 42	40 between tenons
13	Back Slats	½ x 2 x 11¹⁵⁄₁₆	10¹⁵⁄₁₆ between tenons
2	Corbels	⅞ x 1⅝ x 6¹¹⁄₁₆	

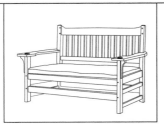

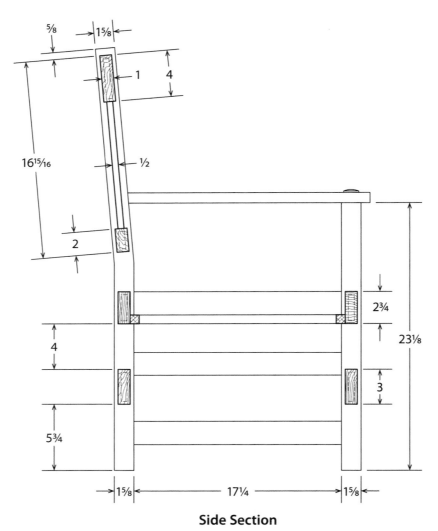

5/8   1 5/8

1   4

16 15/16   1/2

2

2 3/4

23 1/8

4

3

5 3/4

1 5/8   17 1/4   1 5/8

Side Section

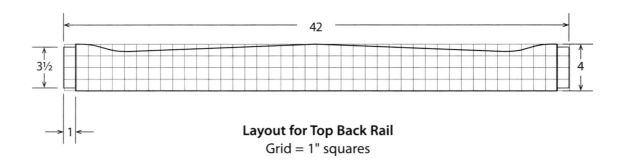

42

3 1/2   4

1

Layout for Top Back Rail
Grid = 1" squares

L. & J. G. STICKLEY NO. 516 TABLE WITH OPEN BOOKCASE

27" x 27" x 29" high

Also known as an encyclopedia table, this is a great place to store a collection of fine books, and a wonderful opportunity for purchasing a hollow-chisel mortiser. When laying out the slats, work from the center out to the ends, and be precise. There are enough slats and spaces for tiny errors to accumulate.

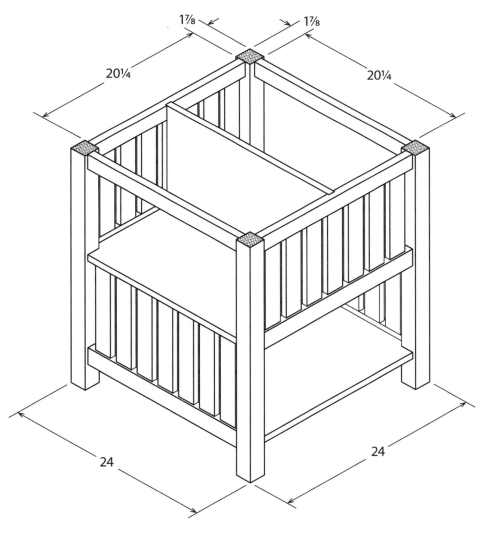

Assembly

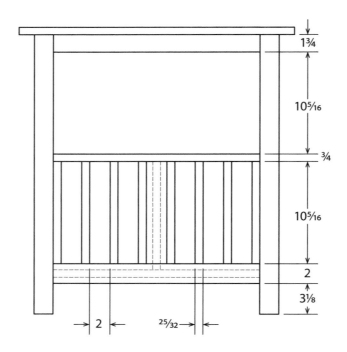

Front

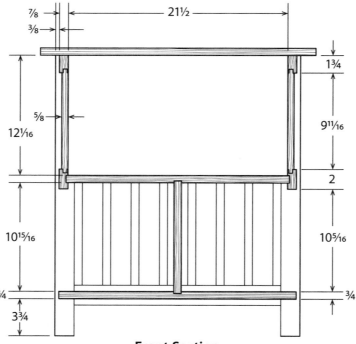

Front Section

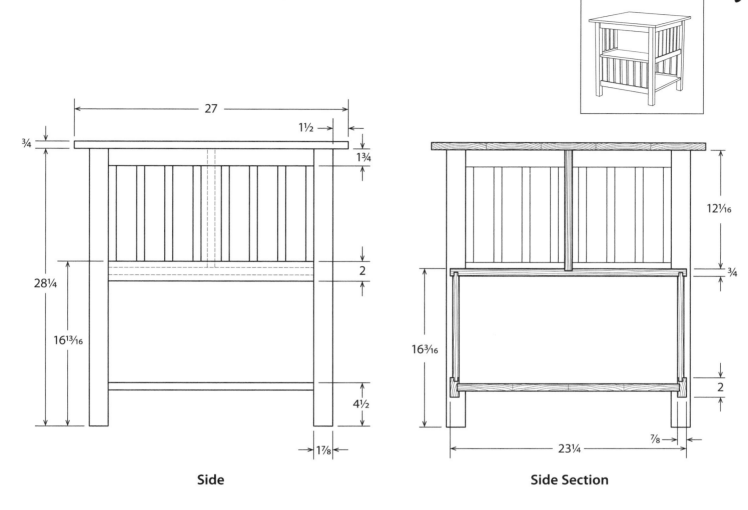

Side

Side Section

L. & J. G. Stickley No.516 Table with Open Bookcase

Qty	Part	Size	Notes
1	Top	¾ x 27 x 27	
4	Leg	1⅞ x 1⅞ x 28¼	
2	Shelves	¾ x 22 x 23¼	21½ exposed width
1	Upper Vertical Divider	¾ x 12⁵⁄₁₆ x 22	12¹⁄₁₆ x 21½ exposed
1	Lower Vertical Divider	¾ x 11⁷⁄₁₆ x 22	10¹⁵⁄₁₆ x 21½ exposed
4	Top Rails	⅞ x 1¾ x 21½	20¼ between tenon shoulders
4	Middle & Bottom Rails	⅞ x 2 x 21½	20¼ between tenon shoulders
14	Upper Slats	⅝ x 2 x 10⁷⁄₁₆	9¹¹⁄₁₆ between tenon shoulders
14	Lower Slats	⅝ x 2 x 11¹⁄₁₆	10⁵⁄₁₆ between tenon shoulders

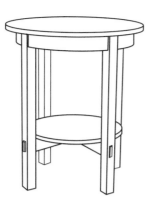

L. & J. G. STICKLEY
NO. 540 OCCASIONAL TABLE

24" diameter x 30" high

Most of the original versions of this type of table had the curved aprons cut from solid stock, leaving very weak short grain where the aprons join the legs. In most of the examples I have seen this joint has failed, with the wood at the end of the apron actually falling apart. A better approach would be to make the aprons from curved plywood, or to laminate them from several thin, solid-wood strips.

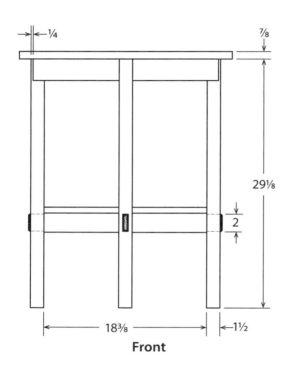

Front

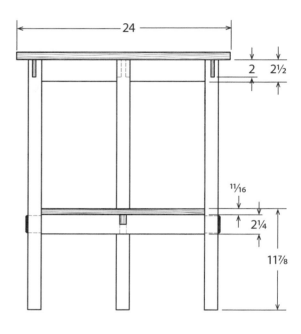

Front Section

Plan

Apron Section

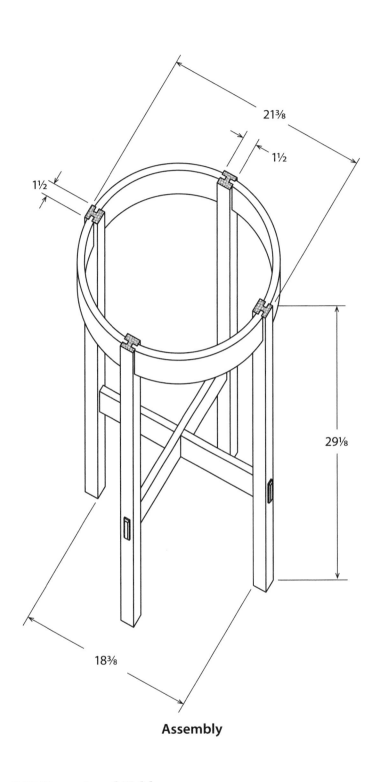

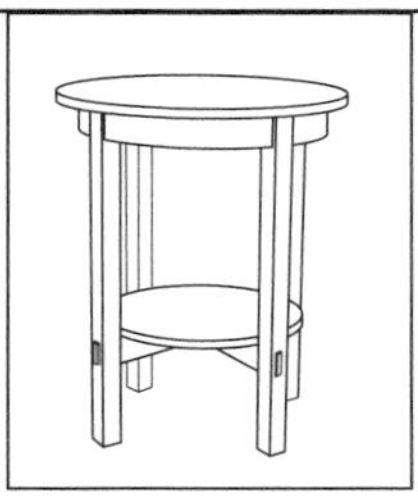

Assembly

L. & J.G. Stickley No. 540 Occasional Table

Qty	Part	Size	Notes
1	Top	⅞ x 24 diameter	
1	Shelf	¾ x 18⁵⁄₁₆ diameter	
4	Legs	1½ x 1½ x 29⅛	Curved
4	Bottom Stretchers	¾ x 2¼ x 21⅞	18⅜ between tenons
4	Top Stretchers	¾ x 2½ x 15⅞	Curved

GUSTAV STICKLEY NO. 603 TABOURET

18" diameter x 20" high

Because of its construction, the tabouret is a very sturdy little piece, suitable for use as an end table, TV table, or plant stand. You could also press it into service as a place to park your lap-top computer, though you might want to increase the height by a few inches.

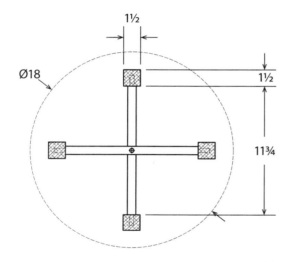

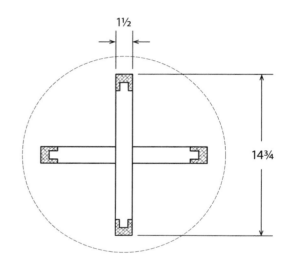

Plan

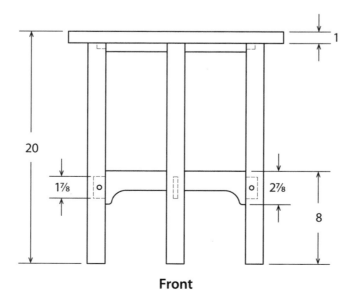

Front

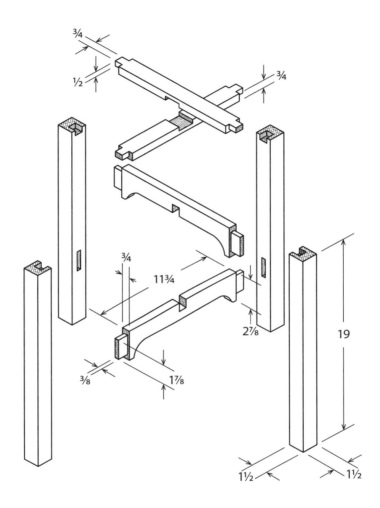

Assembly

Gustav Stickley No. 603 Tabouret

Qty	Part	Size	Notes
1	Top	1 x 18 diameter	
4	Legs	1½ x 1½ x 19	
2	Top Stretchers	¾ x 1½ x 13¼	half lap in middle
2	Bot. Stretchers	¾ x 2⅞ x 13¾	11¾ between tenon shoulders

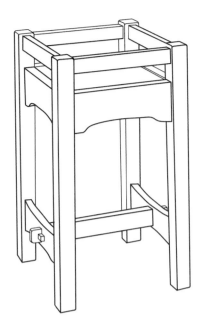

GUSTAV STICKLEY PLANT STAND

26" high x 14" square

The original has a Greuby tile top. If you use tile, finish the stand before setting the tile.

This plan allows for a ⅜" thick tile. If you use a different thickness, adjust the height of the cleats and plywood accordingly (the top of the tile should be ⅛" below the adjacent wood).

I couldn't find this plant stand in any of the old catalogs, but at auction it had a genuine Gustav Stickley tag. L. & J.G. Stickley made a very similar stand, without the arches on the stretchers and without the keyed tenons.

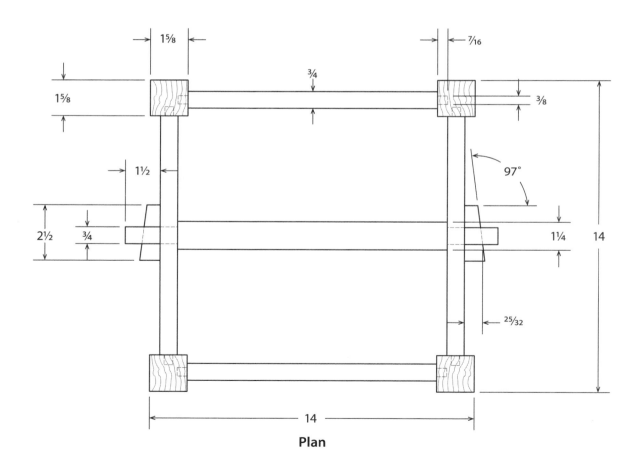

Plan

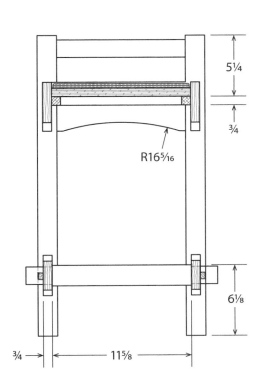

5¼

¾

R16⁵⁄₁₆

6⅛

¾

11⅝

Front Section

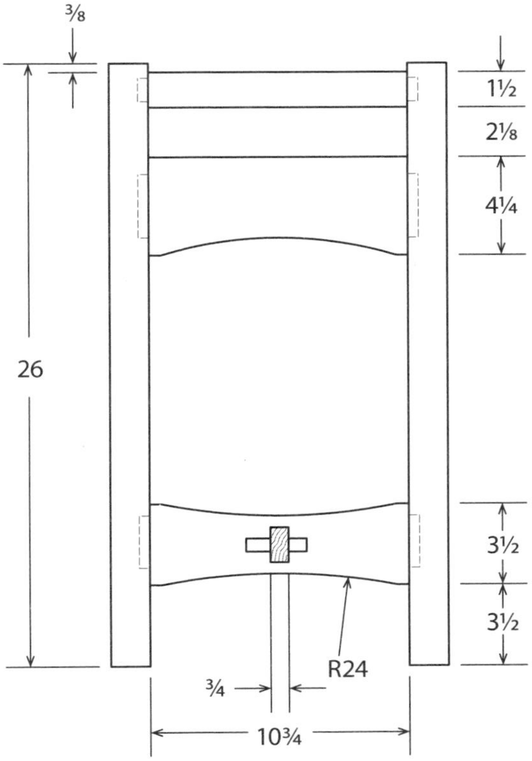

⅜

1½

2⅛

4¼

26

3½

3½

R24

¾

10¾

Side

Gustav Stickley Plant Stand

Qty.	Part	Size	Notes
4	Legs	1⅝ x 1⅝ x 26	
4	Top Rails	¾ x 1½ x 11⅝	10¾ shoulder to shoulder
4	Middle Rails	¾ x 4¼ x 11⅝	10¾ shoulder to shoulder
2	Bottom Rails	¾ x 3½ x 11⅝	10¾ shoulder to shoulder
1	Bottom Stretcher	1¼ x 1⅞ x 16⅝	tenon = ¾ x 1⅝ x 11⅝ shoulder to shoulder
2	Keys	⅝ x ⅞ x 2½	
1	Plywood Top	¾ x 11⅝ x 11⅝	notch corners for legs
4	Cleats	¾ x ¾ x 11⅝	below plywood

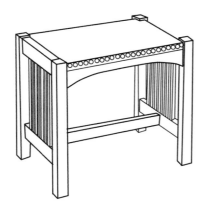

L. & J. G. STICKLEY
NO. 1292 FOOTSTOOL

18" x 13" x 16" high

Note that the leather top is tucked in at the ends, and overlays the arched top rail at the front and back, held down with decorative tacks. Make it as a slip seat, but leave the long edges of the leather loose. After the stool is finished, attach the seat, fold the leather over the edges, trim it straight, and tack it down.

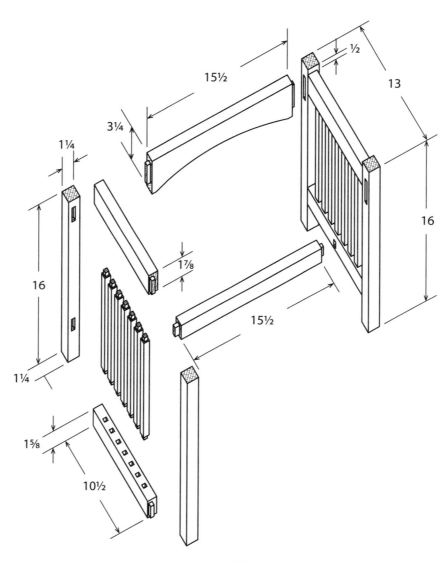

Assembly

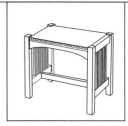

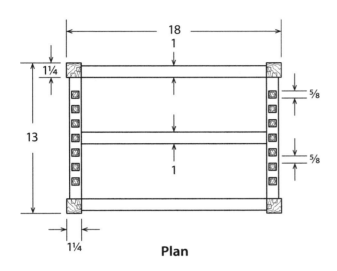

Plan

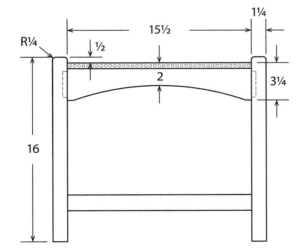

Front Elevation

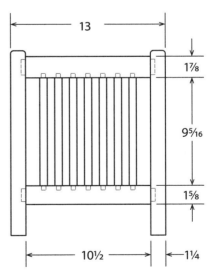

End Elevation

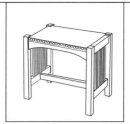

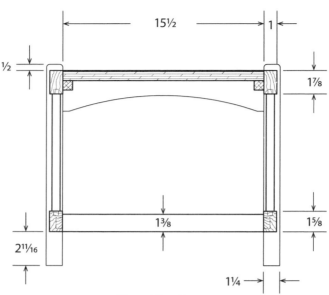

Front Section

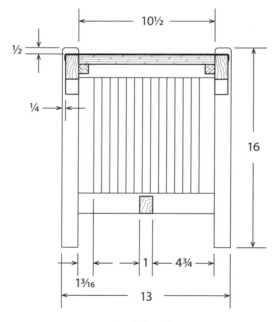

End Section

L & J. G. Stickley No. 1292 Footstool

QTY	PART	SIZE	NOTES
4	Legs	1¼ x 1¼ x 16	
2	Bottom Rails	1 x 1⅝ x 11½	10½ between tenons
2	Top Rails	1 x 1⅞ x 11½	10½ between tenons
14	Spindles	⅝ x ⅝ x 10¹⁄₁₆	9⁵⁄₁₆ between tenons
2	Arched Rails	1 x 3¼ x 16½	15½ between tenons
1	Stretcher	1 x 1⅜ x 16½	15½ between tenons
1	Top	¾ x 10½ x 15½	plywood or assembled frame for upholstery

Craftsman Bedroom Furnishings

Image courtesy University of Wisconsin Digital Collections

A typical Craftsman bedroom. (*The Craftsman*, February 1906.)

Of all rooms in the house, the one where individual taste has the fullest play is the bedroom. The dwelling rooms must necessarily reflect the life of the whole family and the several occupations that are carried on in them, but the bedroom is the inner sanctum of each individual, and is intended above all for privacy, comfort, and repose. It is the place for one's personal belongings, those numberless little things which are such sure indications of individual character and fancy, and it is the one room where purely personal preference may be freely exercised.

In addition to this, it is, or should be, a place where one can go to sleep at night with nothing in the surroundings to depress, distract, or annoy, and awaken in the morning to a first unconscious impression of peace and cheerfulness.

Gustav Stickley
The Craftsman, February 1906

Original examples of Craftsman bedroom furniture are scarcer than furniture from other rooms, perhaps because of the private nature of that space; often the bedroom is last on the list for new furniture. However, the furniture we choose to live with should reflect our lives and meet our needs, not be a means to impress those who only visit. Relaxation, comfort, and rest are as important to our lives as our need to socialize, work, and eat, and well-made furniture can make a mighty contribution to an environment that is both serene and encouraging.

Within this group of furniture are some case pieces designed by Harvey Ellis. These pieces manage to turn the rules of design upside down with graceful dignity and a touch of romance. Within the overall framework of Craftsman design, elegant touches are added to the simple lines we might expect to see; legs that taper toward the top as well as the bottom, and the tallest drawer somewhere other than the bottom. These innovations are subtle at first glance, and they wear well as time goes by, indications of confident talent in the designer.

Bedroom furniture needs to wear well, for unlike a sideboard in the dining room, drawers and doors will be opened on a daily basis.

Finding socks and underwear in the morning is as mundane a task as there can be, but if those necessities are found in a well-built drawer that is part of a handmade piece of Craftsman furniture, that mundane task becomes an opportunity to pause and enjoy the look and feel of honest hardwood and a drawer that moves effortlessly day after day and year after year. If our efforts can provide us with a daily reminder that work done well matters, and a reminder that we are capable of doing that type of work, we've built more than furniture—we've also built character.

Values and character are at the core of Craftsman furniture, and building these pieces and living with them offer far more than a place to put your stuff, or get your sleep. There is an influence on us from the material things that surround us, and that influence is based on the fundamental qualities of those things. In a world of "value engineering," outsourcing, and letting the bottom line rule, it's vital to have a retreat—a quiet and encouraging place—where "value engineering" means producing the best of which we're capable so that the efforts of our labor will meet the needs of, and offer encouragement to, others long after we are gone.

HARVEY ELLIS
NO. 911 DRESSER

33" high (to top of case) x 48" wide x 20" deep

An elegant design by Harvey Ellis. The butterfly keys holding the support for the mirror together stand slightly proud, and the mirror frame is attached with cleats screwed to the back of the case. The mirror pivots on fittings that were common on all types of furniture of the period. Like the 913 dresser, the side panels can be stiles and rails, or a simple veneered panel.

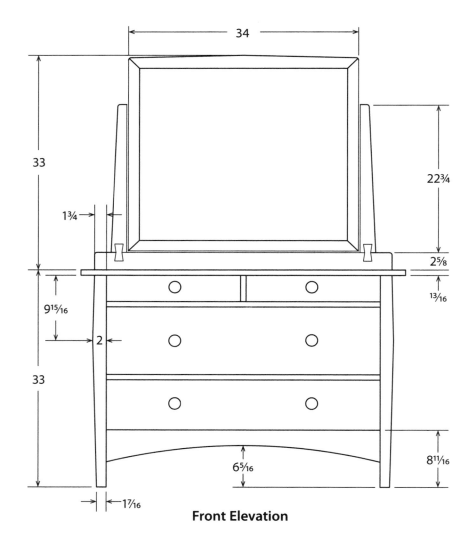

Front Elevation

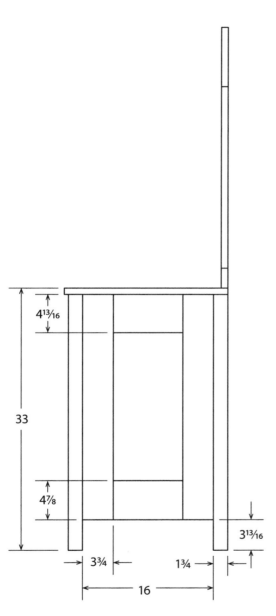

Side Elevation

Side Section

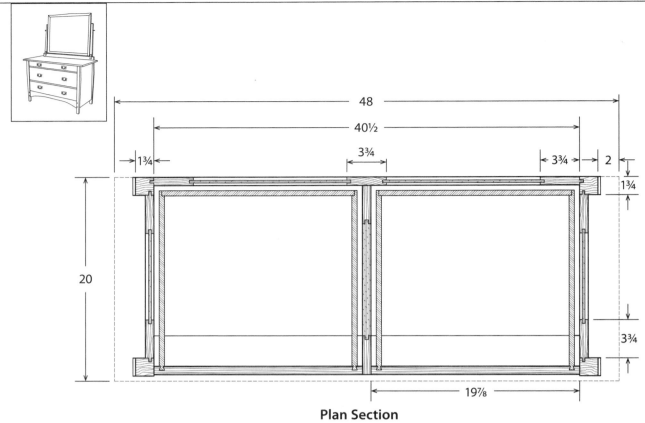

Plan Section

Gustav Stickley No. 911 Dresser

Qty	Part	Size	Notes
1	Top	$^{13}/_{16}$ x 20 x 48	
4	Legs	1¾ x 2 x 32³⁄₁₆	
2	Side Panels	¾ x 16¾ x 28⅜	assembled—16 x 28⅜ exposed—parts detailed below
4	Stiles	¾ x 4⅛ x 28⅜	3¾ exposed
2	Bottom Rails	¾ x 4⅞ x 9½	8½ between tenons
2	Top Rails	¾ x 4¹³⁄₁₆ x 9½	8½ between tenons
2	Panels	¼ x 9½ x 19¹¹⁄₁₆	8½ x 18¹¹⁄₁₆ exposed
1	Back Panel	¾ x 41½ x 28⅜	assembled—40½ exposed—parts detailed below
2	Stiles	¾ x 4⅛ x 28⅜	3¾ exposed
2	Rails	¾ x 3¾ x 33¾	33 between tenons
1	Middle Stile	¾ x 3¾ x 21⅝	20⅞ between tenons
2	Panels	¼ x 15⅜ x 21⅝	14⅝ x 20⅞ exposed
1	Arched Apron	¾ x 4⅞ x 42½	40½ between tenons
1	Bottom Drawer Front	¾ x 7⅝ x 40½	opening
1	Middle Drawer Front	¾ x 10¼ x 40½	opening
2	Top Drawer Fronts	¾ x 4 x 19⅞	opening
1	Bottom Rail	¾ x 2¼ x 42½	40½ between tenons
2	Middle Rails	¾ x 3¼ x 42½	40½ between tenons
2	Top Rails	¾ x 3¼ x 19⅞	add for tenons or pocket screw
1	Vertical Divider	¾ x 18⅝ x 4	vertical grain on front exposed edge
1	Backsplash	¾ x 2⅝ x 44	
2	Mirror Supports	¾ x 2⁵⁄₁₆ x 22¾	
2	Mirror Stiles	¾ x 1⅝ x 29¾	
1	Mirror Bottom Rail	¾ x 1⅝ x 34	
1	Mirror Top Rail	¾ x 2 x 34	taper to 1⅝ at ends

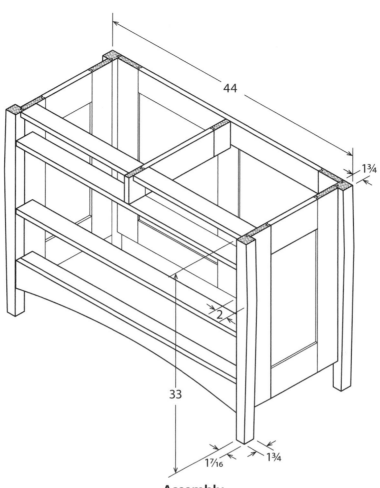

Assembly

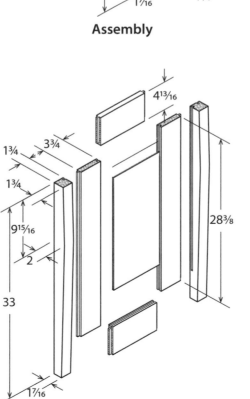

Detail of Side Panel

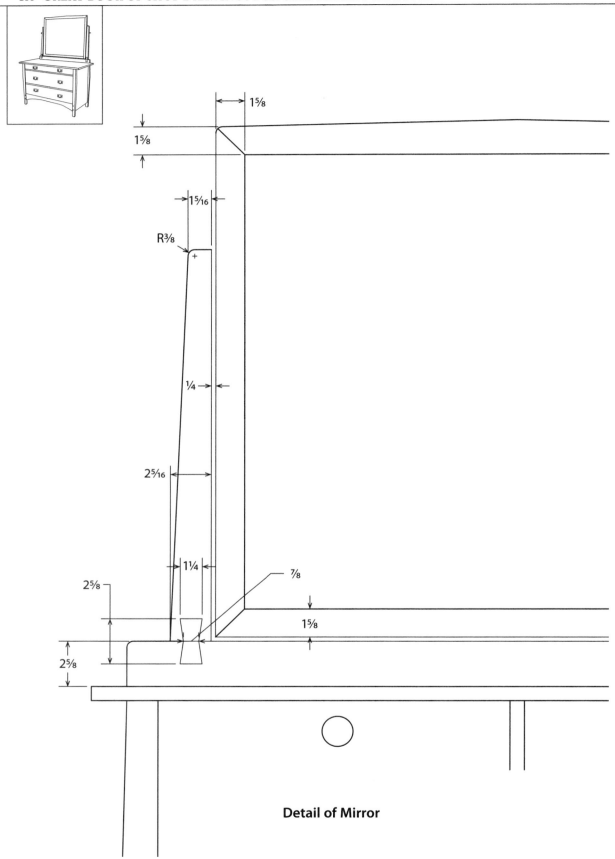

1⁵⁄₈

1⁵⁄₈

1⁵⁄₁₆

R³⁄₈

¹⁄₄

2⁵⁄₁₆

1¹⁄₄

⁷⁄₈

2⁵⁄₈

1⁵⁄₈

2⁵⁄₈

Detail of Mirror

GUSTAV STICKLEY
NO. 913 DRESSER

50" high x 36" wide x 20" deep

Designed by Harvey Ellis, this bureau and several related pieces are among the best-proportioned furniture ever manufactured. Small in stature, its dignified appearance and simple elegance make it seem much larger when viewed in isolation. This piece appeared in the old catalogs in several variations—different types of hardware, and with or without the paneled sides.

The legs have often been described as "bowed," but they are actually tapered toward the top as well as the bottom. In the front elevation there is a dimension indicating where the two lines meet.

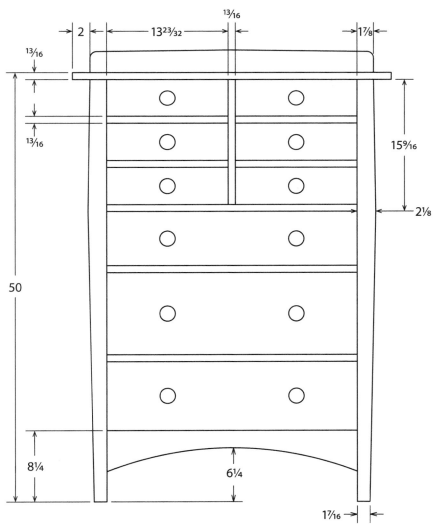

Front

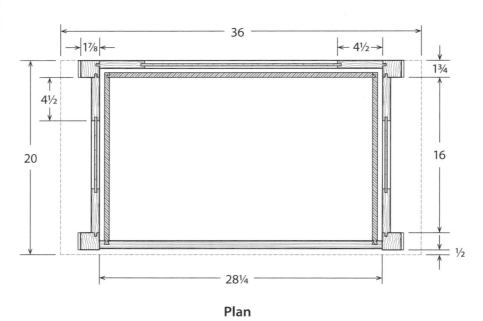

Plan

Gustav Stickley No. 913 Dresser

Qty.	Part	Size	Notes
1	Top	$^{13}/_{16}$ x 20 x 36	
1	Backsplash	$^{13}/_{16}$ x 2⅝ x 32	
4	Legs	1¾ x 2⅛ x 49³/₁₆	
2	Side Panels	$^{13}/_{16}$ x 17 x 45¾	16 exposed between legs—parts detailed below
4	Side Stiles	$^{13}/_{16}$ x 5 x 45¾	4½ exposed
2	Side Top Rails	$^{13}/_{16}$ x 4⅜ x 8	7 between tongues
2	Side Mid Rails	$^{13}/_{16}$ x 3¼ x 8	7 between tongues
2	Side Bottom Rails	$^{13}/_{16}$ x 4¾ x 8	7 between tongues
2	Side Upper Panels	¼ x 8 x 8¹⁵/₁₆	7 x 7¹⁵/₁₆ exposed
2	Side Lower Panels	¼ x 8 x 26⅜	7 x 25⅜ exposed
1	Back Panel	$^{13}/_{16}$ x 29¼ x 45¾	28¼ exposed between legs—parts detailed below
2	Back Stiles	$^{13}/_{16}$ x 5 x 45¾	4½ exposed
1	Back Top Rail	$^{13}/_{16}$ x 4⅜ x 20¼	19¼ between tongues
1	Back Mid Rail	$^{13}/_{16}$ x 4¼ x 20¼	19¼ between tongues
1	Back Bottom Rail	$^{13}/_{16}$ x 4¾ x 20¼	19¼ between tongues
1	Back Upper Panel	¼ x 20¼ x 18¹⁵/₃₂	19¼ x 17¹⁵/₃₂ exposed
1	Back Lower Panel	¼ x 20¼ x 15¹⁹/₃₂	19¼ x 14¹⁹/₃₂ exposed
3	Rails Between Drawers	$^{13}/_{16}$ x 4½ x 29¼	28¼ between tenons
4	Rails Between Drawers	$^{13}/_{16}$ x 4½ x 14¹⁵/₃₂	13²³/₃₂ between tenons
1	Vertical Divider Between Drawers	$^{13}/_{16}$ x 4½ x 14¾	screw through rail below, or add to length for joint
1	Bottom Front Rail	$^{13}/_{16}$ x 3¹¹/₁₆ x 29¼	28¼ between tenons
1	Arched Front Apron	$^{13}/_{16}$ x 4¾ x 30¼	28¼ between tenons
6	Drawer Fronts	$^{13}/_{16}$ x 4⅜ x 13²³/₃₂	opening size—trim for desired gaps
1	Drawer Front	$^{13}/_{16}$ x 6¼ x 28¼	opening size—trim for desired gaps
1	Drawer Front	$^{13}/_{16}$ x 9⁵/₁₆ x 28¼	opening size—trim for desired gaps
1	Drawer Front	$^{13}/_{16}$ x 8 x 28¼	opening size—trim for desired gaps

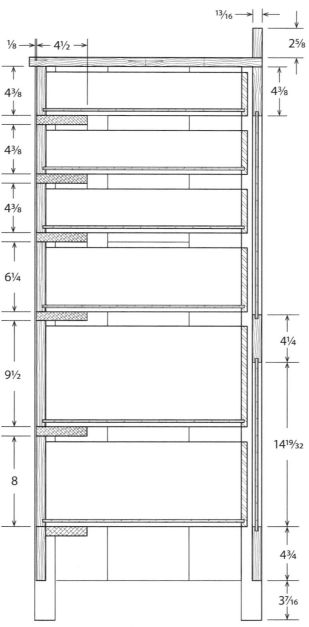

Side Section

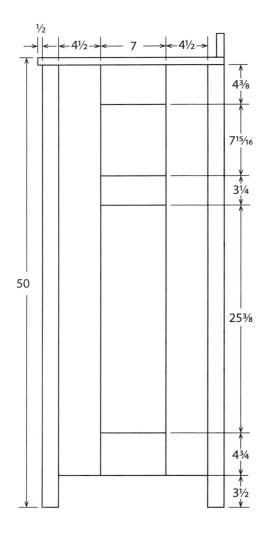

½   4½   7   4½

4⅜

7¹⁵⁄₁₆

3¼

50

25⅜

4¾

3½

Side

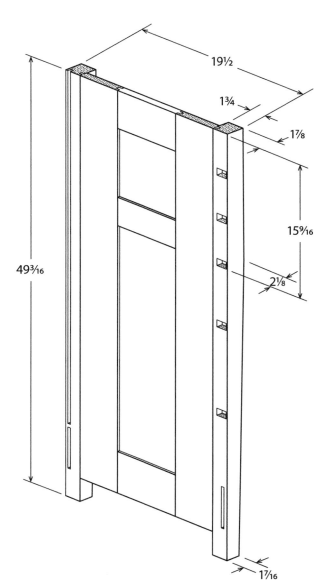

19½

1¾

1⅞

49³⁄₁₆

15⁹⁄₁₆

2⅛

1⁷⁄₁₆

Assembly—Side Panel

L. & J. G. STICKLEY
NO. 112 WARDROBE

60" high x 50" wide x 22½" deep

The hanger slide-out on the right side could be replaced with a rod going from side to side, although there is barely enough room to do so. Because of the width of this cabinet, and the weight of all the drawers, it wouldn't be a bad idea to put in a support in the middle of the bottom, running to the floor. Also note that the door overlays the front of the case and is notched into the sides.

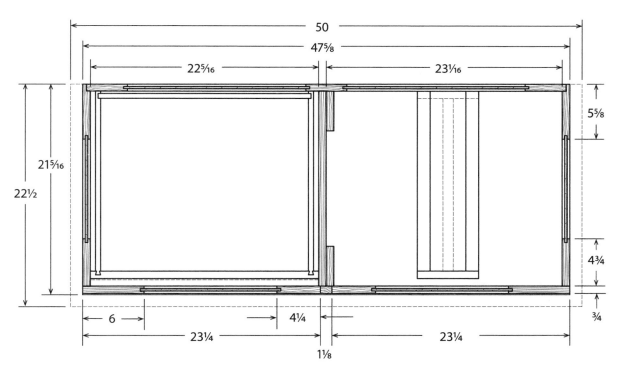

Plan

L. & J.G. Stickley No. 112 Wardrobe

Qty	Part	Size	Notes
1	Top	1 x 22½ x 50	
2	Side Panels	¾ x 21⁵⁄₁₆ x 59	parts detailed below
4	Stiles	¾ x 5⅝ x 59	front stiles notched @ door
2	Top Rails	¾ x 4¾ x 11¹⁄₁₆	10¹⁄₁₆ between tongues
2	Mid Rails	¾ x 2⅝ x 11¹⁄₁₆	10¹⁄₁₆ between tongues
2	Bottom Rails	¾ x 12¹⁄₁₆ x 11¹⁄₁₆	10¹⁄₁₆ between tongues
2	Upper Side Panels	¼ x 11¹⁄₁₆ x 12¼	10¹⁄₁₆ x 11¼ exposed
2	Lower Side Panels	¼ x 11¹⁄₁₆ x 27³⁄₁₆	10¹⁄₁₆ x 26³⁄₁₆ exposed
1	Back Panel	¾ x 46⅞ x 52⅛	46⅛ x 52¾ exposed—parts detailed below
2	Outer Stiles	¾ x 4 x 52⅛	
2	Top & Bottom Rails	¾ x 4 x 39⅞	38⅞ between tongues
1	Middle Stile	¾ x 4 x 45⅛	44⅛ between tongues
2	Middle Rails	¾ x 4 x 17⁷⁄₁₆	16⁷⁄₁₆ between tongues
4	Panels	¼ x 17⁷⁄₁₆ x 21¹⁄₁₆	16⁷⁄₁₆ x 20¹⁄₁₆ exposed
1	Bottom	¾ x 21⁵⁄₁₆ x 46⅛	
1	Vertical Divider	¾ x 20⁹⁄₁₆ x 51¾	
2	Uprights	¾ x 4 x 51¾	
1	Door Divider	¾ x 1⅛ x 51¾	
6	Hor. Div. Bet. Dwrs.	¾ x 19¹³⁄₁₆ x 22⁵⁄₁₆	biscuit or pocket screw to side
1	Ver. Div. Bet. Dwrs	¾ x 3¾ x 19¹³⁄₁₆	
2	Drawer Fronts	¾ x 3¾ x 10²⁵⁄₃₂	opening size—trim for desired gaps
5	Drawer Fronts	¾ x 5⅜ x 22⁵⁄₁₆	opening size—trim for desired gaps
2	Doors	¾ x 23¼ x 51¾	parts detailed below—opening size trim for desired gaps
2	Hinge Stiles	¾ x 6 x 51¾	
2	Inner Stiles	¾ x 4¼ x 51¾	
2	Top Rails	¾ x 4¾ x 14	13 between tongues
2	Middle Rails	¾ x 2⅝ x 14	13 between tongues
2	Bottom Rails	¾ x 7⅜ x 14	13 between tongues
2	Top Panels	¼ x 14 x 12¼	13 x 11¼ exposed
2	Bottom Panels	¼ x 14 x 26¾	13 x 25¾ exposed
2	Arched Aprons	¾ x 4 x 46⅛	add to length for joint or use biscuits or pocket screws
2	Bottom Cleats	¾ x 1½ x 19⁹⁄₁₆	
1	Hanger Slide		parts detailed below
1	Front	¾ x 4 x 6	
2	Cleats @ Top	¾ x 1¼ x 17½	
1	Slide	¾ x 5 x 17½	
1	Back	¾ x 3¼ x 6	
1	Rod	1 diameter x 19	

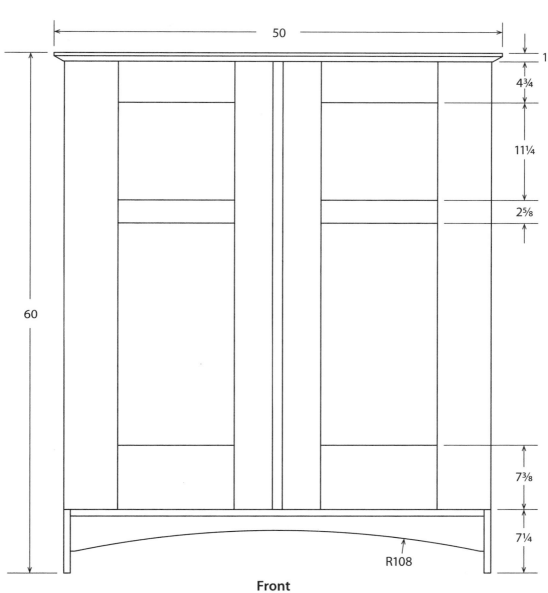

Front

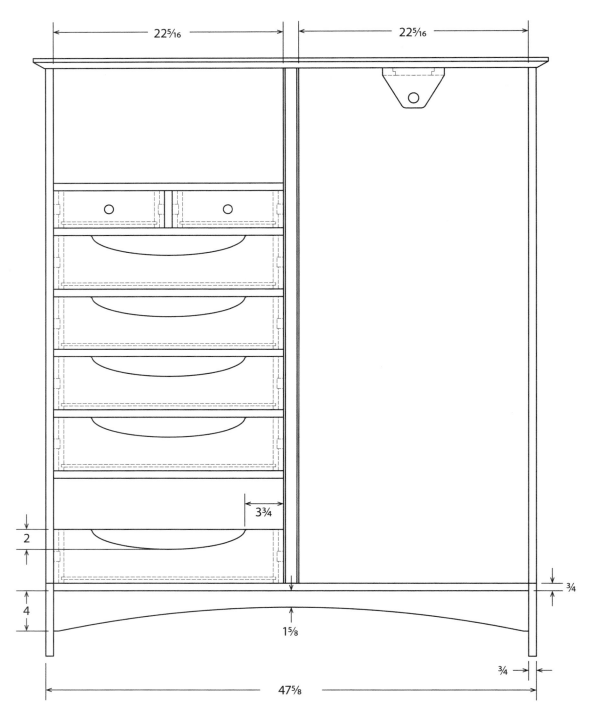

22⁵⁄₁₆

22⁵⁄₁₆

3¾

2

¾

4

1⁵⁄₈

¾

47⁵⁄₈

Front Section

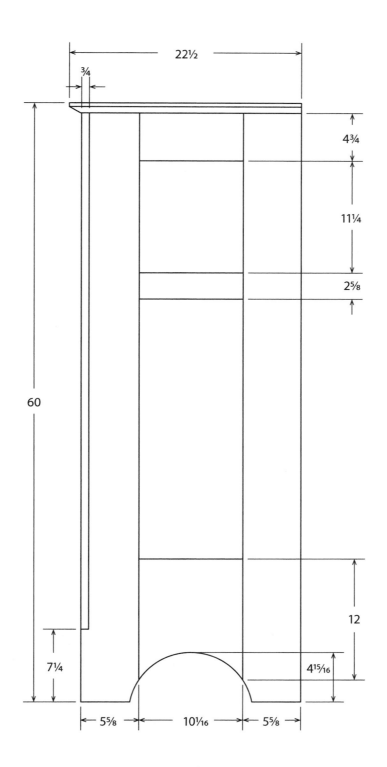

Side

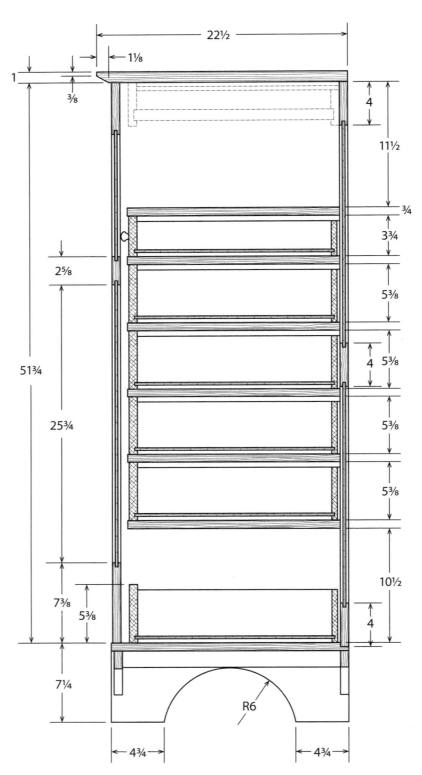

Side Section

BED BY GUSTAV STICKLEY

87½" long x 65" wide x 42½" high

A different approach to fastening the rails to the head and footboard—the removable pegs lock the through tenons of the rails to the head and footboard. These joints should not be glued. The head and foot board are identical. Dimensions have been modified slightly to accommodate a modern queen size mattress—before you begin construction, check the fit of the particular mattress you will be using.

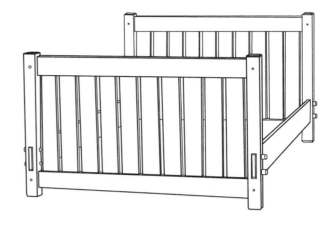

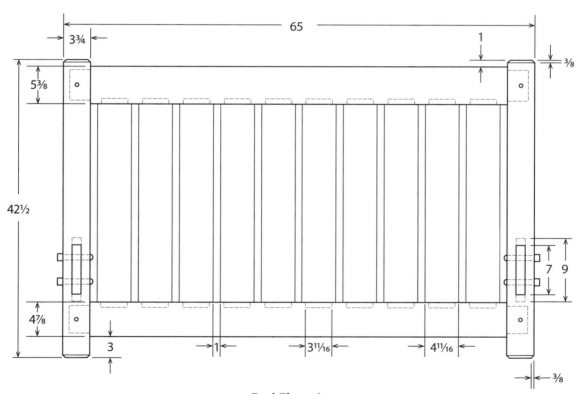

End Elevation

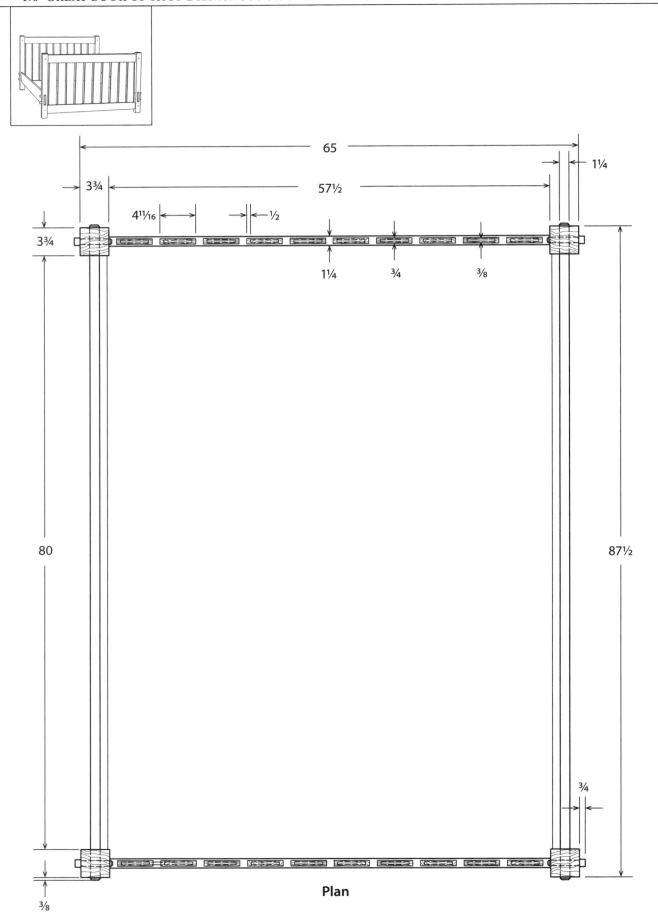

Plan

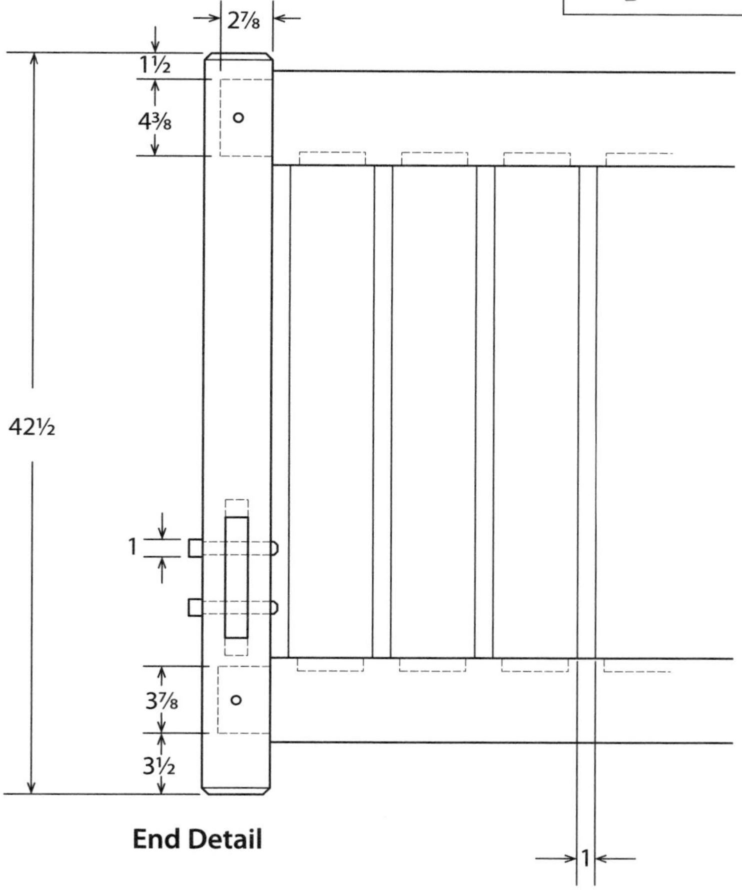

$2\frac{7}{8}$

$1\frac{1}{2}$

$4\frac{3}{8}$

$42\frac{1}{2}$

1

$3\frac{7}{8}$

$3\frac{1}{2}$

1

End Detail

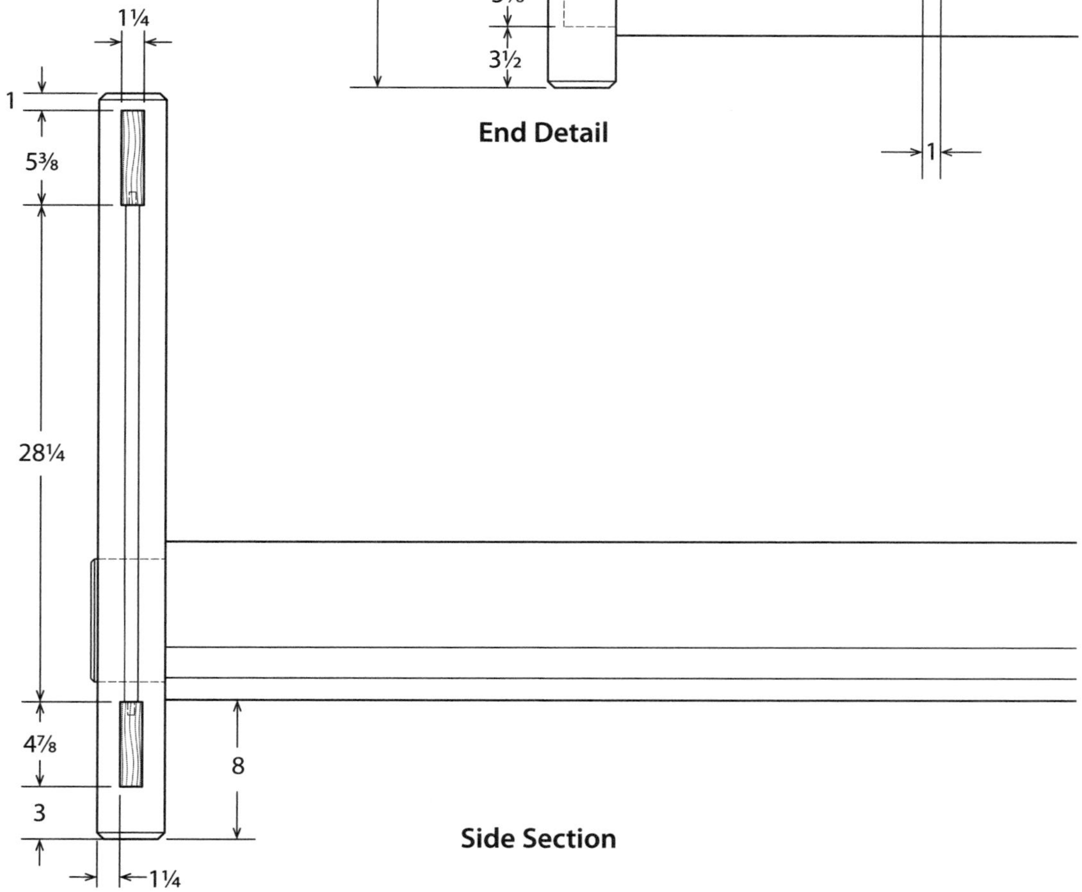

$1\frac{1}{4}$

1

$5\frac{3}{8}$

$28\frac{1}{4}$

$4\frac{7}{8}$

8

3

$1\frac{1}{4}$

Side Section

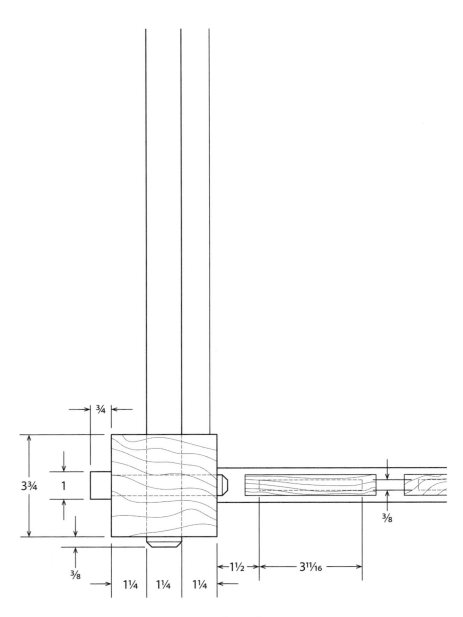

Joint Details—Plan View

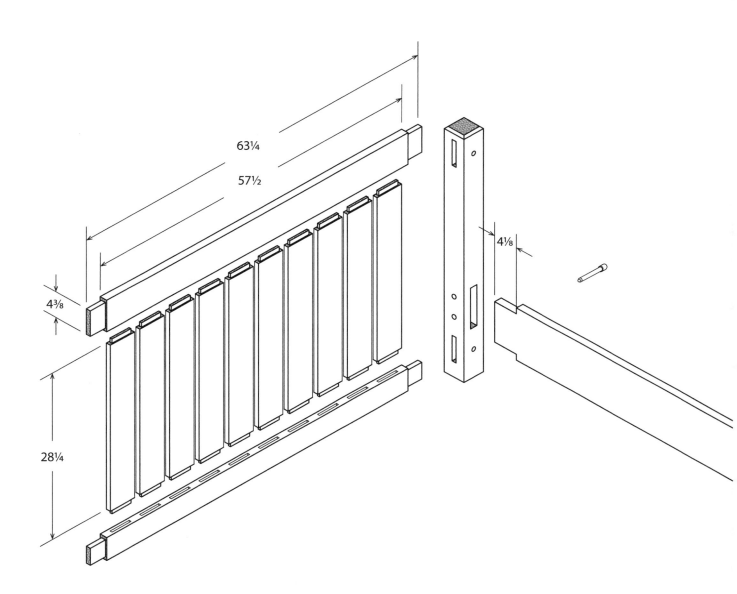

Assembly

Bed by Gustav Stickley

Qty	Part	Size	Notes
4	Posts	3¾ x 3¾ x 42½	
2	Bottom Rails	1¼ x 4⅞ x 63½	57½ between tenons
2	Top Rails	1¼ x 5⅜ x 63½	57½ between tenons
20	Vertical Slats	¾ x 4¹¹⁄₁₆ x 29¾	28¼ between tenons
2	Rails	1¼ x 9 x 87½	80 between tenons—check length against mattress

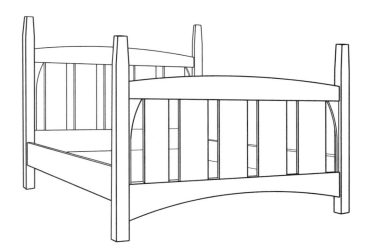

HARVEY ELLIS QUEEN-SIZE BED

The original of this bed had inlays in the slats on the head and foot boards, and apparently never went into production. The size has been modified slightly to accommodate a modern queen-size mattress and box spring.

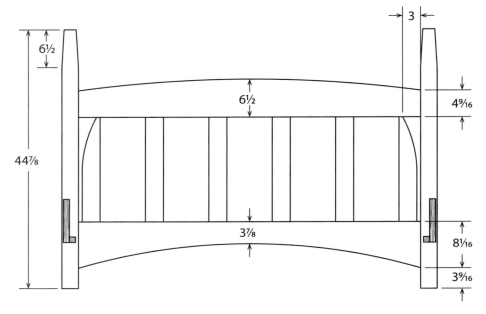

3

6½

6½

4⁹⁄₁₆

44⅞

3⅞

8¹⁄₁₆

3⁹⁄₁₆

Foot

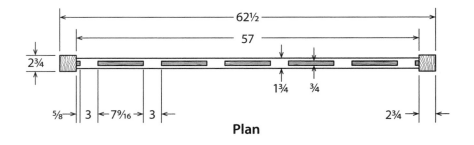

62½

57

2¾

1¾   ¾

⅝   3   7⁹⁄₁₆   3   2¾

Plan

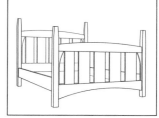

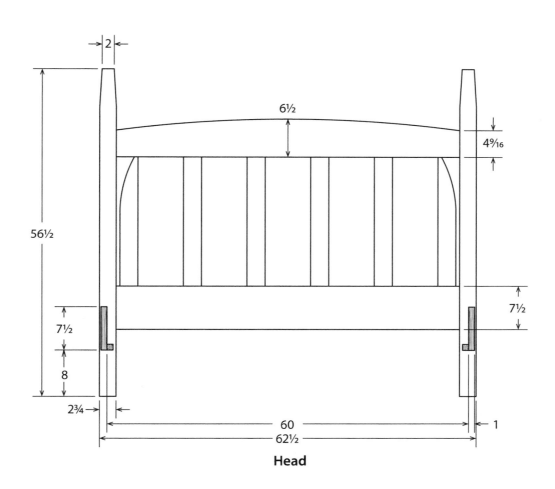

Head

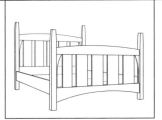

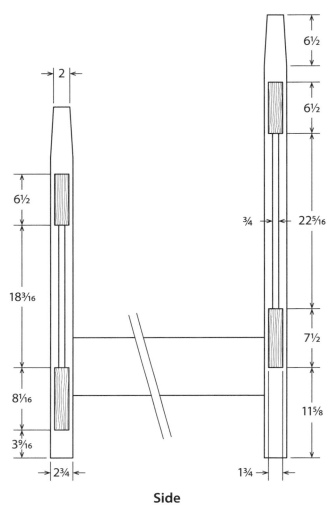

Side

Gustav Stickley Queen-Size Bed

Qty	Part	Size	Notes
2	Headboard Legs	2¾ x 2¾ x 56½	
2	Footboard Legs	2¾ x 2¾ x 44⅞	
2	Top Rails	1¾ x 6½ x 60	57 between tenon shoulders
1	Headboard Bottom Rail	1¾ x 7½ x 60	57 between tenon shoulders
1	Footboard Bottom Rail	1¾ x 8¹⁄₁₆ x 60	57 between tenon shoulders
2	Headboard Corbels	¾ x 3 x 22⁵⁄₁₆	cut to curve
2	Footboard Corbels	¾ x 3 x 18³⁄₁₆	cut to curve
5	Headboard Slats	¾ x 7⁹⁄₁₆ x 24¹³⁄₁₆	22⁵⁄₁₆ between tenon shoulders
5	Footboard Slats	¾ x 7⁹⁄₁₆ x 19¹¹⁄₁₆	18³⁄₁₆ between tenon shoulders
2	Bed Rails	1 x 7½ x 80	double check length with mattress
2	Bed Slat Supports	1 x 1 x 80	double check length with mattress

CHARLES LIMBERT DRESSING TABLE

30" high x 36" wide x 24" deep

All of the exposed edges are rounded over, a look that became newly popular in the 1970s. The exposed tenons are also rounded, with a smaller radius. The top is stepped in, and sits in a ⅛"-deep rabbet around the top edge of the frame.

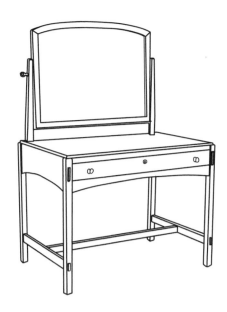

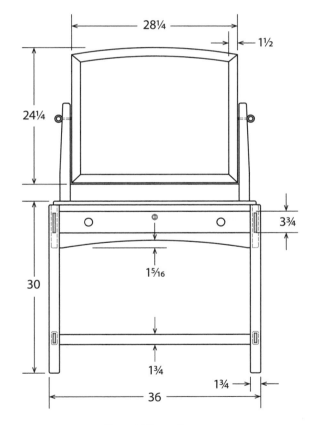

Front Elevation

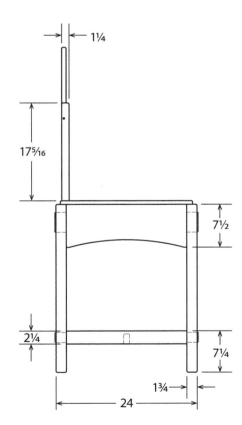

Side Elevation

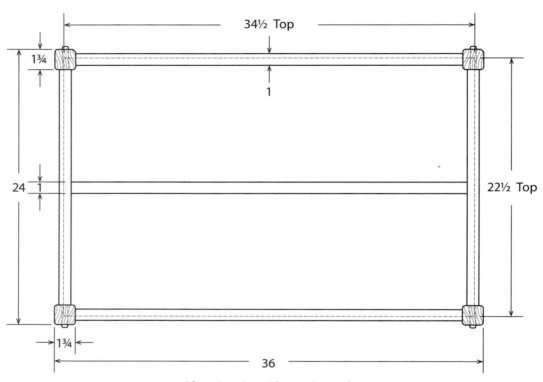

34½ Top

1¾

1

24   1

22½ Top

1¾

36

Plan Section Above Stretcher

Charles Limbert Dressing Table

Qty	Part	Size	Notes
4	Legs	1¾ x 1¾ x 29⅜	
2	Side Stretchers	1 x 2¼ x 24½	20½ between tenons
1	Stretcher	1 x 1¾ x 34¼	33¼ between tenons
2	Arched Side Rails	1 x 7½ x 24½	20½ between tenons
1	Back Rail	1 x 7½ x 34¼	33¼ between tenons
1	Arched Front Rail	1 x 2⅝ x 34¼	33¼ between tenons
1	Top	¾ x 22½ x 34½	
1	Drawer Front	1 x 3¾ x 33¼	opening
1	Front Rail	1 x 1⅛ x 34¼	33¼ between tenons
2	Mirror Support Uprights	1¼ x 1¾ x 17⁵⁄₁₆	
1	Mirror Support Rail	1 x 3 x 29¾	28¾ between tenons
2	Mirror Frame Stiles	¾ x 1½ x 22¾	
1	Mirror Frame Bottom Rail	¾ x 1½ x 28¼	
1	Mirror Frame Arched Top Rail	¾ x 1½ x 28¼	bent to 79¼ radius, or cut from 2½ wide piece

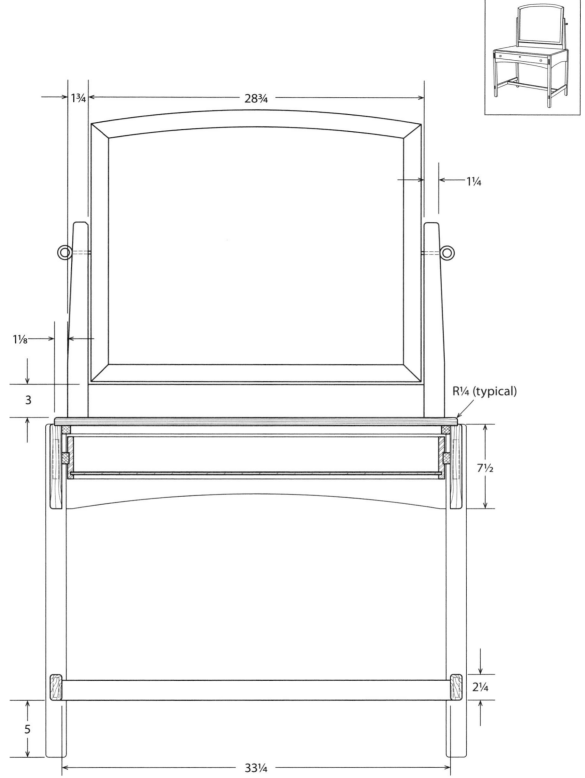

Front Section Through Drawer

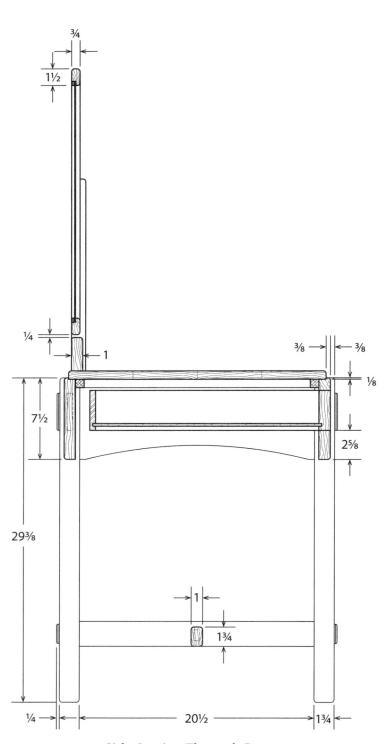

Side Section Through Drawer

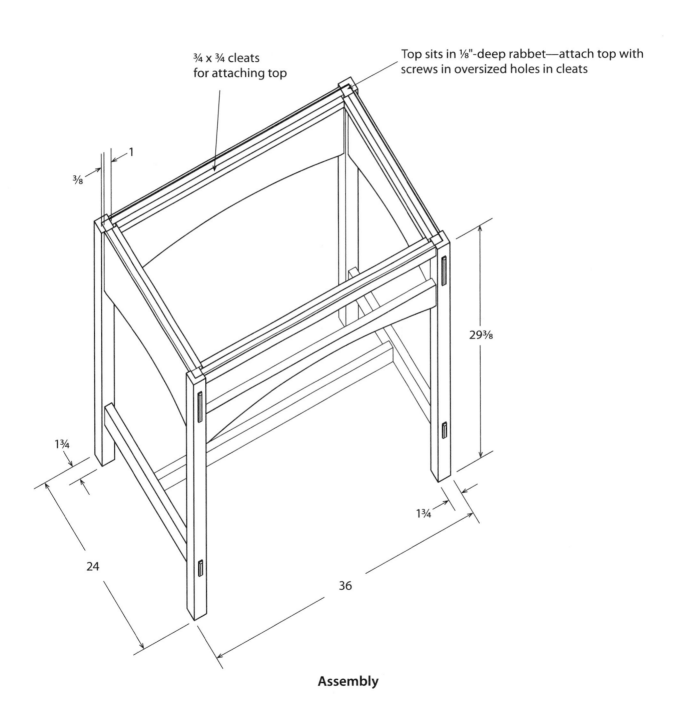

¾ x ¾ cleats
for attaching top

Top sits in ⅛"-deep rabbet—attach top with
screws in oversized holes in cleats

1

⅜

29⅜

1¾

1¾

24

36

Assembly

L. & J. G. STICKLEY
NO. 110 NIGHTSTAND

29" x 14" x 18"

Note that the arcs that form the feet at the bottom of the sides extend into the rails. The dimension given is to the line between the radii when the cut is finished. Make the bottom rail a little wider and cut the curves after the side panel is assembled. The arch in the apron under the drawers starts 1/2" in from the ends.

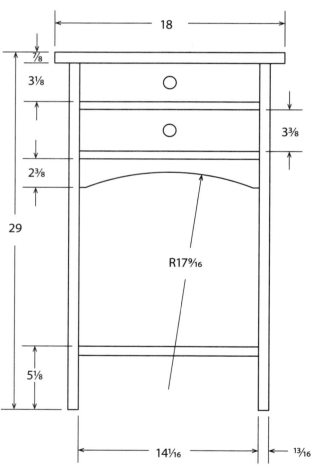

Front Elevation

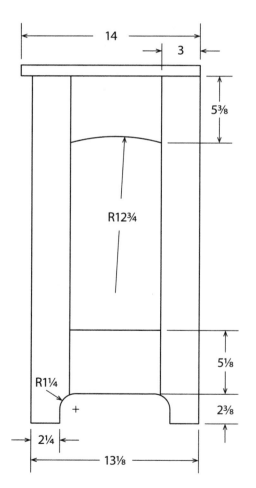

Side Elevation

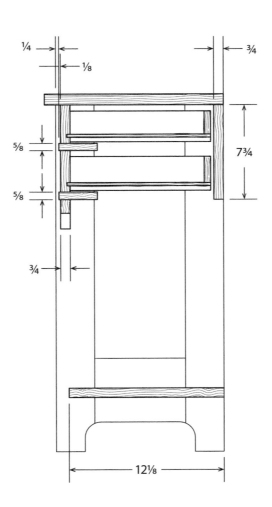

Section

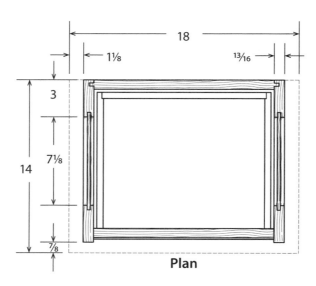

Plan

L. & J. G. Stickley No. 110 Nightstand

Qty	Part	Size	Notes
1	Top	⅞ x 14 x 18	
2	Sides	¹³⁄₁₆ x 13⅛ x 28⅛	assembled—parts detailed below
4	Stiles	¹³⁄₁₆ x 3 x 28⅛	
2	Bottom Rails	¹³⁄₁₆ x 5⅛ x 8⅛	7⅛ between tenons
2	Top Rails	¹³⁄₁₆ x 5⅜ x 8⅛	7⅛ between tenons
1	Bottom Shelf	¹³⁄₁₆ x 12⅛ x 14¹³⁄₁₆	14¹⁄₁₆ between tenons
1	Back	¾ x 7¾ x 14¹³⁄₁₆	14¹⁄₁₆ between tenons
1	Arched Apron	¾ x 2⅜ x 14¹³⁄₁₆	14¹⁄₁₆ between tenons
2	Rails	⅝ x 3 x 14¹³⁄₁₆	14¹⁄₁₆ between tenons
1	Bottom Drawer Front	¾ x 3⅜ x 14¹⁄₁₆	opening
1	Top Drawer Front	¾ x 3⅛ x 14¹⁄₁₆	opening
1	Panel	¼ x 7⅞ x 16½	7⅛ x 15¾ exposed

GUSTAV STICKLEY NO. 641 NIGHTSTAND

29" high x 20" wide x 18" deep

This simple little stand will work very well with the Ellis bed and No. 913 bureau (page 187). The nightstand could also be used as an end-table, with or without its backsplash.

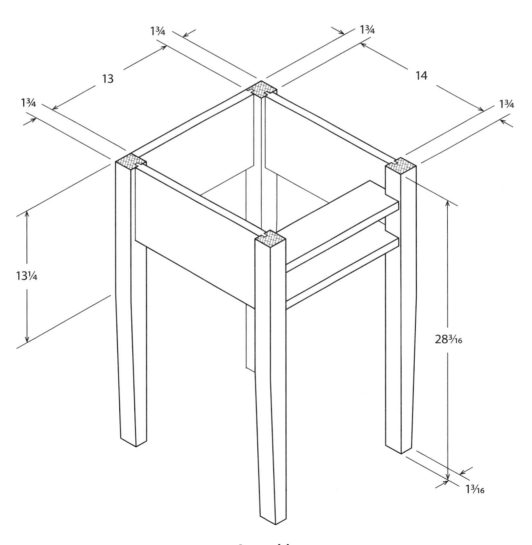

Assembly

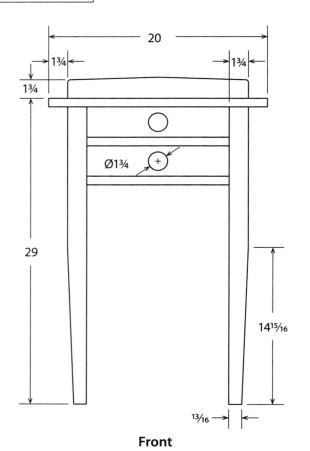

Front

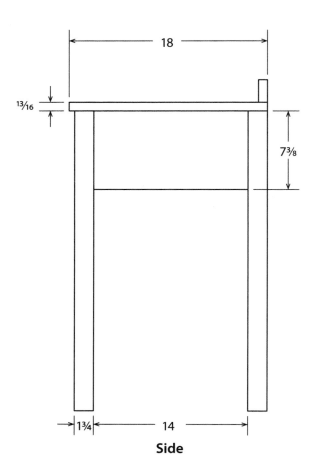

Side

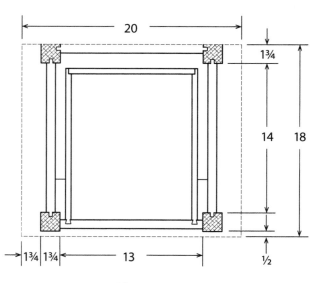

Plan

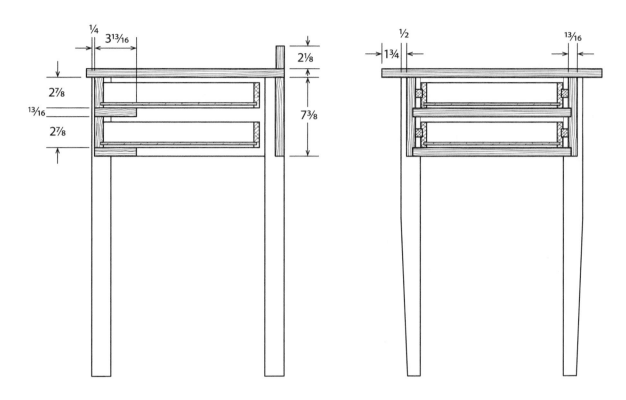

Side Section   **Front Section**

Gustav Stickley No. 641 Nightstand

Qty	Part	Size	Notes
1	Top	$^{13}/_{16}$ x 18 x 20	
4	Legs	$1^{3}/_{4}$ x $1^{3}/_{4}$ x $28^{3}/_{16}$	
2	Sides	$^{13}/_{16}$ x $7^{3}/_{8}$ x 15	14 between tenon shoulders
1	Back	$^{13}/_{16}$ x $7^{3}/_{8}$ x 14	13 between tenon shoulders
2	Rails	$^{13}/_{16}$ x $3^{13}/_{16}$ x $13^{7}/_{8}$	biscuit or pocket screw to sides or add for tenons
2	Drawer Fronts	$^{13}/_{16}$ x $2^{7}/_{8}$ x 13	opening size—trim for desired gaps
1	Backsplash	$^{13}/_{16}$ x $2^{1}/_{8}$ x $16^{1}/_{2}$	

Craftsman Office, Den & Library Furnishings

Image courtesy University of Wisconsin Digital Collections

In one sense, a workroom is always a library. (*The Craftsman*, December 1905.)

No room in the house represents more unmistakably the character and calling of its owner than his workroom. It is also a sign of the present healthy tendency to return to simple things known by their right names, that the name "workroom" is beginning to be used for the room formerly known as library, study, or den. The adoption of the simpler and more expressive word is evidence that the true character of the room is beginning to be recognized and insisted upon—that this room is being made increasingly a place where the love of work is constantly aroused by the evidences of work.

Gustav Stickley
The Craftsman, December 1905

In Stickley's log home at Craftsman Farms, a large library table occupied a central location in the living room. That great room takes up half of the first floor, served several purposes, and was divided into distinct areas defined by groups of furniture. If you stand in the room today, you can easily imagine Gustav at his table, with papers spread across its broad surface. But work in the midst of family is not done in isolation. Looking up from his ledgers, he would see an inlaid Craftsman piano directly ahead, and a grouping of settles around the fireplace to his right. If he needed a break, or wanted to satisfy his ever-present desire to read, an Eastwood chair was nearby, and bookcases are but a few steps away from any location in the room. The evidence of his work is impossible to miss.

These pieces are more personal in nature than the social pieces of the living room and dining room. A dining table appeals to a group; here is where we gather, but a desk defines a personal space; here is where I can concentrate on the task at hand, and the bookcase contains my resources. If you work at a desk, or store your books in furniture that you made, the result of your physical effort can be an inspiration on a daily basis. There aren't many ways in our modern world to leave behind evidence of what we do, and what we have a passion for.

When work encroaches on our family time, the right piece of furniture, in the right place, will keep us from isolation, and when the task is finished it will be evidence of our good efforts, and of good things yet to come, not a reminder of the things we have not accomplished. The furniture we make serves as a connection on many levels. It joins us with craftsmen of earlier times and those who will follow us, who we were with what we learned, and who we are now with who we will become. The evidence of our work connects us to our homes and our families, both now and in the future.

GUSTAV STICKLEY
NO. 503 DESK

42" x 28" x 30"

With drawers on opposite sides, this can be used as a partner's desk. If placing against a wall, eliminate the back drawer, and substitute a solid panel. The drawer could easily be replaced with a pull-out tray for a computer keyboard, or for a lap-top computer.

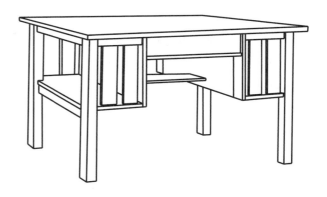

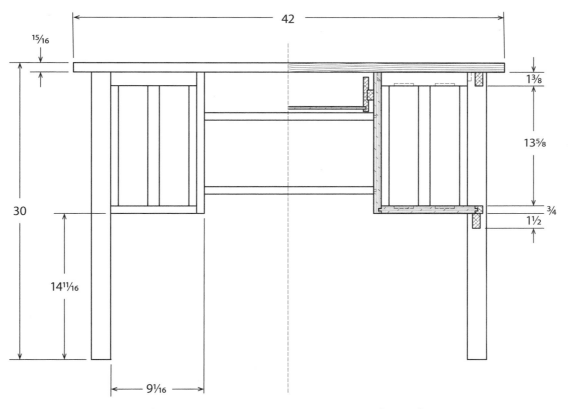

Front Elevation   **Section Through Center**

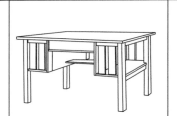

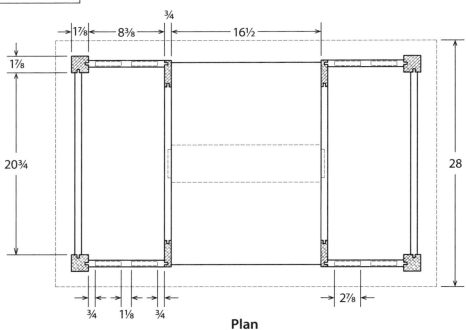

Plan

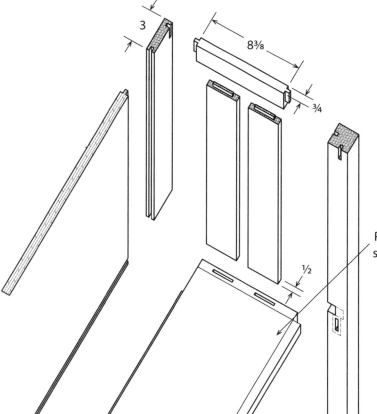

Plywood shelf with ¾" x ¾"
solid wood edges

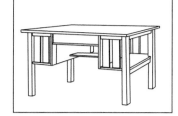

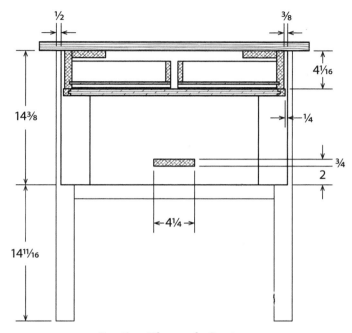

½   ⅜

4¹⁄₁₆

14³⁄₈

¼

¾

2

←4¼→

14¹¹⁄₁₆

Section Through Center

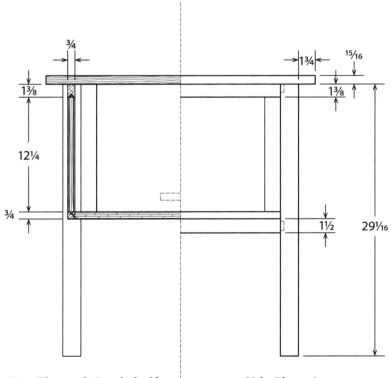

¾

15⁄16

1¾

1³⁄₈   1³⁄₈

12¼

29¹⁄₁₆

¾

1½

Section Through Bookshelf   **Side Elevation**

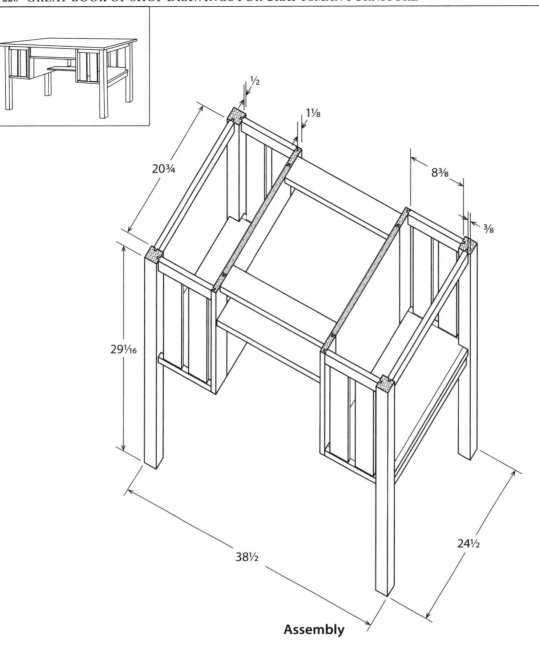

Assembly

Gustav Stickley No. 503 Desk

Qty	Part	Size	Notes
4	Legs	1⅞ x 1⅞ x 29¹⁄₁₆	
1	Top	¹⁵⁄₁₆ x 28 x 42	
2	Shelves	¾ x 10⅛ x 23½	plywood with solid wood edges
2	Backs	¾ x 15¾ x 17½	plywood
4	Back Edges	¾ x 3 x 15¾	
1	Stretcher	¾ x 4¼ x 17¼	
4	Bookshelf Side Rails	¾ x 1⅜ x 9⅛	8⅜ between tenons
2	Bookshelf End Rails	¾ x 1⅜ x 21½	20¾ between tenons
2	Bookshelf Bottom Rails	¾ x 1½ x 21½	20¾ between tenons
1	Shelf Below Drawers	¾ x 23 x 16½	plywood with solid wood edges
2	Drawer Rails	¾ x 3½ x 16½	
8	Shelf Slats	½ x 2⅞ x 13	12¼ between tenons
2	Drawer Fronts	¾ x 4¹⁄₁₆ x 16½	opening size

GUSTAV STICKLEY
NO. 706
DROP-FRONT DESK

44" high x 30" wide x 11" deep

This is truly an elegant little desk, and a challenge to build.

Make the pigeonholes as a separate section, and secure that with screws to the sides of the cabinet. The writing surface can be hinged with pivot hinges. Locate them so that when opened, this surface stops against the bottom of the pigeonhole insert.

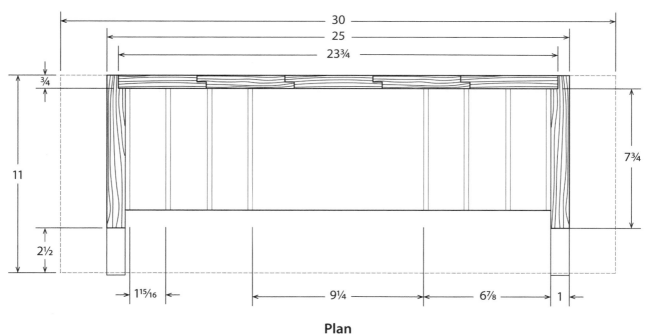

Plan

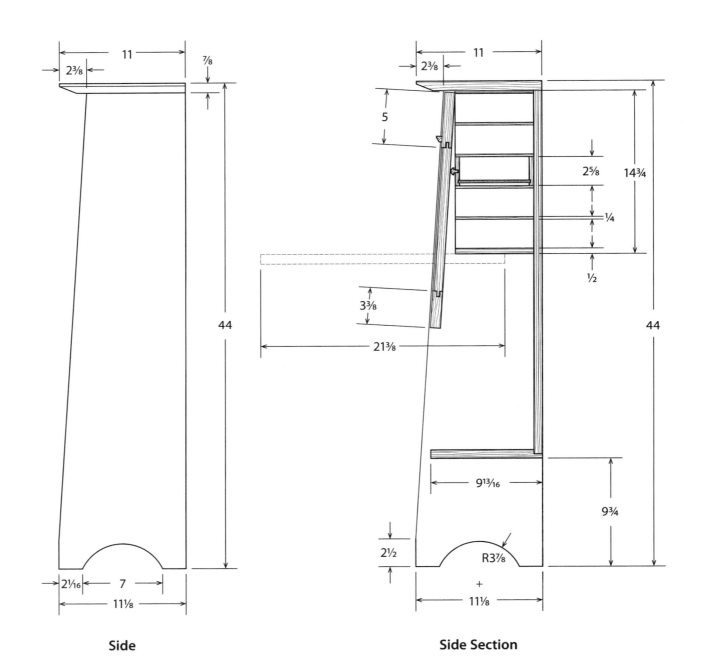

Side

Side Section

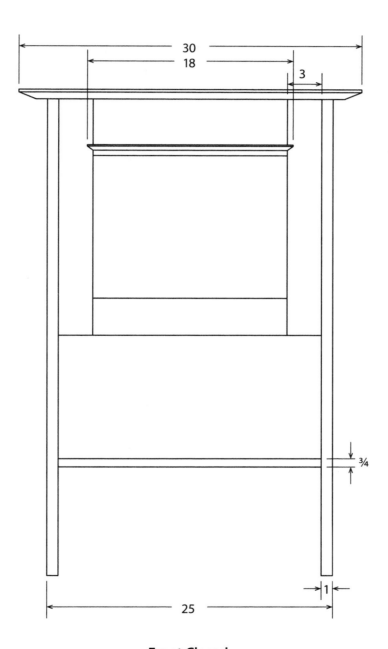

Front Closed

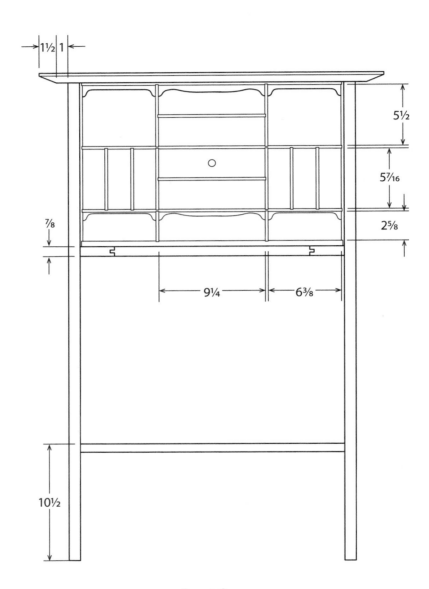

Front Open

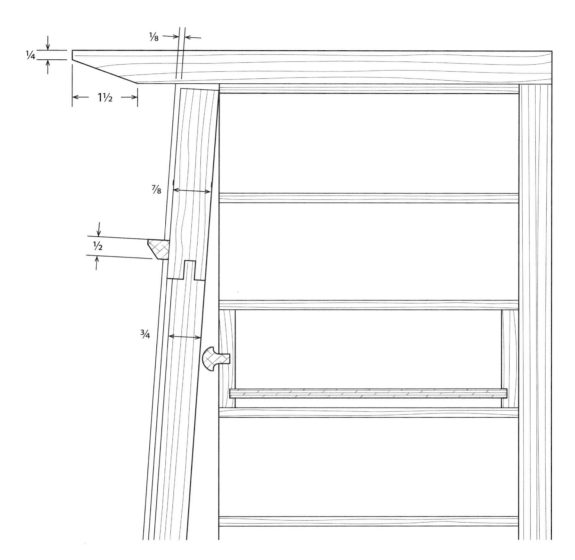

Section Through Pigeonhole Insert

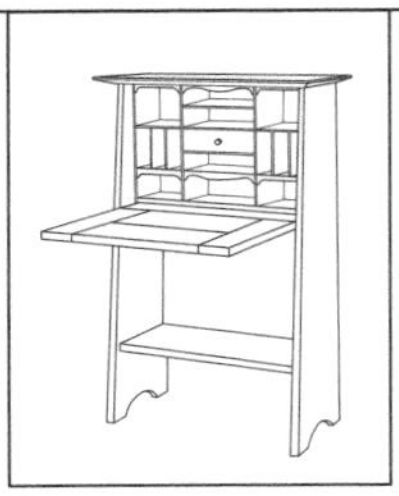

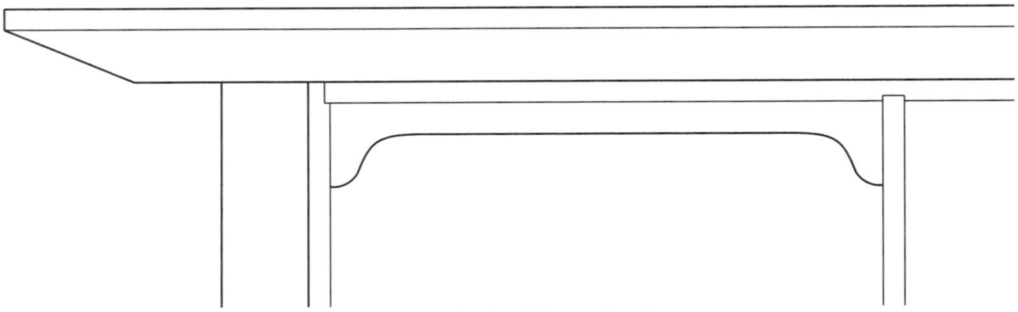

Pigeonhole Trim—End

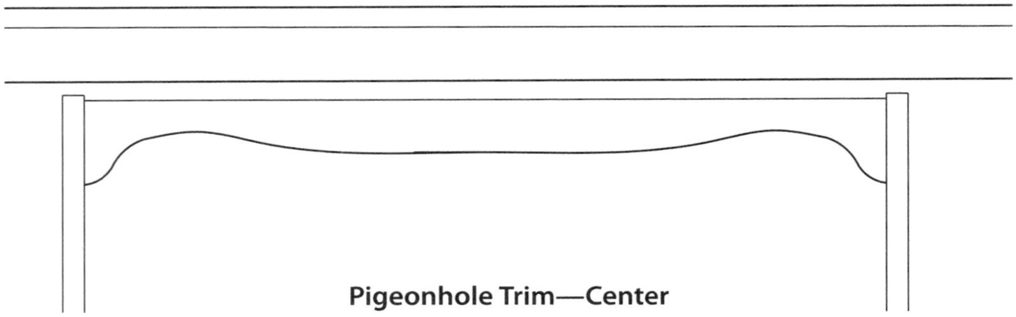

Pigeonhole Trim—Center

Gustav Stickley No. 706 Drop-Front Desk

QTY	PART	SIZE	NOTES
2	Sides	1 x 11⅛ x 43⅛	
1	Top	⅞ x 11 x 30	
1	Lower Shelf	¾ x 9 13/16 x 23¾	23 exposed between sides
1	Drop Front	⅞ x 23 x 21⅜	Width of opening—trim for desired gaps—parts detailed below
2	Stiles	⅞ x 3 x 21⅜	
1	Top Rail	⅞ x 5 x 18	17 exposed
1	Bottom Rail	⅞ x 3⅜ x 18	17 exposed
1	Panel	¾ x 18 x 14	17 x 14 exposed
1	Applied Trim	½ x ½ x 18	
1	Back	¾ x 23¾ x 33⅜	23 exposed between sides—33 exposed between top & shelf parts for "shiplap" back listed below
5	Back Planks	¾ x 5 3/16 x 33⅜	⅜ rabbets as detailed will yield back 23 11/16 wide planks should be NO wider, narrower if humid
	Pigeonhole Insert		
2	Outer Uprights	¼ x 7¾ x 14¾	
1	Bottom	½ x 7¾ x 22¾	22½ exposed between outer uprights
3	Top & Shelves	¼ x 7¾ x 22¾	22½ exposed between outer uprights
2	Upper Vertical Dividers	¼ x 7¾ x 5⅝	5½ exposed between top & shelf
6	Middle Vertical Dividers	¼ x 7¾ x 5 9/16	5 7/16 exposed between shelves
2	Lower Vertical Dividers	¼ x 7¾ x 2¾	2⅝ exposed between bottom & shelf
3	Horizontal Dividers	¼ x 7¾ x 9⅜	9¼ exposed between vertical dividers
4	End Trim	¼ x 1 x 6⅜	
2	Middle Trim	¼ x 1 x 9¼	

GUSTAV STICKLEY NO. 708 DESK WITH TWO DRAWERS

36" high x 40" wide x 22" deep

People don't write letters with pen and paper any more, probably because they don't have a terrific desk like this one. It would also make a good home for a laptop computer—good design is timeless.

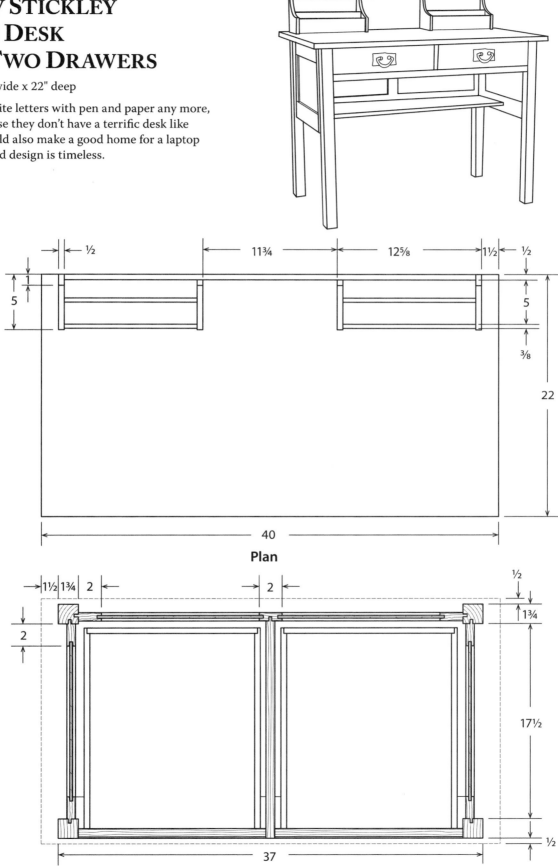

Plan

Plan Section

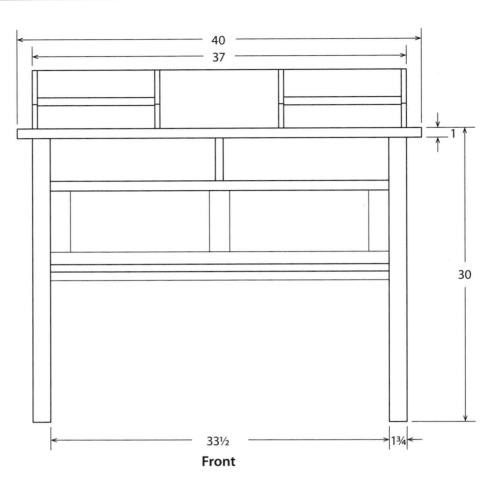

40

37

1

30

33½

1¾

Front

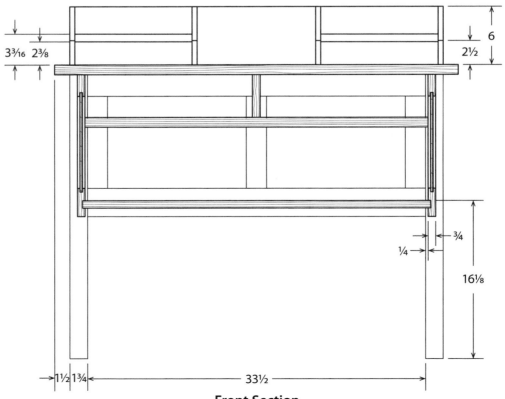

3³⁄₁₆ 2³⁄₈

6

2½

¾

¼

16⅛

1½ 1¾

33½

Front Section

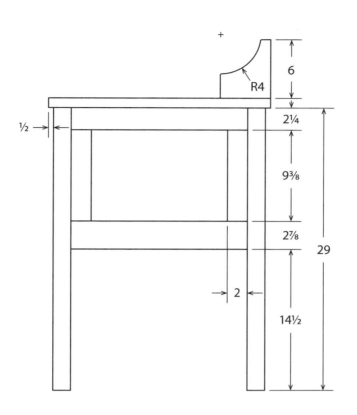

Side

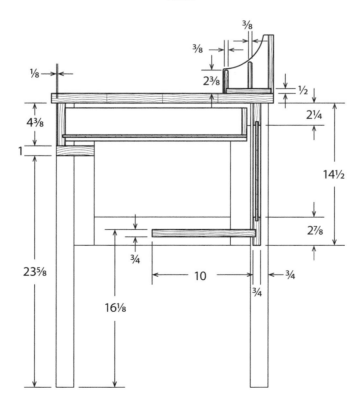

Side Section

Gustav Stickley No. 708 Desk with Two Drawers

QTY	PART	SIZE	NOTES
1	Top	1 x 22 x 40	
4	Legs	1¾ x 1¾ x 29	
2	Side Panels	¾ x 18½ x 14½	parts detailed below—17½ exposed between legs
4	Stiles	¾ x 2½ x 10⅜	2 x 9⅜ exposed
2	Top Rails	¾ x 2¼ x 18½	17½ exposed
2	Bottom Rails	¾ x 2⅞ x 18½	17½ exposed
2	Panels	¼ x 14½ x 10⅜	13½ x 9⅜ exposed
1	Back Panel	¾ x 34½ x 14½	parts detailed below—33½ exposed between legs
2	End Stiles	¾ x 2½ x 10⅜	2 x 9⅜ exposed
1	Middle Stile	¾ x 2 x 10⅜	9⅜ exposed
1	Top Rail	¾ x 2¼ x 34½	33½ exposed between legs
1	Bottom Rail	¾ x 2⅞ x 34½	33½ exposed between legs
2	Panels	¼ x 14¾ x 10⅜	13½ x 9⅜ exposed
1	Shelf	¾ x 10 x 34½	34 exposed between side panels
1	Rail Below Drawers	¾ x 3¾ x 34½	33 exposed between side panels
1	Drawer Divider	¾ x 4⅜ x 19⅝	19¼ exposed
2	Drawer Fronts	¾ x 4⅜ x 16⅜	opening size—trim for desired gaps
	Letter Rack		
1	Back	½ x 6 x 36	add to length for joints if desired
2	Outer Ends	½ x 5 x 6	cut out radius
2	Inner Ends	½ x 4½ x 6	add to width for joints if desired—cut out radius
2	Middle Dividers	⅜ x 2¾ x 11⅝	add to length for joints if desired
2	Fronts	⅜ x 2⅜ x 11⅝	add to length for joints if desired
2	Bottoms	½ x 4½ x 11⅝	4 exposed

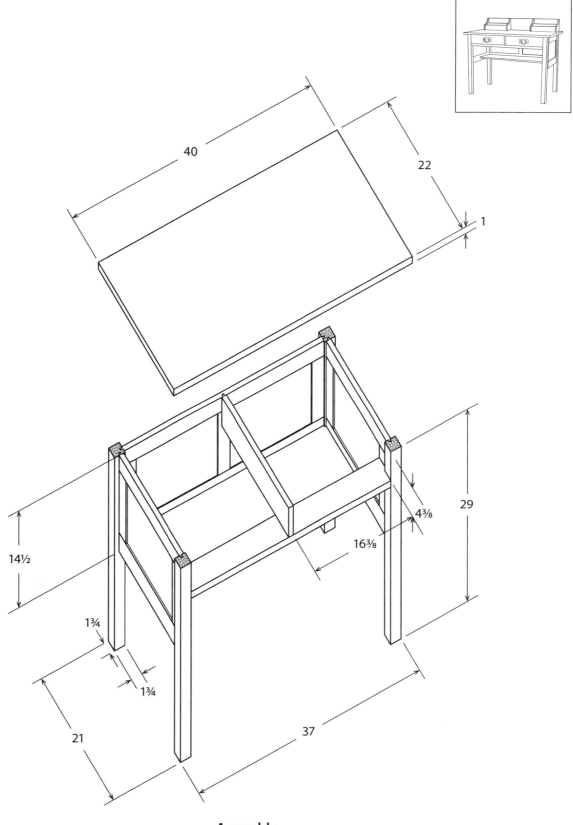

Assembly

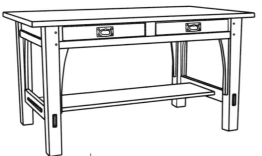

GUSTAV STICKLEY NO. 616 LIBRARY TABLE

30" high x 32" deep x 54" wide

Many variations of this table were made—it was available with a leather top or a wooden top, and appeared in some catalogs with three drawers instead of two as shown in this example. Similar tables were also manufactured in different sizes with different model numbers.

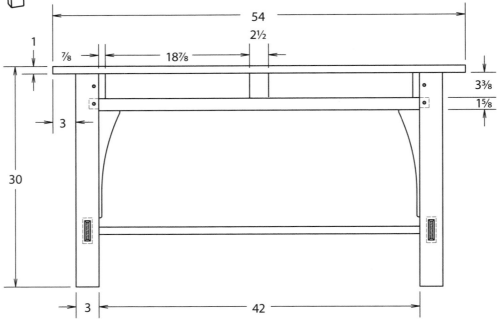

Front Elevation

Plan Section Above Shelf

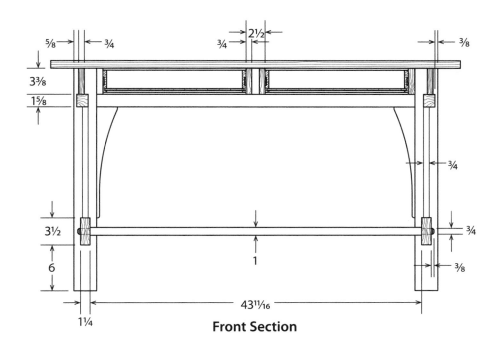

Front Section

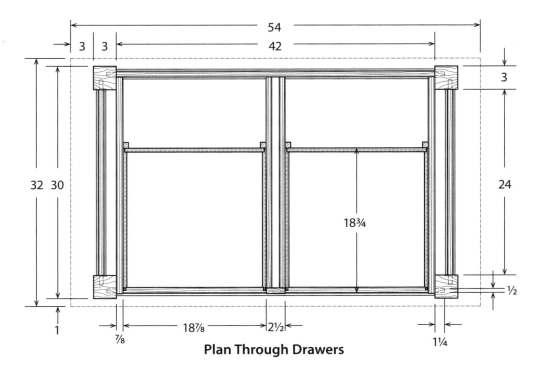

Plan Through Drawers

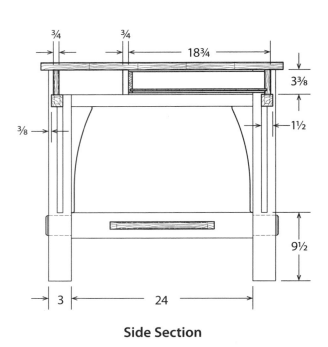

Side Section

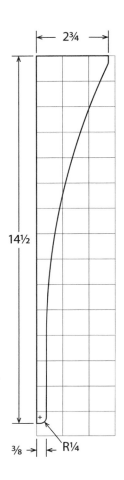

**Corbel Detail
1" Grid**

Gustav Stickley No. 616 Library Table

Qty	Part	Size	Notes
1	Top	1 x 32 x 54	
4	Legs	3 x 3 x 29	
2	Lower Rails	1¼ x 3½ x 30¾	24 between tenons
2	Upper Rails	1½ x 1⅝ x 26½	24 between tenons
2	Panels Below Top	¾ x 3⅜ x 26½	24 between tenons
1	Shelf	1 x 13¾ x 46⅞	43⅝ between tenons
2	Front & Back Rails	1½ x 1⅝ x 43½	42 between tenons
1	Back Panel Below Top	¾ x 3⅜ x 43½	42 between tenons
2	Vertical Trim @ Drawers	¾ x ⅞ x 3⅜	
1	Vertical Trim @ Drawers	¾ x 2½ x 3⅜	
4	Drawer Stretchers	¾ x 3⅜ x 27½	
2	Drawer Fronts	¾ x 3⅜ x 18⅞	opening
8	Corbels	¾ x 2¾ x 14½	

NO. 637 LIBRARY TABLE

29" high x 30" wide x 48" long

Here is a robust library table that could be used as a computer desk, a conference table, or a dining table. It would be easy to adjust the length and width to your particular purpose. The keyed tenons make an especially attractive detail.

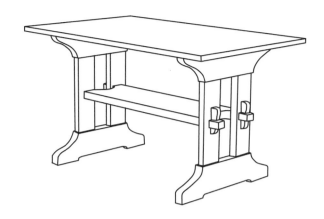

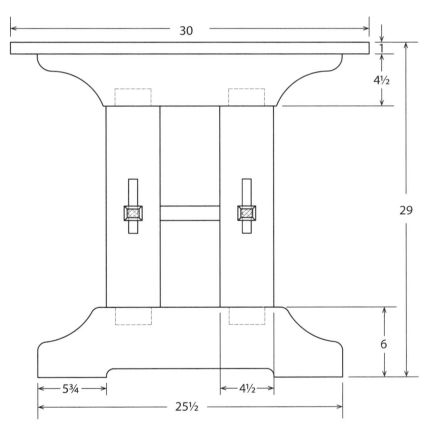

End Elevation

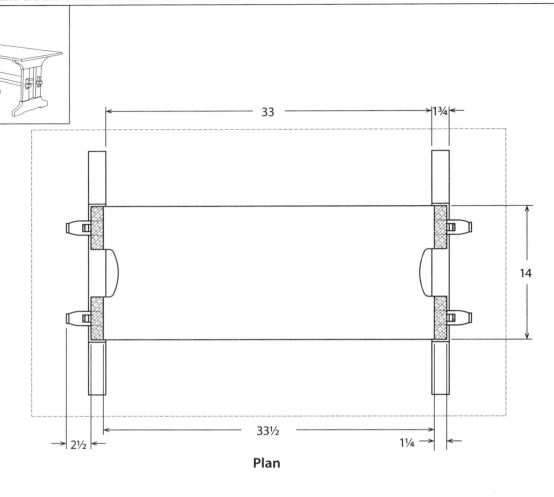

Plan

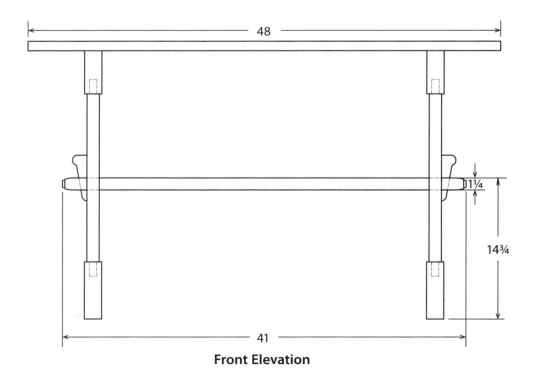

Front Elevation

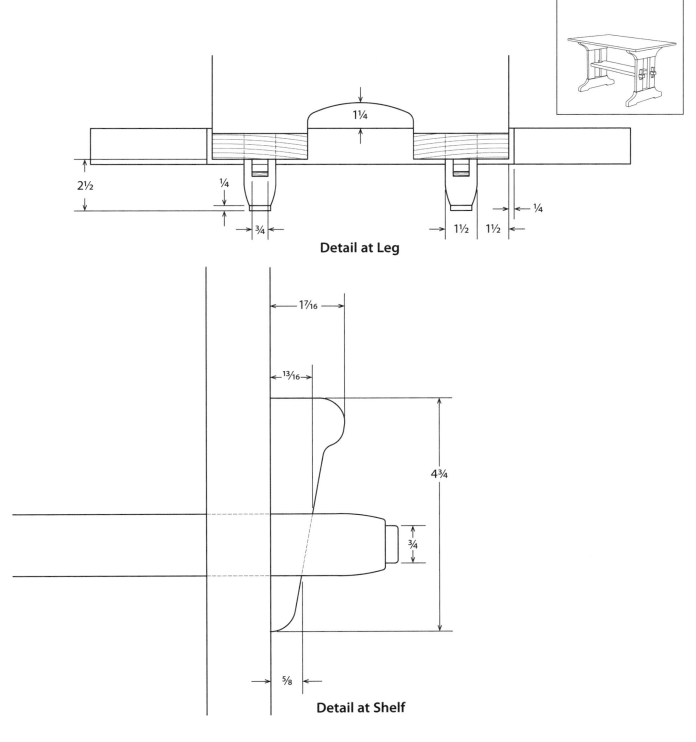

Detail at Leg

1¼

2½

¼

¾

1½

1½

¼

Detail at Shelf

1⁷⁄₁₆

1³⁄₁₆

4¾

¾

⁵⁄₈

Gustav Stickley No. 637 Library Table

QTY	PART	SIZE	NOTES
2	Feet	1¾ x 6 x 25½	
2	Top Rails	1¾ x 4½ x 25½	
4	Uprights	1¼ x 4½ x 21½	18½ between tenons
1	Shelf	1¼ x 14 x 41	33½ between tenons
1	Top	1 x 30 x 48	
4	Keys	¾ x 1⁷⁄₁₆ x 4¾	

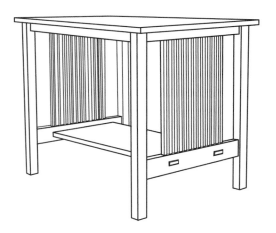

GUSTAV STICKLEY
NO. 655 LIBRARY TABLE

29" high x 48" wide x 30" deep

The No. 655 library table would be an elegant addition to your library, if you had one, and if you added a keyboard tray, an excellent computer desk in the Arts & Crafts style.

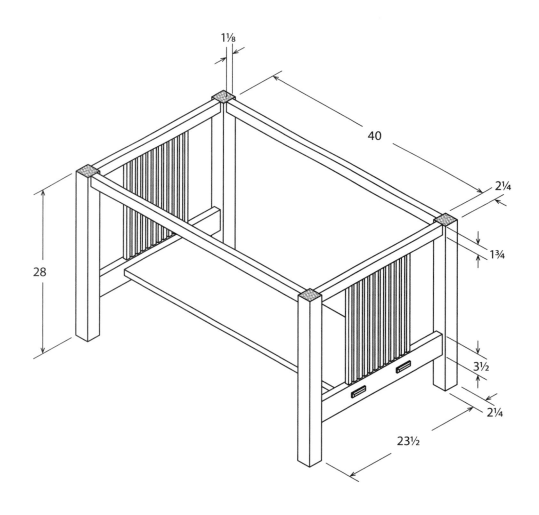

1⅛

40

2¼

1¾

28

3½

2¼

23½

Assembly

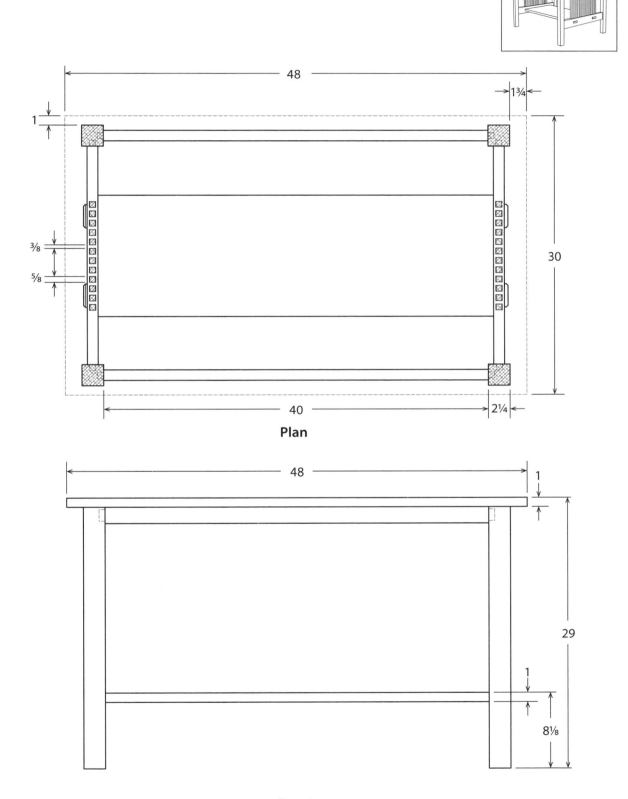

Plan

Front

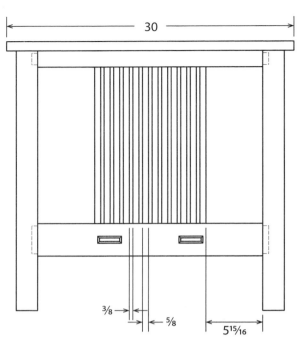

Side

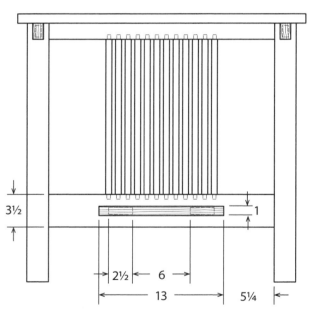

Side Section

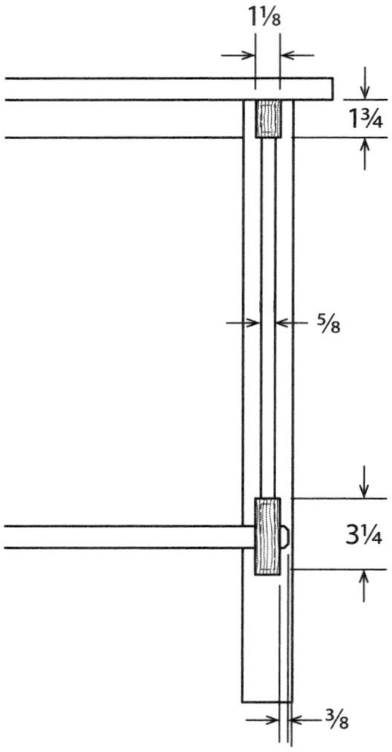

Front Section

Gustav Stickley No. 655 Library Table

Qty	Part	Size	Notes
1	Top	1 x 30 x 48	
4	Legs	2¼ x 2¼ x 28	
2	Long Top Rails	1⅛ x 1¾ x 41½	40 between tenon shoulders
2	Short top Rails	1⅛ x 1¾ x 25	23½ between tenon shoulders
2	Bottom Rails	1⅛ x 3¼ x 25	23½ between tenon shoulders
1	Shelf	1 x 13 x 44⅛	41⅛ between tenon shoulders
24	Spindles	⅝ x ⅝ x 18⅞	18⅛ between tenon shoulders

L. & J. G. STICKLEY
NO. 644 BOOKCASE

55" high x 36" wide x 12" deep

This bookcase was made in several widths, 30", 36", 49", and 70" wide. It could easily be made any width desired. The widest version had two vertical dividers, but the sides and basic construction of all four versions was the same. The shelves could be made fixed, but the rest of the structure is so stout that there is no reason not to have them be adjustable. Gustav Stickley made bookcases very similar to this, but the sides were not as thick as in this example.

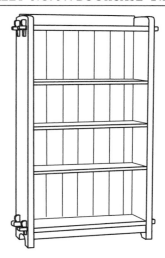

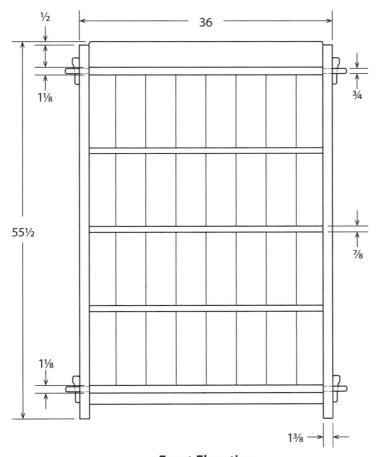

Front Elevation

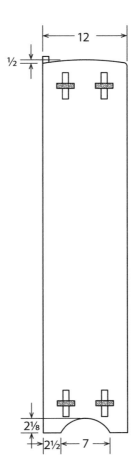

Side Elevation

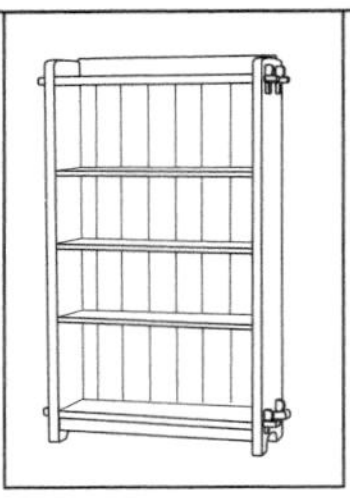

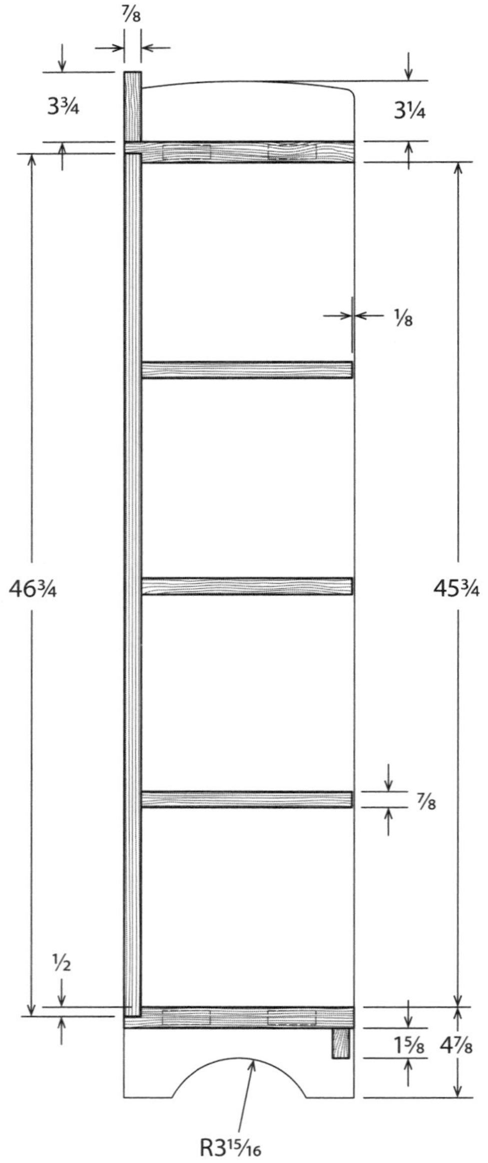

Side Section

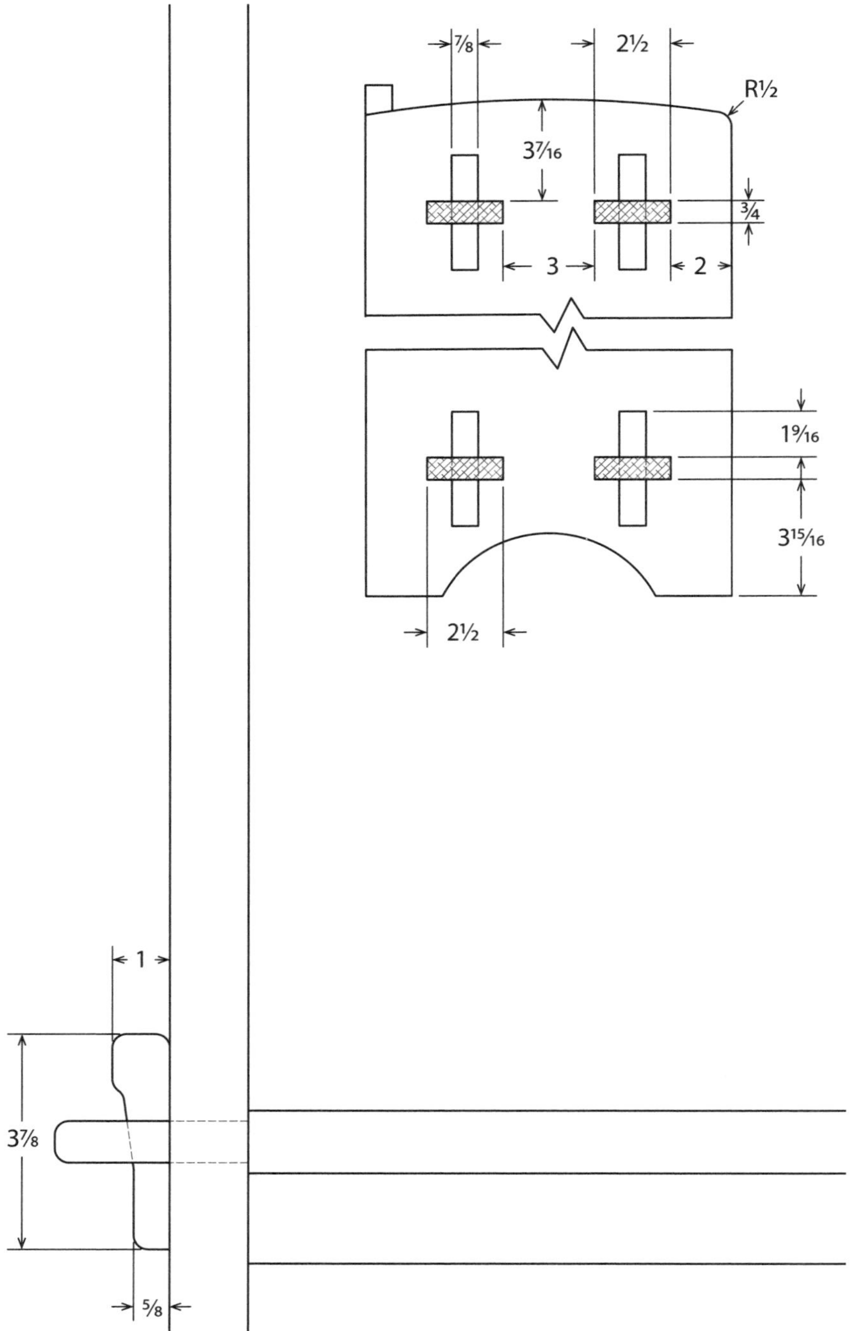

Detail of Tusk Tenon

L. & J. G. Stickley No. 644 Bookcase

Qty	Part	Size	Notes
2	Sides	1⅜ x 12 x 55	
2	Top & Bottom	1⅛ x 12 x 40	33¼ between tenons
3	Shelves	⅞ x 11 x 33¼	opening
8	Back Planks	¾ x 4⁵⁄₁₆ x 46¾	
8	Keys	⅞ x 1 x 3⅞	
1	Backsplash	⅞ x 3¾ x 33¼	

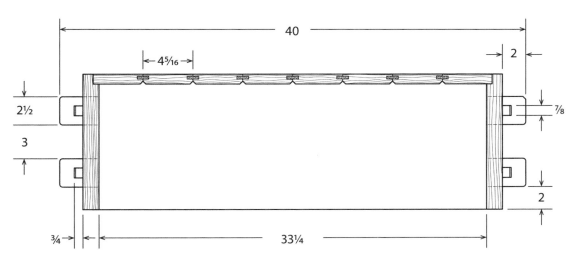

Plan Section Above Top Shelf

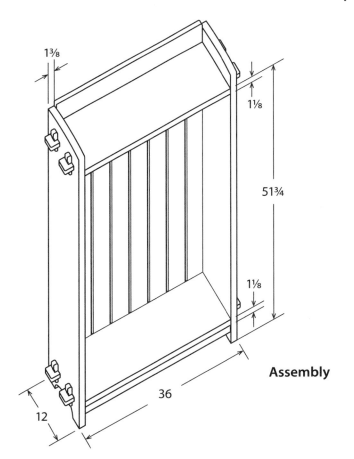

Assembly

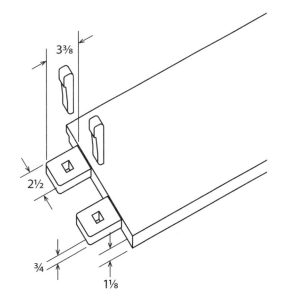

GUSTAV STICKLEY NO. 700 BOOKCASE

58" high x 36" wide x 14" deep

One of Harvey Ellis' finest designs, it has a commanding presence even though it is actually rather small.

The original has four panes of leaded glass in each of the top lights. There also was no knob or handle on the original, only a small escutcheon for a key a little more than half-way up the left-hand door stile.

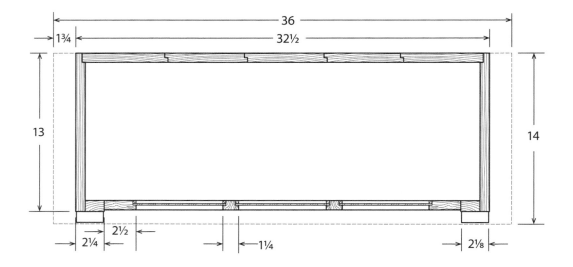

Plan

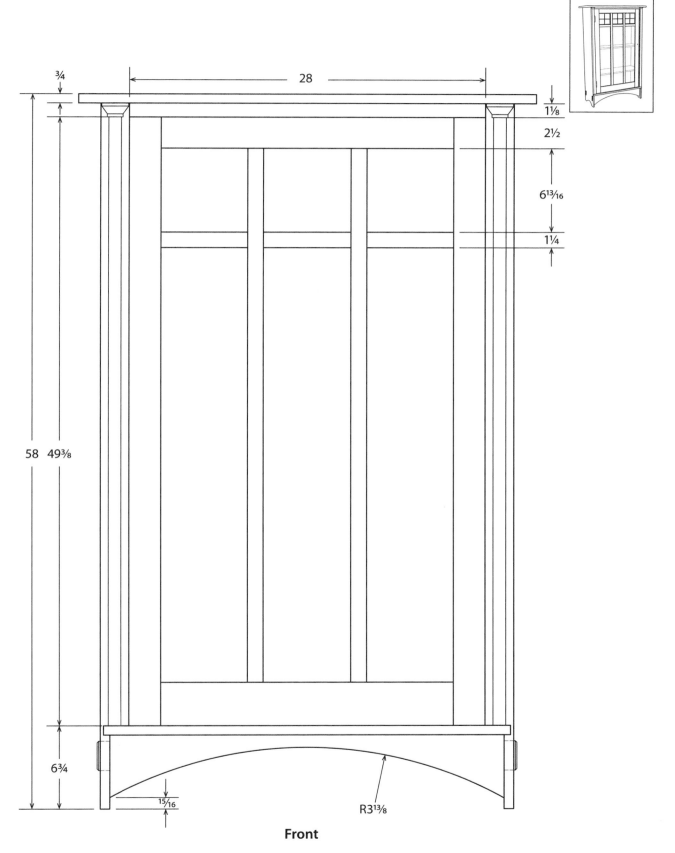

Front

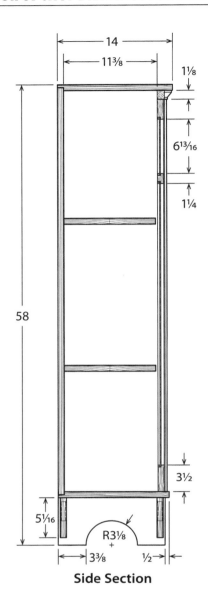

Side Section

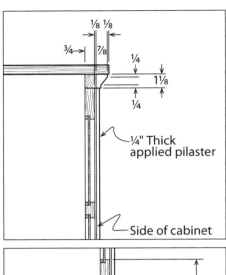

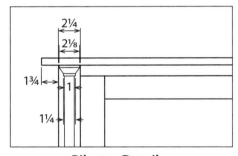

Details

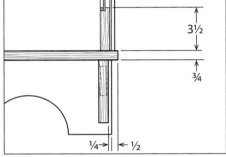

Pilaster Detail

Gustav Stickley No. 700 Bookcase

Qty	Part	Size	Notes
1	Top	¾ x 14 x 36	
2	Sides	¾ x 13 x 57¼	
1	Bottom	¾ x 13½ x 32	notched @ front of sides, dado into sides, 31 exposed between sides
1	Back	¾ x 31½ x 51¼	31 exposed between sides, 50½ exposed between top & bottom
2	Shelves	¾ x 11⅛ x 30⅞	size for adjustable shelves—smaller than opening
2	Front & Back Toe Boards	¾ x 5¹⁄₁₆ x 33¼	31 between tenons—tenons extend ⅜ beyond sides
2	Stiles	⅞ x 1½ x 50½	
1	Top Rail	⅞ x 1⅛ x 29	28 between tenon shoulders into stiles
2	Applied Pilaster	¼ x 1 x 49⅜	
2	Pilaster Head Trim Blocks	⅞ x 2⅛ x 1⅛	see detail
1	Door	¾ x 28 x 49⅜	opening size, trim for desired gaps—parts detailed below
2	Door Stiles	¾ x 2½ x 49⅜	
1	Door Top Rail	¾ x 2½ x 25	23 between tenon shoulders
1	Door Bottom Rail	¾ x 3½ x 25	23 between tenon shoulders
2	Mullions	¾ x 1¼ x 44⅜	43⅜ between tenon shoulders
3	Muntins	¾ x 1¼ x 7¹⁹⁄₃₂	6²⁷⁄₃₂ between tenon shoulders
32LF	Glass Stop	¼ x ¼	

GUSTAV STICKLEY
NO. 719 BOOKCASE

Glass doors are a dust-proof luxury rarely seen on a bookcase today. Though designed as a floor-standing piece, you could mount the case to the wall, and you could use it for curios or china as readily as for books. This piece was also made in different widths, and the doors could be divided into three vertical sections as in the sketch at right, or two as in the drawings below.

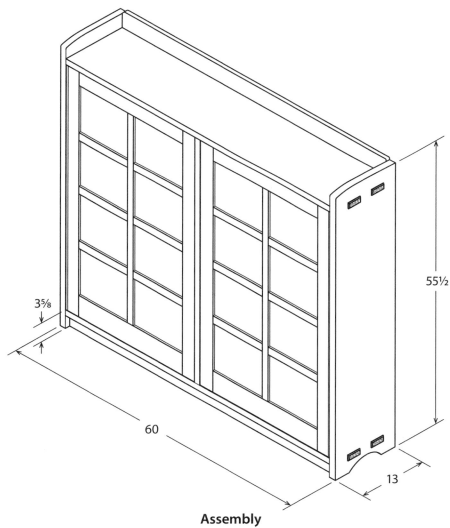

3⅝

55½

60

13

Assembly

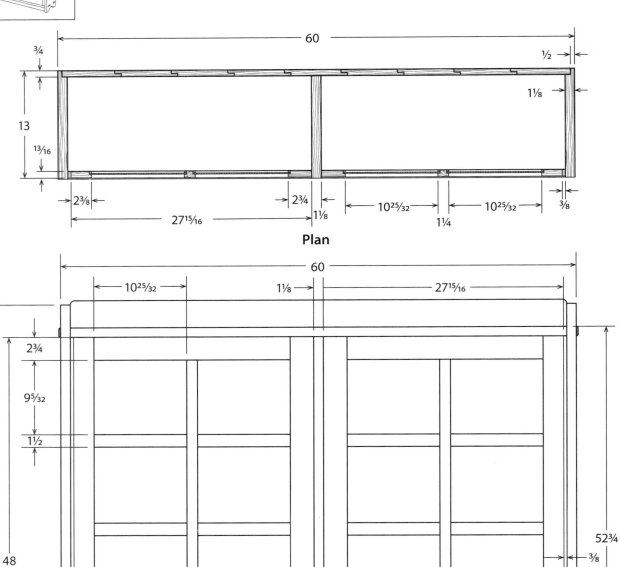

Plan

Front

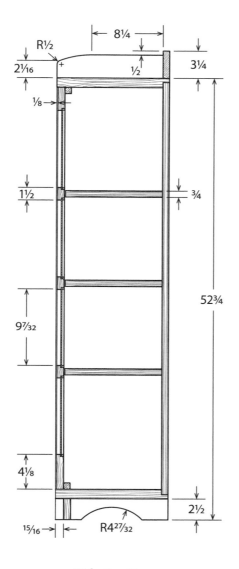

Side Section

Side

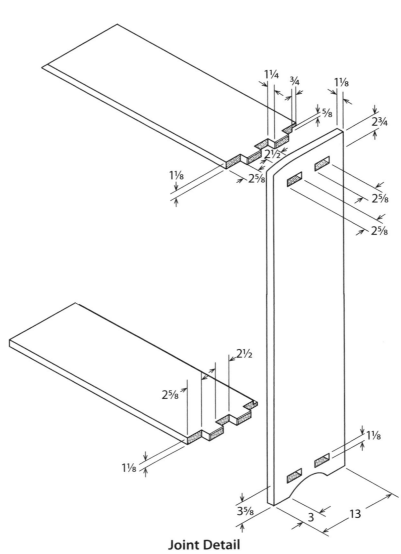

Joint Detail

Gustav Stickley No. 719 Bookcase

Qty	Part	Size	Notes
2	Sides	1⅛ x 13 x 55½	
1	Vertical Divider	1⅛ x 12¼ x 48	add to width & length for joints @ bottom & back
6	Adjustable Shelves	¾ x 11³⁄₁₆ x 28³⁄₁₆	size is for adjustable shelves—smaller than opening
2	Top & Bottom	1⅛ x 13 x 60¾	57¾ between tenons—tenons extend beyond sides ⅜
1	Back	¾ x 59 x 49¼	57¾ x 48 exposed—shiplap parts listed below
9	Back Planks	¾ x 7³⁄₃₂ x 49¼	will make back 58²⁷⁄₃₂ wide—make planks narrower if humid
1	Backsplash	¾ x 3¼ x 57¾	
1	Toe Board	¾ x 2½ x 57¾	
2	Hinge Strips	⅜ x ¹³⁄₁₆ x 48	
4	Door Stops	¾ x ¾ x 27¹⁵⁄₁₆	
2	Doors	1³⁄₁₆ x 27¹⁵⁄₁₆ x 48	opening size—trim for desired gaps—parts detailed below
2	Hinge Stiles	1³⁄₁₆ x 2⅜ x 48	
2	Middle Stiles	1³⁄₁₆ x 2¾ x 48	
2	Top Door Rails	1³⁄₁₆ x 2¾ x 23¹³⁄₁₆	22¹³⁄₁₆ between tongues
2	Bottom Door Rails	1³⁄₁₆ x 4⅛ x 23¹³⁄₁₆	22¹³⁄₁₆ between tongues
2	Mullions	1³⁄₁₆ x 1¼ x 42⅛	41⅛ between tongues
12	Muntins	1³⁄₁₆ x 1½ x 11²⁵⁄₃₂	10²⁵⁄₃₂ between tongues
64lf	Glass Stop	¼ x ¼	

GUSTAV STICKLEY
NO. 724 LADIES' BOOKCASE

46" high x 32" wide x 12" deep

The prototype of this small desk had floriform inlays on the narrow front panels. The inlaid furniture never went into full production, but this handsome little desk was produced as shown for several years. Make the pigeonholes as a separate unit, and attach that inside the upper case.

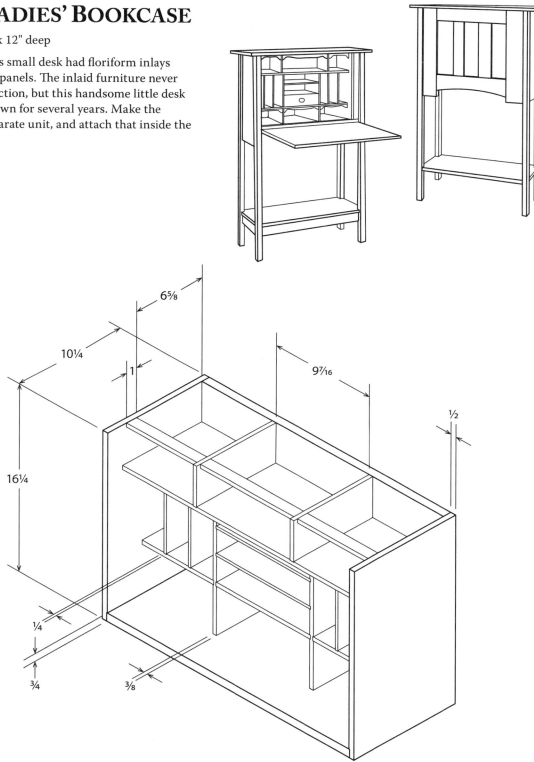

Pigeonhole Detail

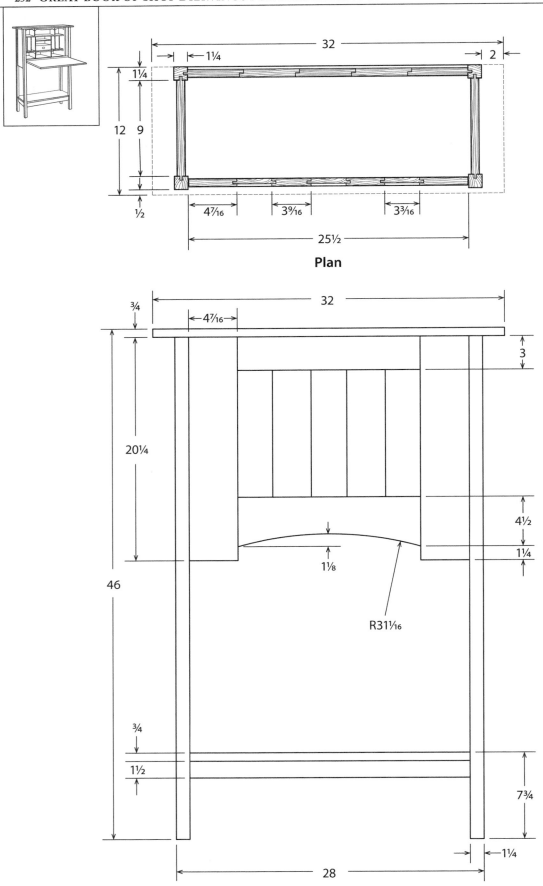

Plan

Front Elevation

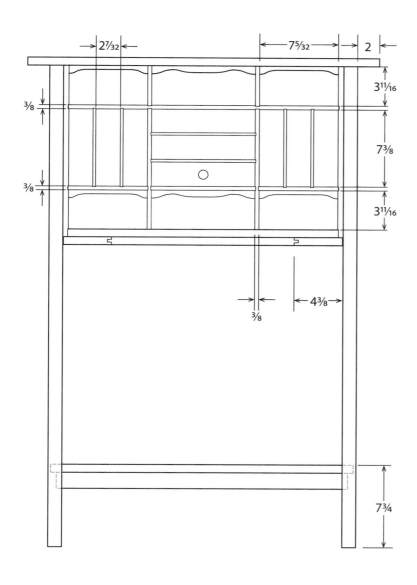

Front Elevation—Open

Side Elevation

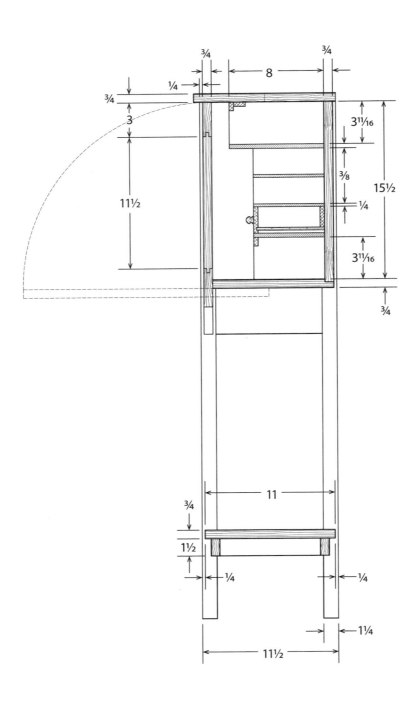

Side Section

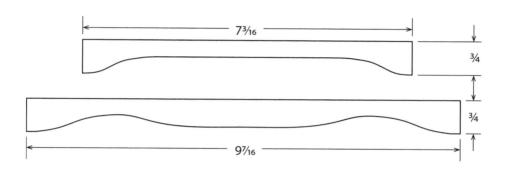

Trim Details

Gustav Stickley No. 724 Ladies' Bookcase

QTY	PART	SIZE	NOTES
4	Legs	1¼ x 1¼ x 45¼	
1	Top	¾ x 12 x 32	
2	Front & Back Shelf Rails	¾ x 1½ x 26½	
2	Shelf End Rails	¾ x 1½ x 10	
1	Lower Shelf	¾ x 11 x 27½	
2	Side Panels	¾ x 10 x 20¼	9 between tenons
1	Door	¾ x 25½ x 20¼	opening—parts detailed below
2	Stiles	¾ x 4⁷⁄₁₆ x 20¼	
1	Bottom Door Rail	¾ x 4½ x 17⅝	16⅝ between tenons
1	Top Door Rail	¾ x 3 x 17⅝	16⅝ between tenons
2	Inner Door Stiles	¾ x 3⁹⁄₁₆ x 12½	11½ between tenons
3	Door Panels	½ x 4⁹⁄₁₆ x 12½	3⁹⁄₁₆ x 11½ exposed
1	Cabinet Bottom	¾ x 10¼ x 24	
1	Cabinet Back	¾ x 15¾ x 25½	
2	Cabinet Sides	¾ x 10¼ x 17	
1	Cabinet Shelf	⅜ x 8 x 24	
2	Vertical Dividers	⅜ x 6 x 11½	
2	Upper Vertical Dividers	⅜ x 8 x 3¾	
1	Shelf	⅜ x 8 x 24⅝	
2	Shelves	⅜ x 6 x 7⁹⁄₃₂	
1	Shelf	⅜ x 6 x 9⁹⁄₁₆	
2	Shelves	¼ x 6 x 9⁹⁄₁₆	
4	Vertical Dividers	¼ x 6 x 7½	
1	Drawer Front	⅜ x 2⁹⁄₁₆ x 9⁷⁄₁₆	opening
2	Center Curved Trim	⅜ x ¾ x 9⁷⁄₁₆	
4	Outer Curved Trim	⅜ x ¾ x 7⁵⁄₃₂	

ROYCROFT "LITTLE JOURNEYS" BOOK STAND

26" high x 26" wide x 14" deep

Produced after Elbert Hubbard's death to hold the complete set of his "Little Journeys" books, this piece was shipped knocked down from the Aurora, N.Y., giftshop. Four screws through table irons attach the top. Existing antiques are often a little wobbly, probably due to having been assembled by the customer. A ¾" x ¾" cleat along the inside of the legs at the top would be a structural improvement.

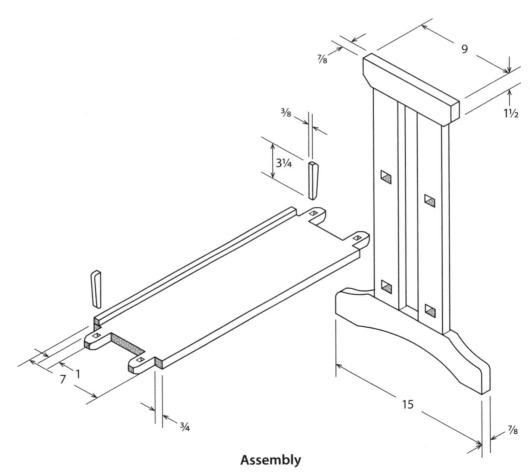

Assembly

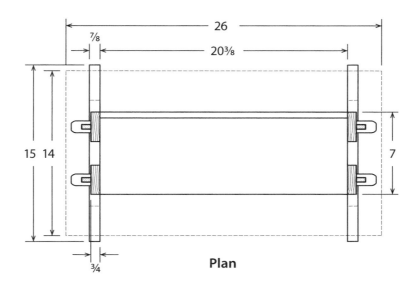

Plan

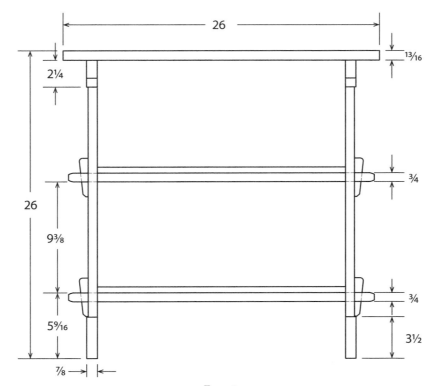

Front

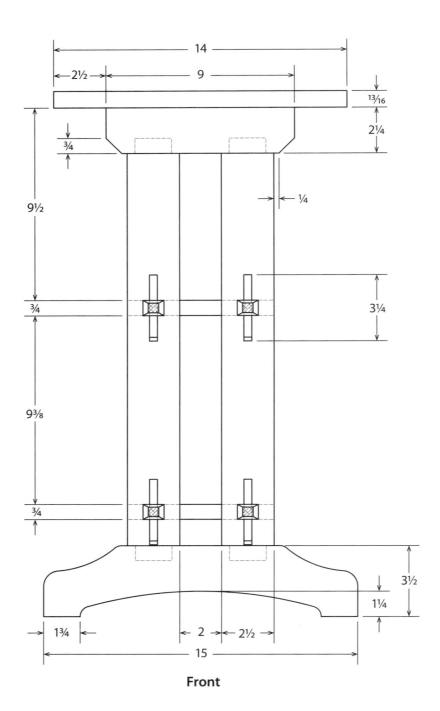

Front

Roycroft "Little Journeys" Stand

Qty	Part	Size	Notes
1	Top	$^{13}/_{16}$ x 14 x 26	
2	Feet	$^{7}/_{8}$ x $3^{1}/_{2}$ x 15	
2	Side Top Rails	$^{3}/_{4}$ x $2^{1}/_{4}$ x 9	
4	Legs	$^{3}/_{4}$ x $2^{1}/_{2}$ x $20^{15}/_{16}$	$19^{7}/_{16}$ between tenon shoulders
2	Shelves	$^{3}/_{4}$ x 7 x $25^{1}/_{4}$	$20^{3}/_{8}$ between tenon shoulders
2	Shelf Backs	$^{1}/_{2}$ x $^{1}/_{2}$ x $20^{3}/_{8}$	
4	Keys	$^{3}/_{8}$ x $^{7}/_{8}$ x $3^{1}/_{4}$	

HARVEY ELLIS
NO. 72 MAGAZINE CABINET

42" x 22" x 13"

An excellent example of Harvey Ellis' design motifs. Note that the shelves are dadoed only into the side panels, not the legs. This simplifies the construction by reducing the number of mortises to cut into the legs (although it does make the shelves a little trickier). Assemble each side as a unit, then assemble the shelves and stretchers. The top goes on last, held down by table irons.

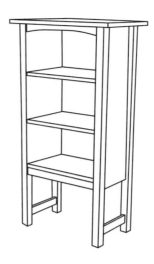

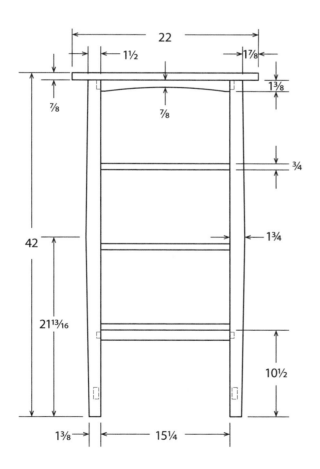

Front Elevation

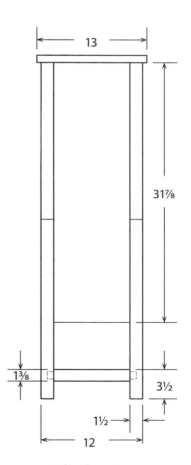

Side Elevation

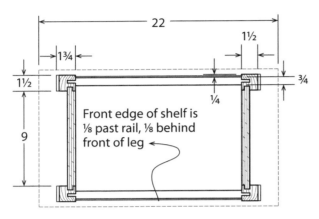

Plan Section Through Rails

Front edge of shelf is ⅛ past rail, ⅛ behind front of leg ←

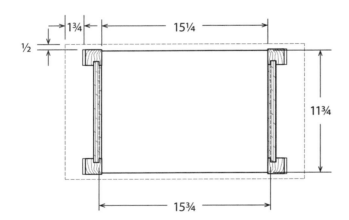

Plan Section Above Shelf

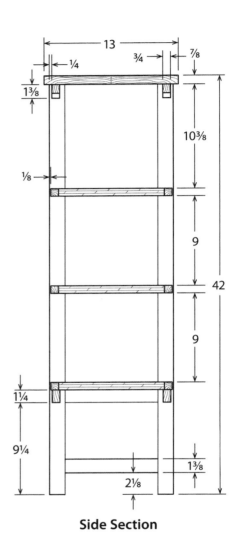

Side Section

Gustav Stickley No. 72 Magazine Cabinet

Qty	Part	Size	Notes
4	Legs	1½ x 1¾ x 41⅛	
2	Side Stretchers	⅝ x 1⅜ x 10½	9 between tenons
2	Side Panels	¾ x 9¾ x 31⅞	9 between tenons
2	Rails Below Bottom Shelf	¾ x 1¼ x 16¾	15¼ between tenons
2	Arched Rails Below Top	¾ x 1⅜ 16¾	15¼ between tenons
3	Shelves	¾ x 11¾ x 15¾	15¼ exposed
1	Top	⅞ x 13 x 22	

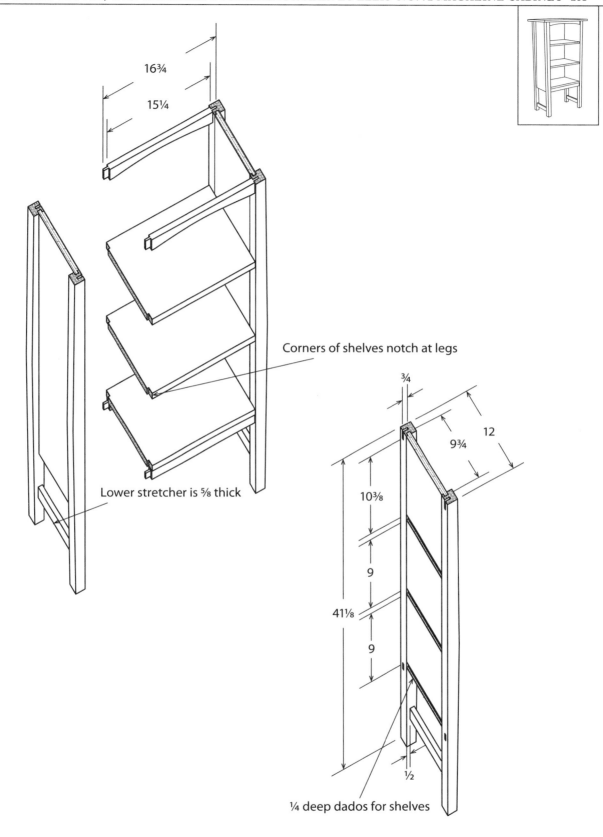

16¾

15¼

Corners of shelves notch at legs

Lower stretcher is ⅝ thick

¾

9¾

12

10⅜

9

41⅛

9

½

¼ deep dados for shelves

Assembly

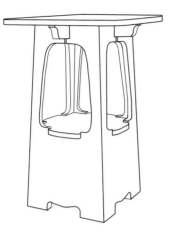

CHARLES LIMBERT LAMP TABLE

19" x 19" x 29"

Mitering the four sides together can be intimidating. The angles work out to barely more than 45° for the miter, and a little more than 2° for the taper at the saw. Practice on some scrap to get the settings right. When putting the whole thing together, assemble two sets of the sides, and then the shelf, before gluing on the last two sides.

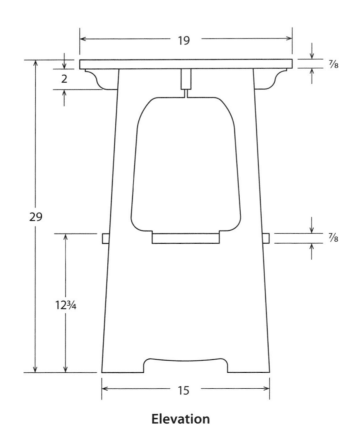

Elevation

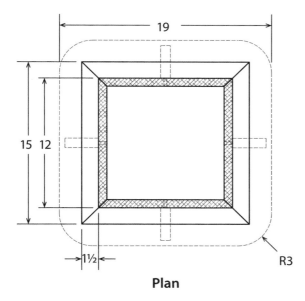

Plan

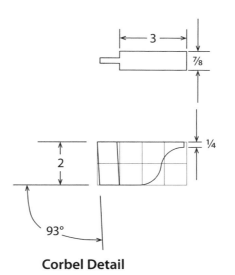

Corbel Detail

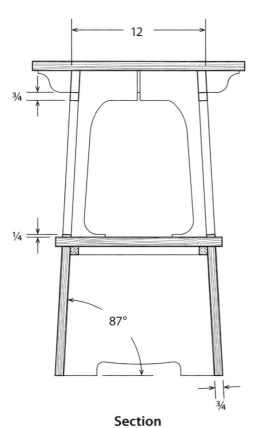

Section

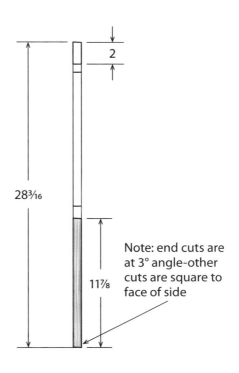

Note: end cuts are at 3° angle-other cuts are square to face of side

True Length of Sides

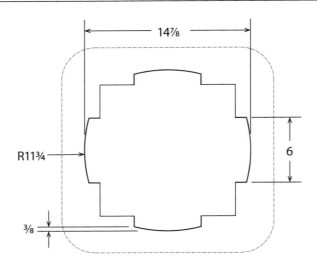

Section at Shelf

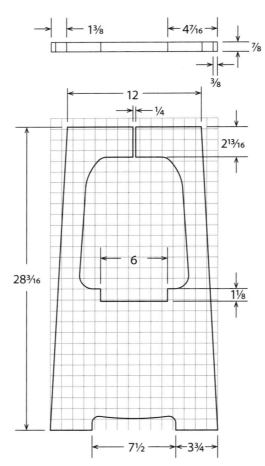

True Elevation of Side
grid = 1" [25.4] squares

Charles Limbert Lamp Table

Qty	Part	Size	Notes
4	Sides	¾ x 15 x 28³⁄₁₆	3° angle on ends
1	Shelf	⅞ x 14⅞ x 14⅞	
1	Top	⅞ x 19 x 19	
4	Corbels	⅞ x 2 x 4	

GUSTAV STICKLEY
NO. 74 BOOKCASE

31" high x 30" wide x 10" deep

Practice making keyed mortise and tenon joints with this small piece. The angled top shelf is good for easy access to reference books, without having to bend over to see the titles.

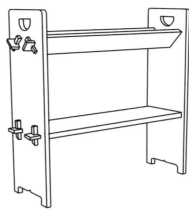

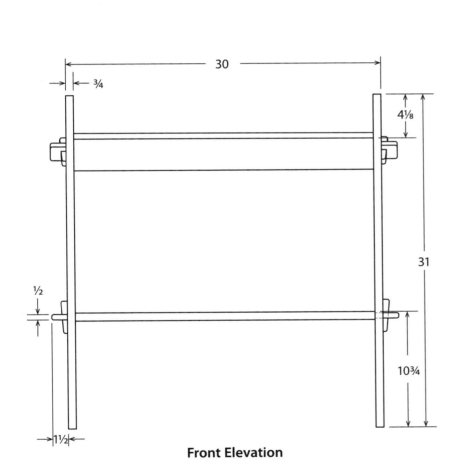

Front Elevation

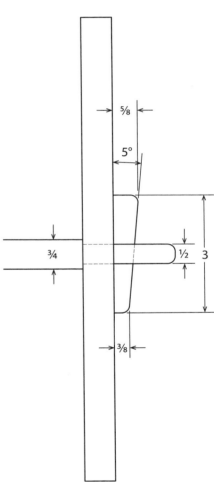

Tusk Tenon Detail

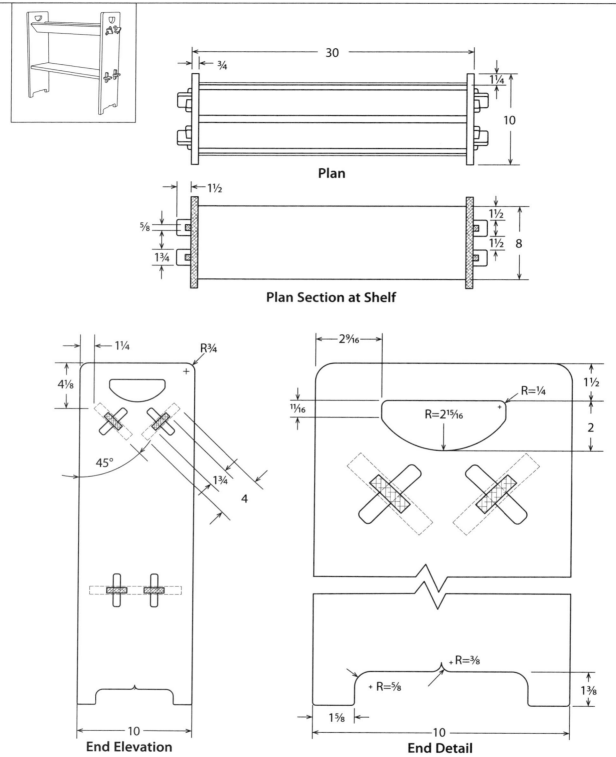

Plan

Plan Section at Shelf

End Elevation

End Detail

Gustav Stickley No. 74 Bookcase

Qty	Part	Size	Notes
2	Sides	¾ x 10 x 31	
2	Top Shelves	¾ x 4 x 33	28½ between tenons
1	Bottom Shelf	¾ x 8 x 33	28½ between tenons
8	Keys	¾ x ⅝ x 3	

Inlays

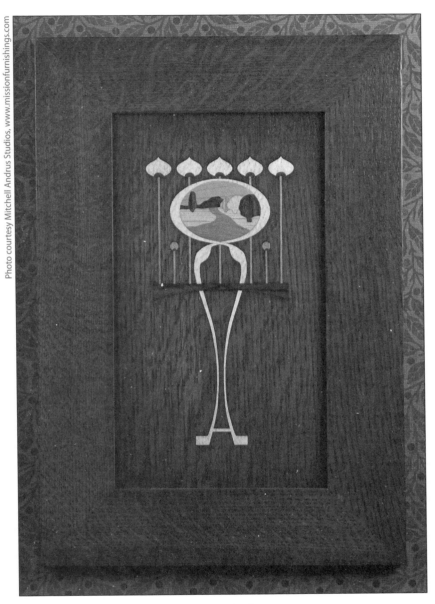

The inlay designs of Harvey Ellis are as fresh and interesting today as they were in 1903. This photo of a reproduction inlay by Mitch Andrus is one of the classic examples of Ellis' lyrical style.

The inlay designs of Harvey Ellis are often spoken of as an anachronism in the broader world of Gustav Stickley's furniture, and Stickley's explanation of how they fit in with his overall scheme has been described as backpedalling on his principles of simple, unadorned forms. Yet, they are the perfect complement, and as Stickley said, "appear to proceed from within outward." Following the example of nature, both the inlays and the furniture upon which they appeared represent harmonious structures in simple forms. Seen one at a time, it is clear that someone with a deep sense of harmony and proportion has created each part. Seen together, they combine to become something greater than the component parts.

Most of the designs on the following pages, and certainly the best examples, are the work of Harvey Ellis. His talent as an artist is shown in the breadth and depth of his work. Today, these small ornaments are his testament, but he was equally talented in work on a grander scale, a talented architect working in pen and ink as well as a watercolor painter and furniture designer. He truly was "one who possessed the sacred fire of genius."

The hardware drawings that close this book are also an example of simple ornaments that complement excellent designs, as opposed to gaudy attachments to inferior designs. The color, shape, and texture of hand-hammered copper hardware adds an interesting element to quartersawn oak—elements of dignity and not distraction.

ARM CHAIR INLAY
CENTER SLAT

This inlay, and the one on the next page, were originally shown on the back slats of an arm chair in the January 1904 issue of *The Craftsman*. This larger pattern was on the center slat, and the smaller version on the following page was on each of the two outer slats.

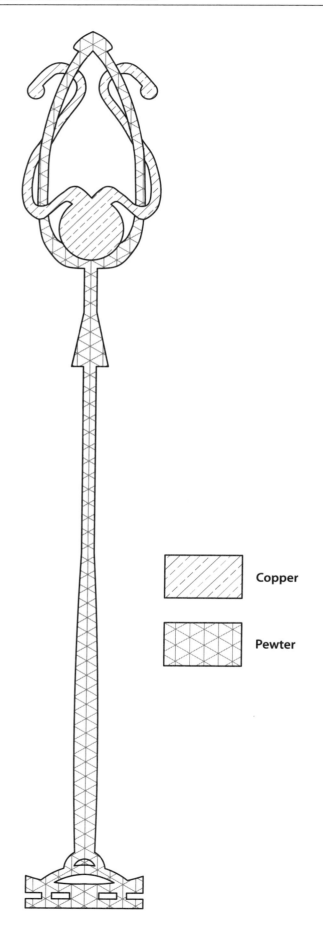

Copper

Pewter

ARM CHAIR INLAY
OUTER SLAT

This slightly smaller version of the inlay on the preceding page flanks that pattern. These two designs are shown entirely in metal, but these same patterns are also seen in veneer in many combinations. This widely used pattern is also seen on the panels of fall-front desks, and on the back slats of many chairs.

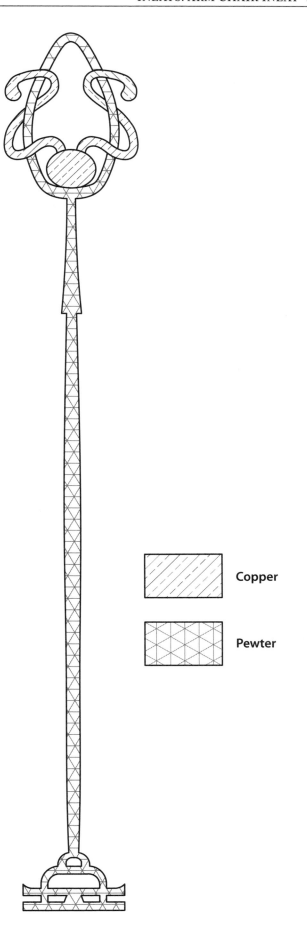

Copper

Pewter

CHAIR SLAT

Less commonly seen, this variation also was used
on chair back slats. It could be made from either a
combination of metals, or entirely from veneer.

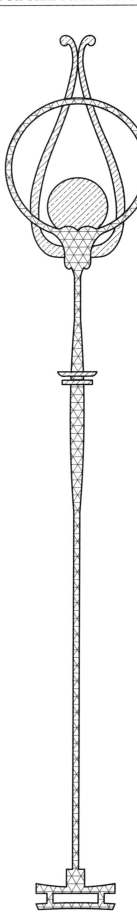

Copper

Pewter

CHAIR SLAT

FULL SIZE

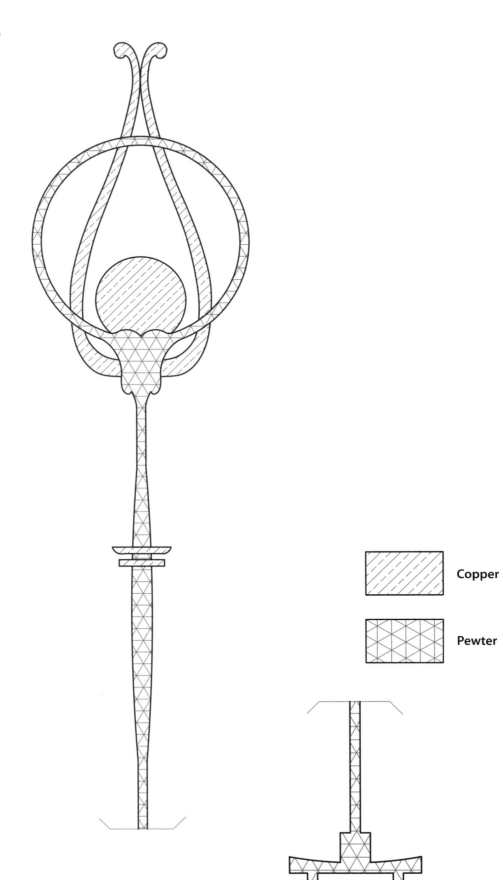

Copper

Pewter

FALL FRONT DESK

The January 1904 issue of *The Craftsman* showed this design on the front panels of an Ellis-designed fall front desk. This illustration has been reduced in size to fit on the page, full size details are on the following page. This pattern could also be made shorter for use on a chair slat.

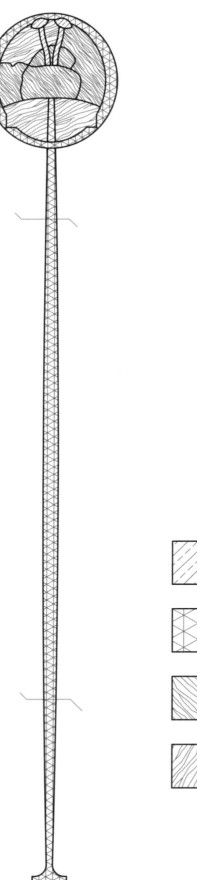

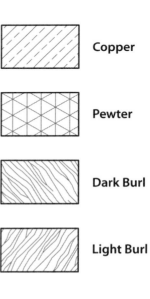

Copper

Pewter

Dark Burl

Light Burl

FALL FRONT DESK
FULL SIZE

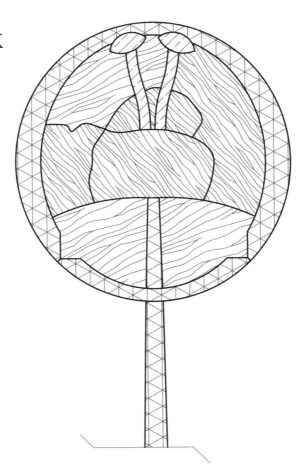

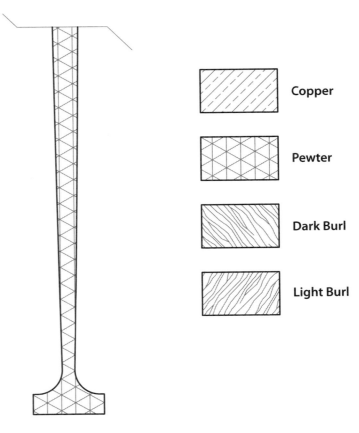

Copper

Pewter

Dark Burl

Light Burl

LARGE CHAIR SLAT

This design also appeared on a chair back, on the middle of three slats. Unlike the previous patterns used for chairs, this design was flanked by two plain slats. Full size details appear on the next page.

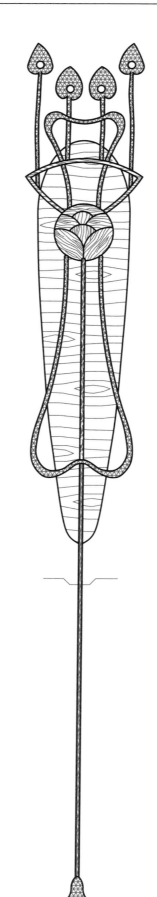

	Pewter
	Light Burl
	Medium Burl
	Medium

LARGE CHAIR SLAT

FULL SIZE

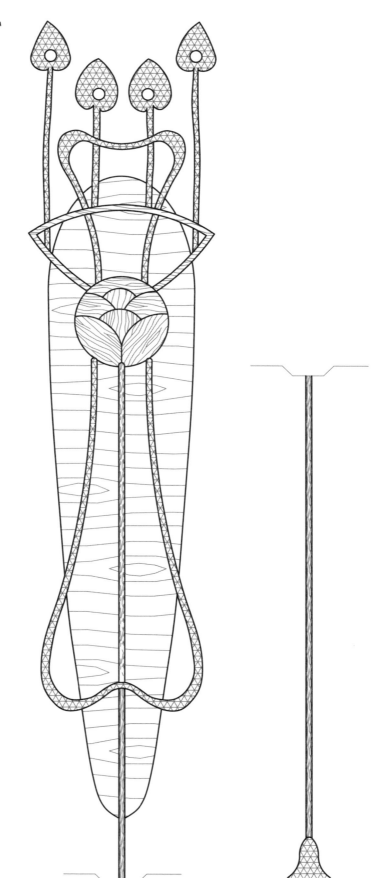

▦	**Pewter**
▨	**Light Burl**
▤	**Medium Burl**
▥	**Medium**

LIBRARY TABLE LEG

In the January 1904 issue of *The Craftsman* this design was found on the wide leg of a library table. Full size details appear on the next page.

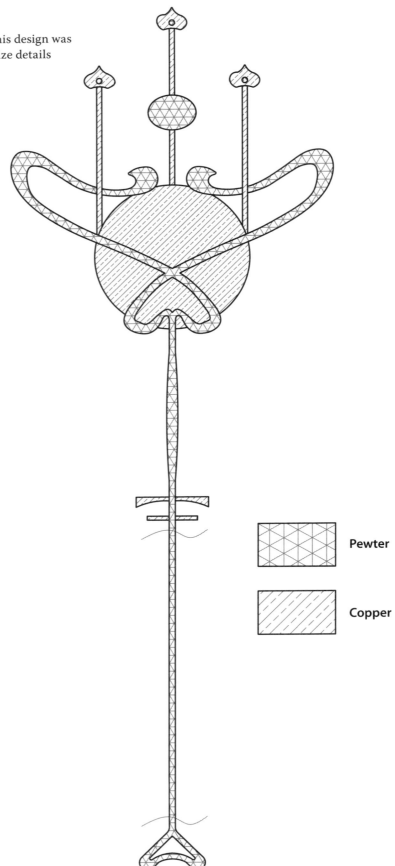

Pewter

Copper

LIBRARY TABLE LEG
FULL SIZE

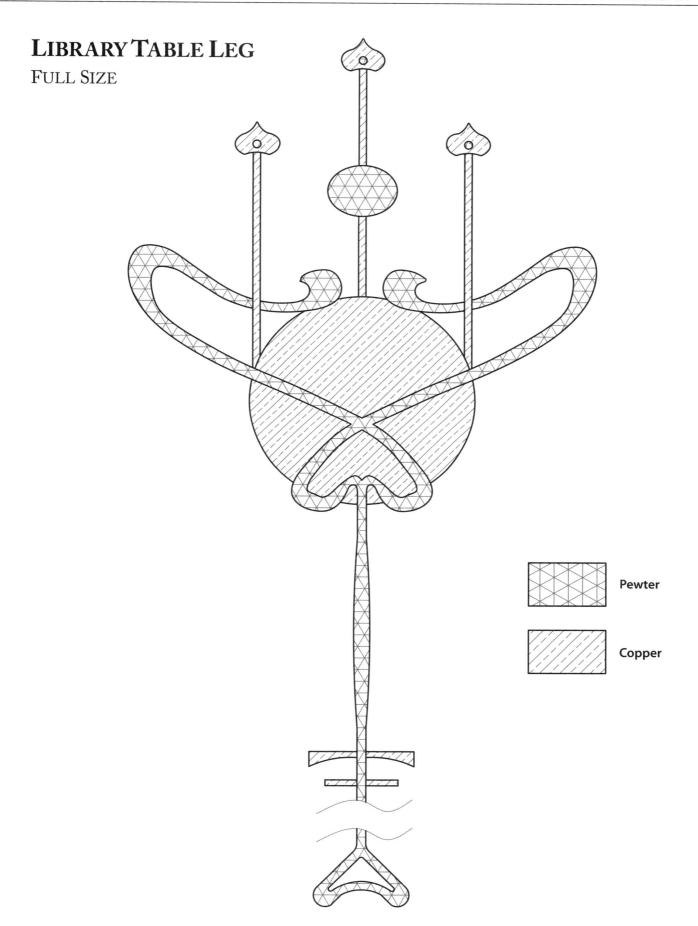

Pewter

Copper

LIBRARY TABLE
ALTERNATE LEG

This pattern appeared on a library table similar in size to the one in the January 1904 issue of *The Craftsman* with four legs instead of the two wide posts in the magazine illustration. The vertical line at the bottom of the pattern was much longer: it was shortened in this drawing to fit the page, and it should be extended to suit the piece on which it is used.

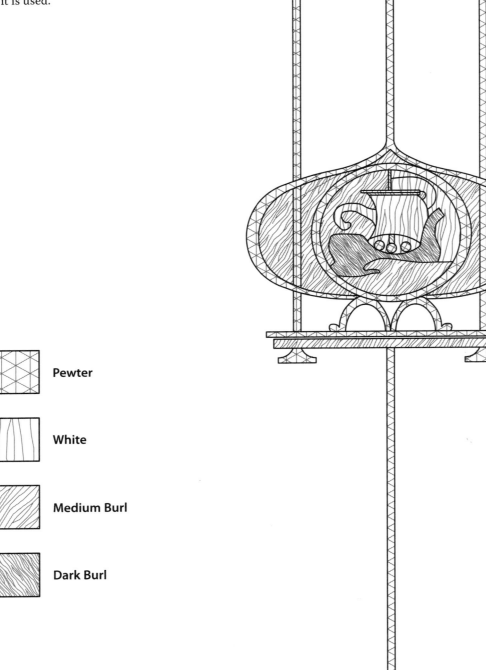

Pewter

White

Medium Burl

Dark Burl

THREE-LOBE SETTLE BACK

This pattern was seen in versions with three, four, or five lobes above the scene of a road winding through trees, most often on the wide slats on the backs of settles, but also on case pieces and pianos. It's reproduced here at 75% of actual size.

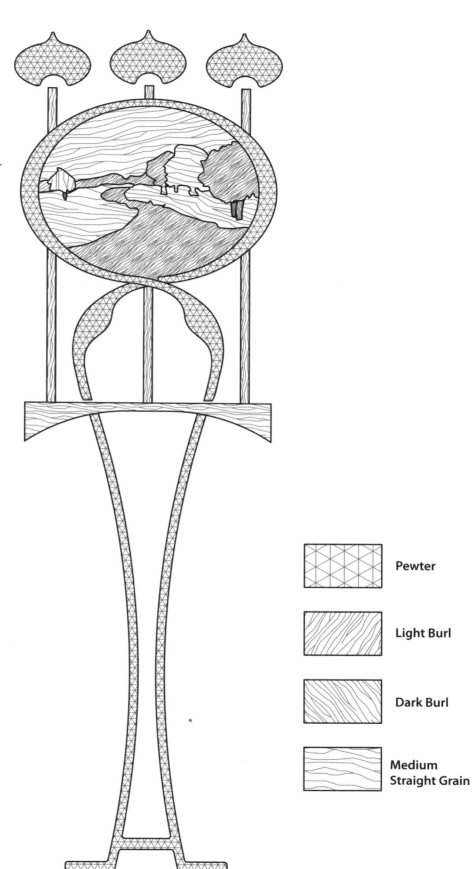

Pewter

Light Burl

Dark Burl

Medium Straight Grain

FOUR-LOBE SETTLE BACK

These designs appeared not only in various combinations of wood veneers and metals, but also with varying levels of detail in the central cameo. This design has also been found on the backs of large chairs. This reproduction is 75% of actual size.

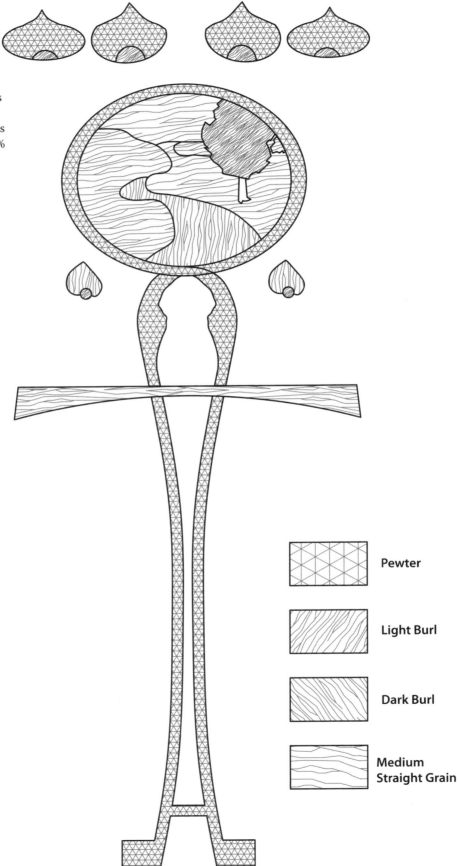

Pewter

Light Burl

Dark Burl

Medium Straight Grain

FIVE-LOBE SETTLE BACK

This is the largest and most complex variation of this pattern, and would be seen flanked by smaller variations.

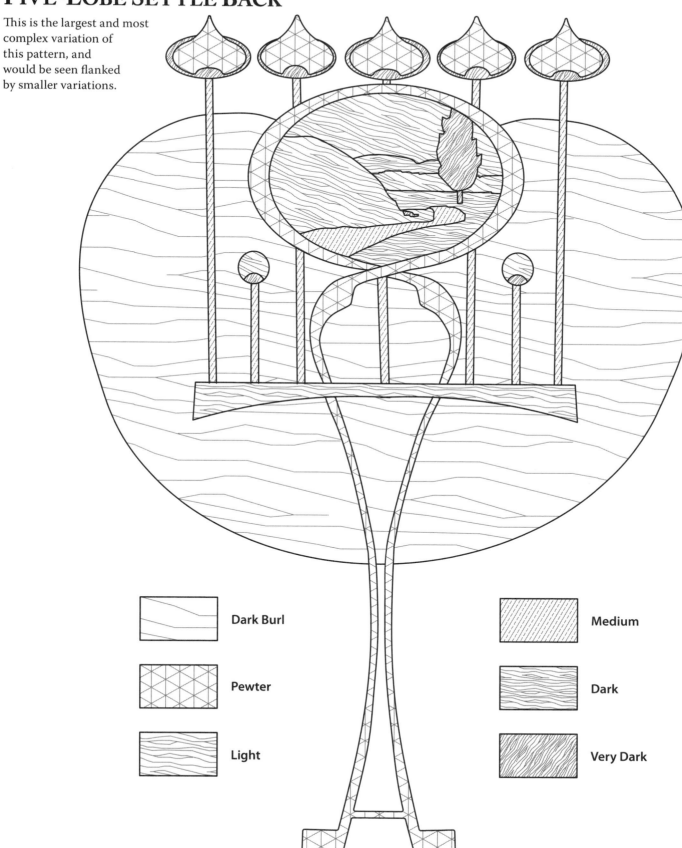

Dark Burl

Pewter

Light

Medium

Dark

Very Dark

TABLE LEG CREST

Another variation found on the leg of a "shoe foot" library table or desk. These shoe foot designs appeared in many of Ellis' magazine illustrations, but were never manufactured in any quantity.

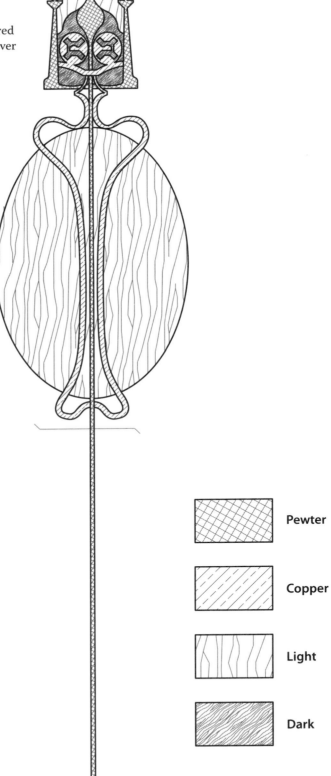

	Pewter
	Copper
	Light
	Dark

TABLE LEG CREST
FULL SIZE

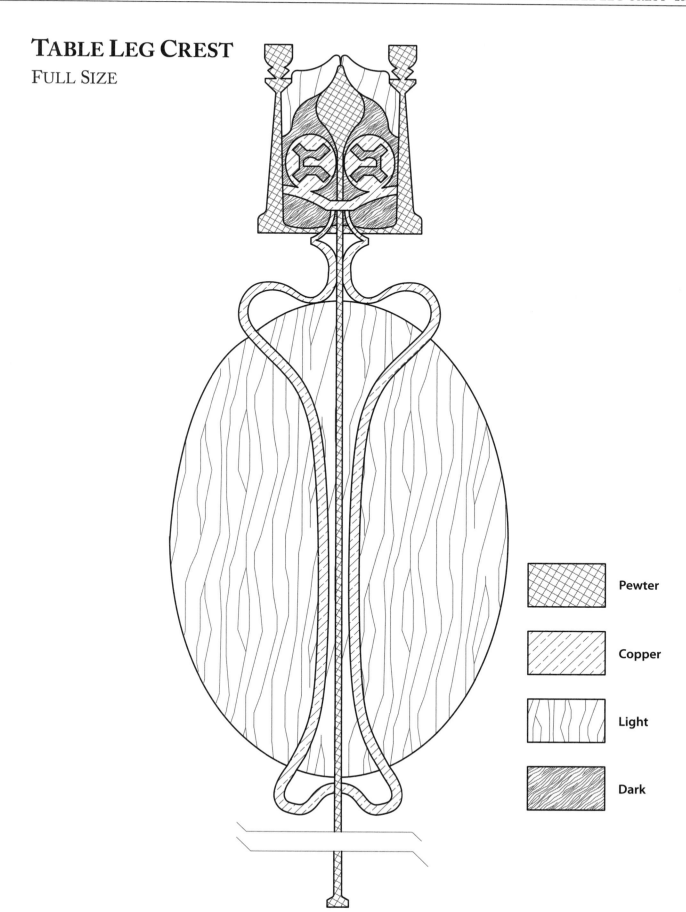

Pewter

Copper

Light

Dark

HORIZONTAL DESIGN

This design is found in many maple pieces, apparently made around 1909. It is seen on the top of chests, as well as on bed rails, including the beds in the girls' room at Stickley's house at Craftsman Farms.

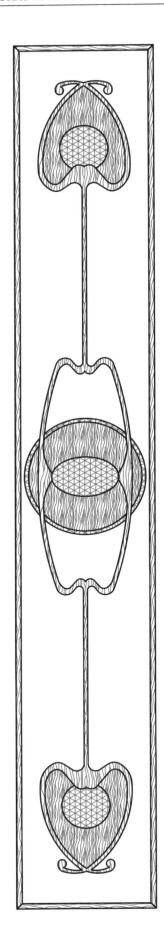

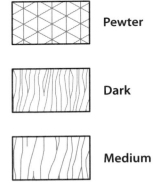

Pewter

Dark

Medium

HORIZONTAL DESIGN

FULL SIZE

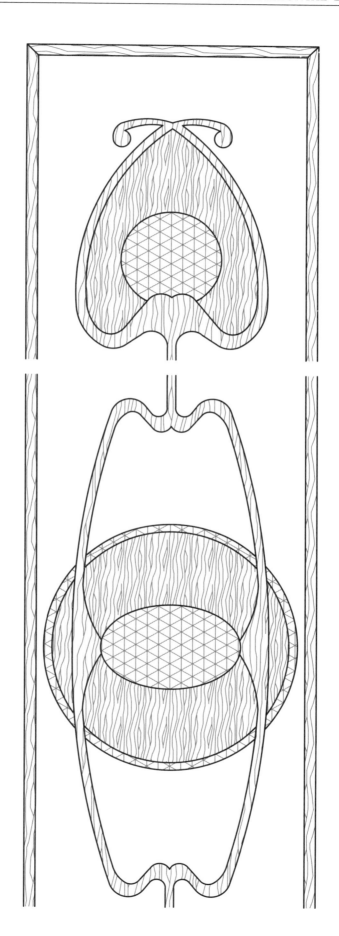

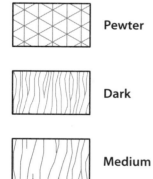

Pewter

Dark

Medium

LARGE CHAIR SLAT

The wide slats on some chair designs
lend themselves to large patterns
such as this. The inlay and
background would be assembled
and veneered to the slat as one piece.

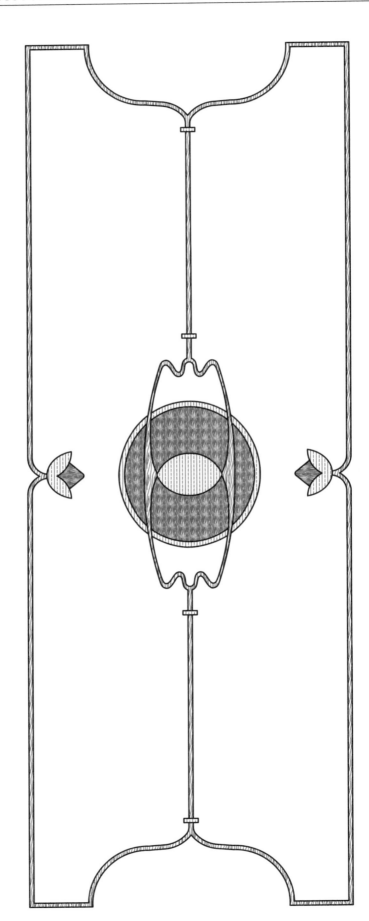

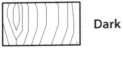 Dark

 Light

 Copper

 Dark Burl

LARGE CHAIR SLAT

FULL SIZE

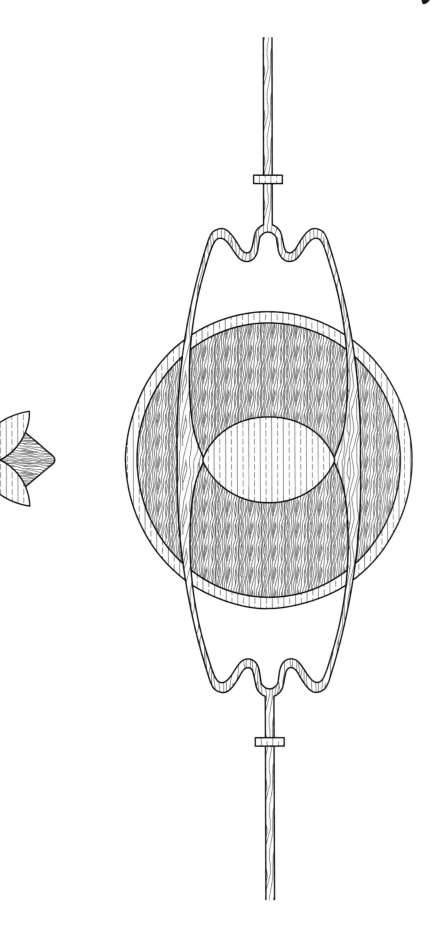

Dark

Light

Copper

Dark Burl

PIANO INLAY

This design was the first inlay photograph to be published in *The Craftsman*, in the October issue of 1903. It was seen on a piano that was among the contents of Stickley's residence in Syracuse.

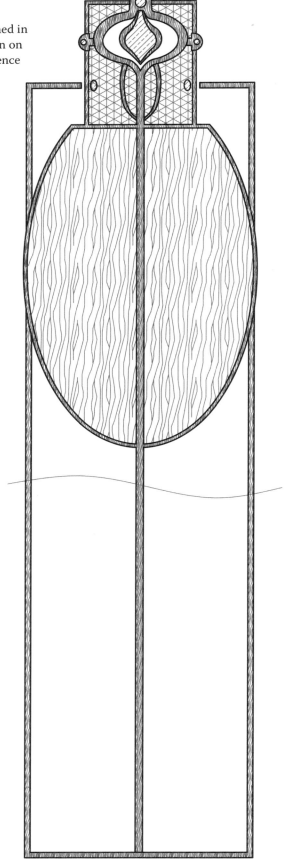

Olive

Black

Pewter

Copper

PIANO INLAY

FULL SIZE

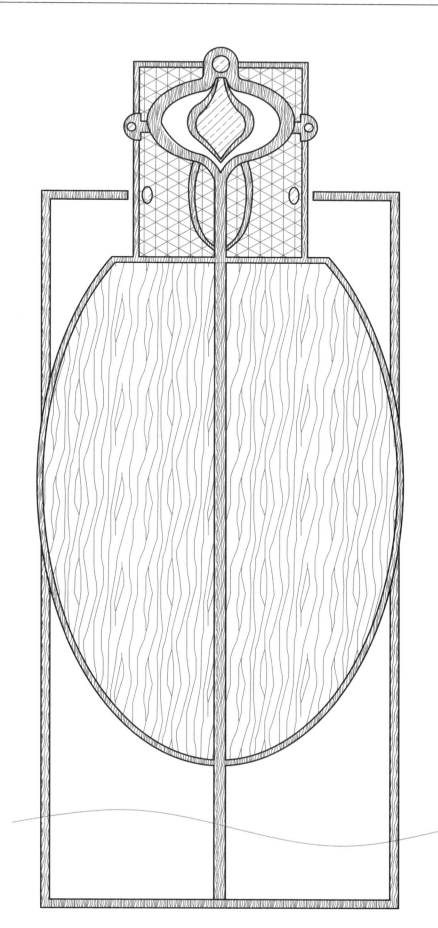

Olive

Black

Pewter

Copper

Unhatched areas are
same as background

SMALL SQUARE MOTIF

Many variations of the Ellis designed No. #700 bookcase (page 244) were produced. Some of the prototypes were adorned with this small inlay on the door stiles. Enlarge or reduce the motif to fit the piece being built.

 Medium

 Light

 Dark

GRAPE CLUSTER

A pair of these patterns was placed on each door of an Ellis designed music cabinet. This drawing is 75% of actual size.

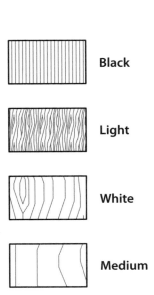

Black

Light

White

Medium

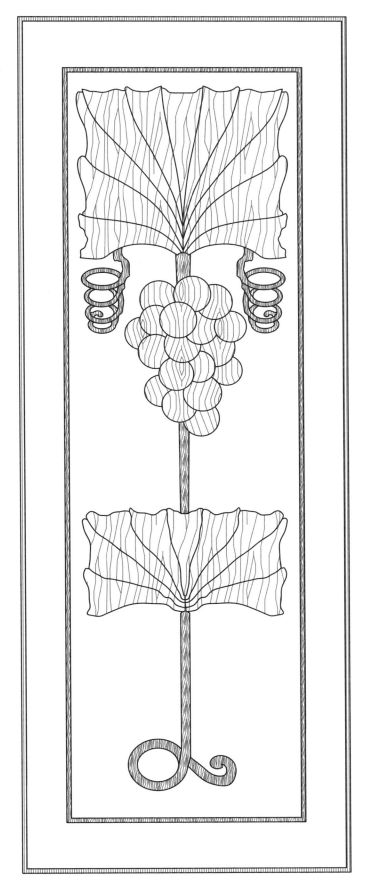

ALL-VENEER CHAIR BACK

Another chair slat detail, one of the few inlays to contain no metal.

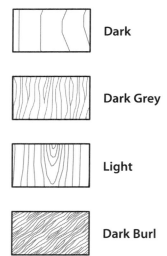

Dark

Dark Grey

Light

Dark Burl

ALL-VENEER CHAIR BACK

FULL SIZE

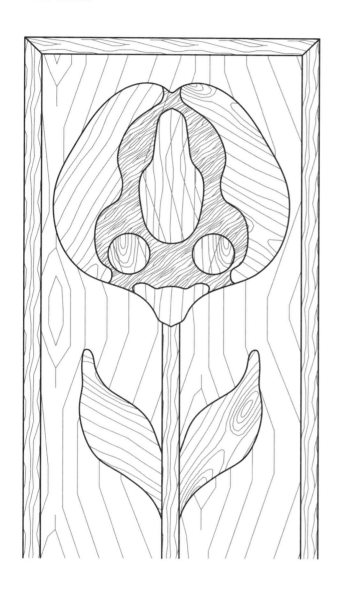

 Dark

 Light

Dark Grey

 Dark Burl

NON-ELLIPTICAL CHAIR SLAT

This design differs from the preceding designs in that the curves are not parts of ellipses. It is not known if these differences are the result of different designers, or different artisans preparing drawings or inlays.

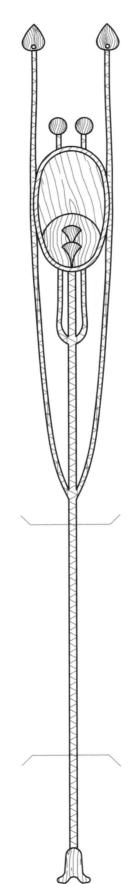

Dark Burl

Light

White

Pewter

Copper

NON-ELLIPTICAL CHAIR SLAT

FULL-SIZE

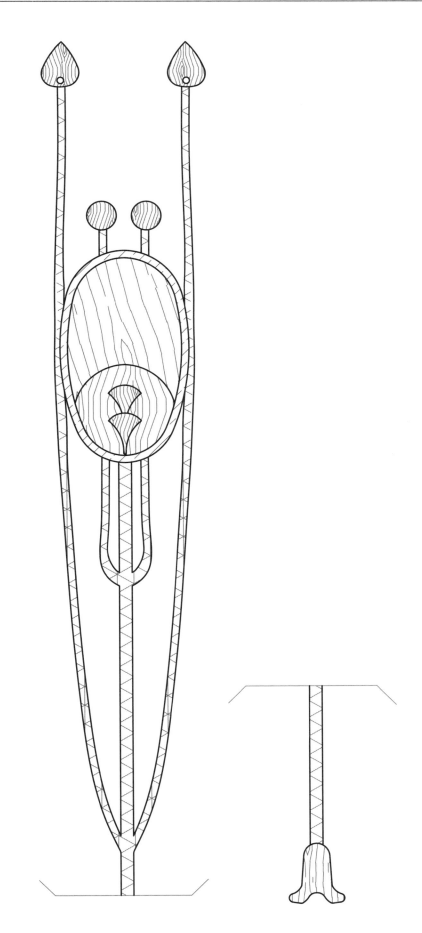

Dark Burl

Light

White

Pewter

Copper

TABLE LEG IN METAL

This design was among the group of pieces introduced in *The Craftsman* in January 1904. The designs in pewter and copper were on each of the four legs of a round shoe foot table.

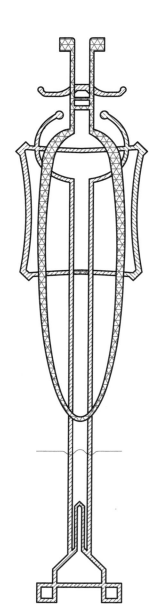

 Pewter

 Copper

TABLE LEG IN METAL
FULL SIZE

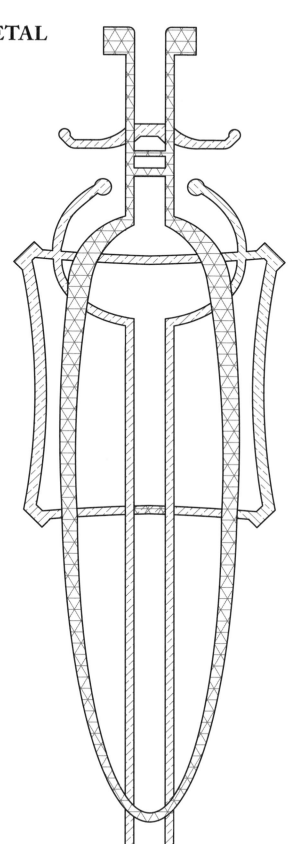

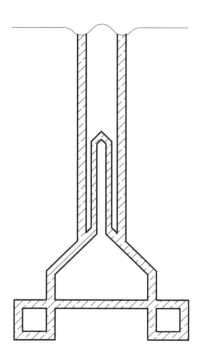

 Pewter

 Copper

SCREEN INLAYS

A three-panel screen in *The Craftsman* featured these inlays at the top of the arched panels. The large motif on this page was centered between two of the designs on the facing page.

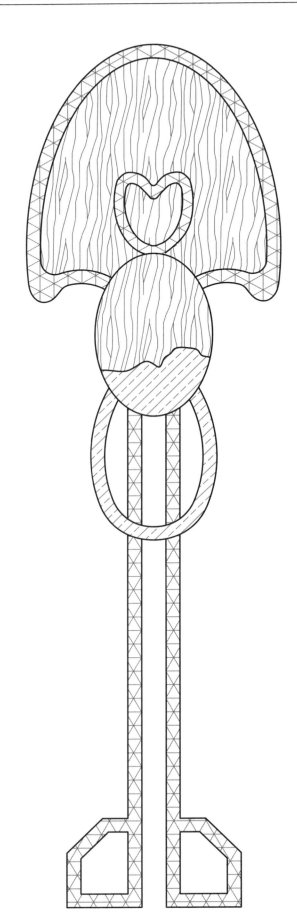

Light Burl

Copper

Pewter

SCREEN INLAYS

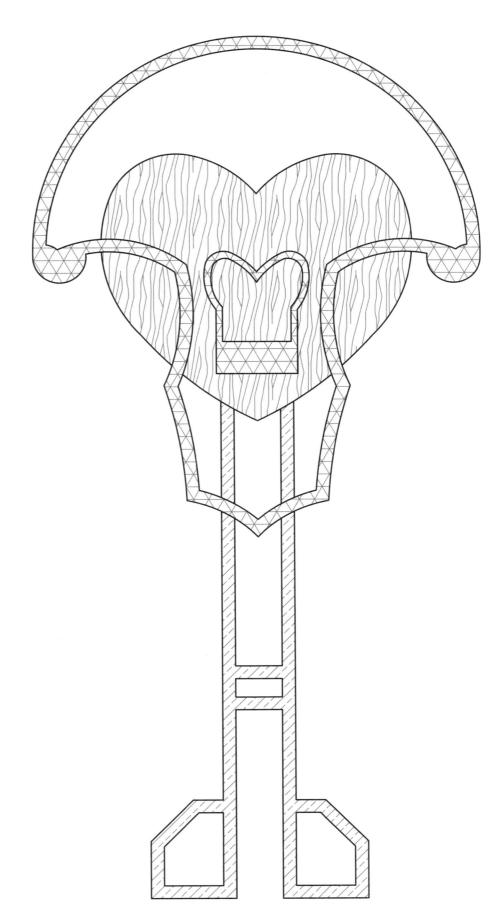

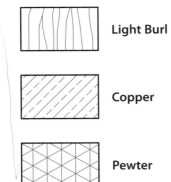

Light Burl

Copper

Pewter

MUSIC CABINET FLORAL INLAY

A single-door music cabinet had this floral design centered in the door. This drawing is actual size.

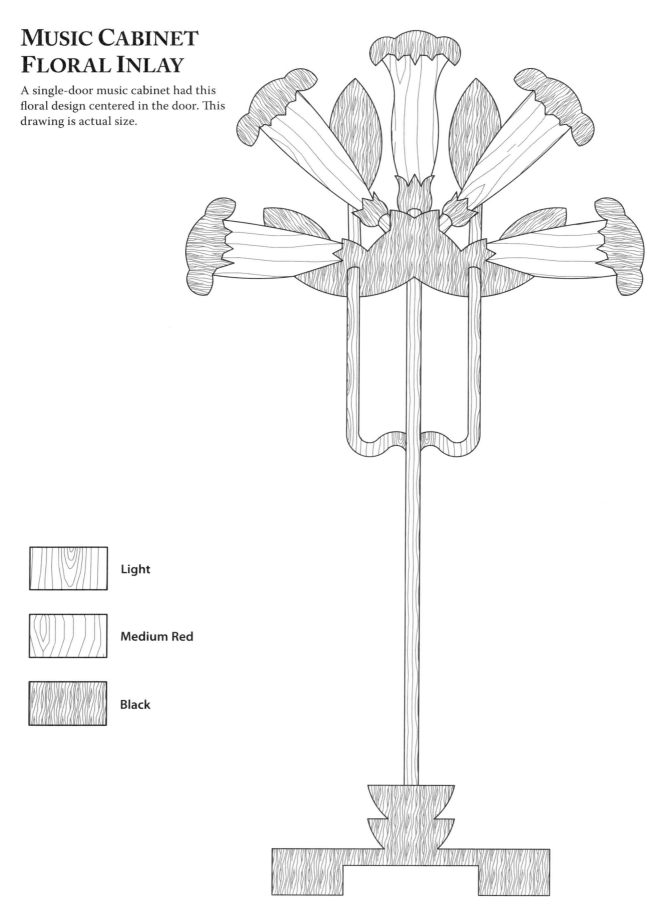

Light

Medium Red

Black

STICKLEY BROTHERS SETTLE BACK

This floral design, while reminiscent of those found on Gustav Stickley's furniture, was actually the product of Albert Stickley's company in Grand Rapids, Michigan. The drawing is 75% of actual size.

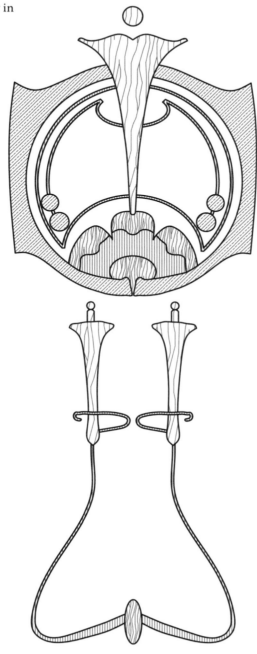

Light

Brass

Dark

Black

STICKLEY BROTHERS SETTLE BACK

TOP DETAIL, FULL SIZE

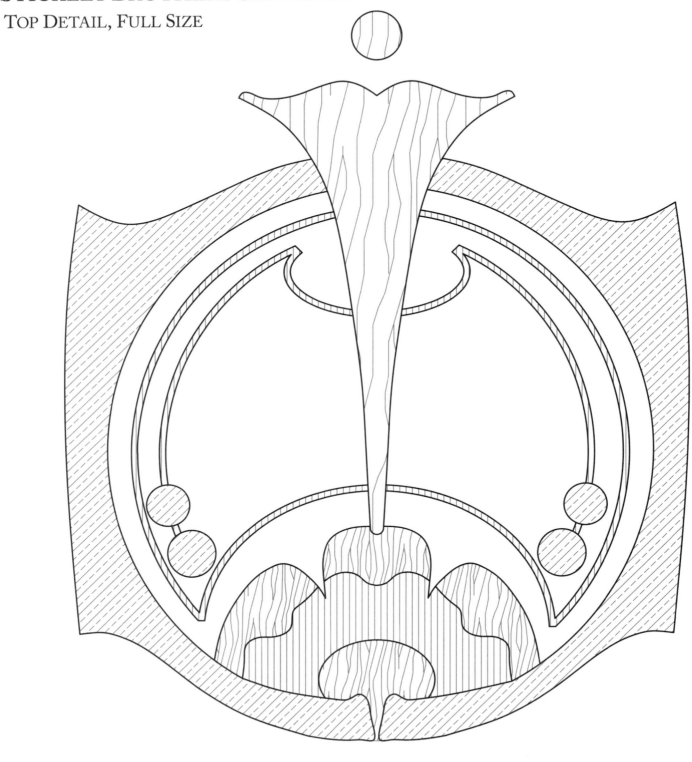

 Light

 Brass

 Dark

 Black

STICKLEY BROTHERS SETTLE BACK

BOTTOM DETAIL, FULL SIZE

 Light

Brass

 Dark

Black

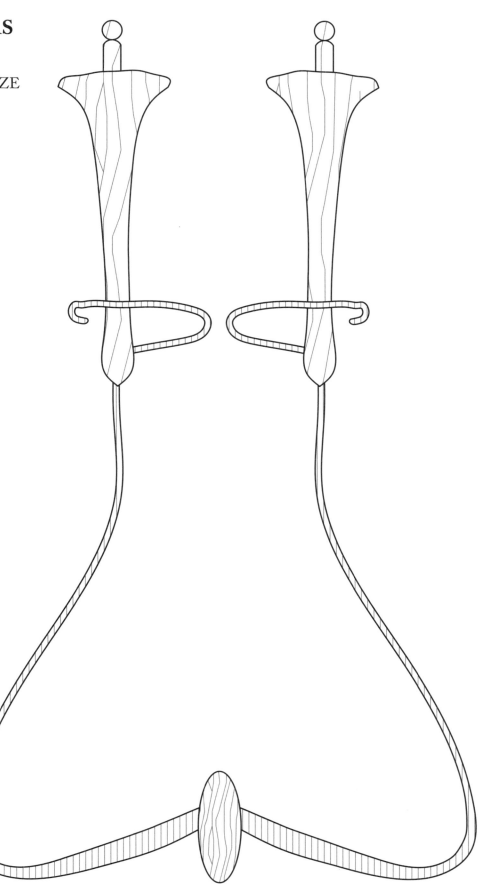

STICKLEY BROTHERS LARGE FLORAL

This large design was placed on two panels of a tall-backed settle.

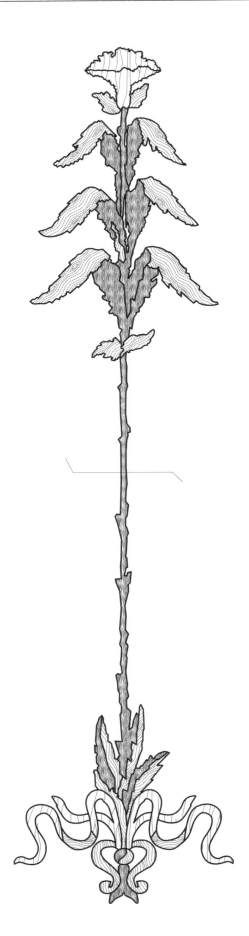

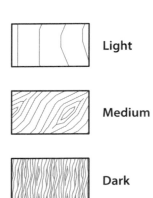

Light

Medium

Dark

STICKLEY BROTHERS
LARGE FLORAL
FULL-SIZE DETAILS

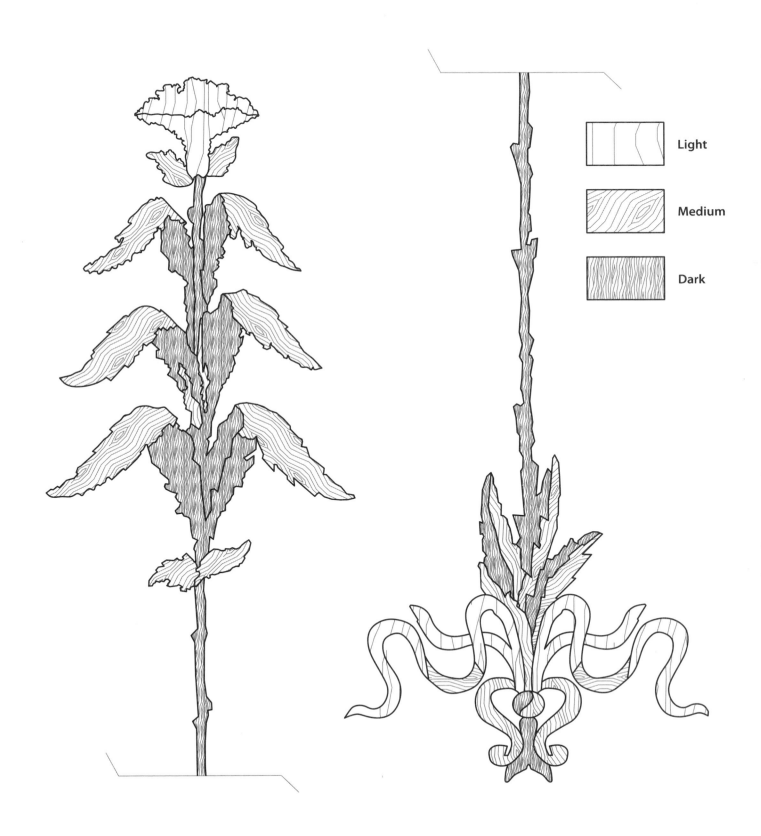

Light

Medium

Dark

STICKLEY BROTHERS SETTLE LEG

This vertical design was set in a recess in the leg of a leather-cushioned settle.

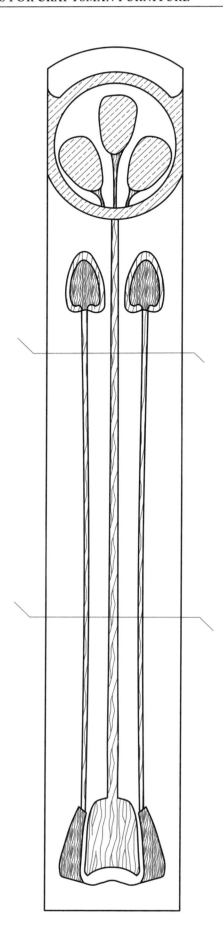

 Copper or Brass

 Black

 Dark

STICKLEY BROTHERS SETTLE LEG

FULL-SIZE DETAILS

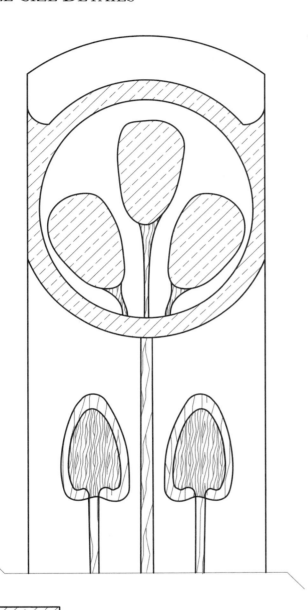

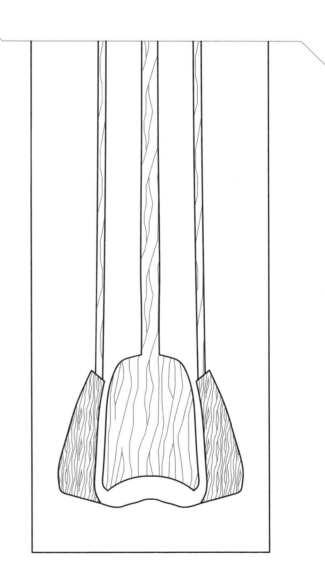

 Copper or Brass

 Black

 Dark

STICKLEY BROTHERS SMALL MOTIF

Reminiscent of a Celtic knot, this small design reflects the English
roots of the Stickley Brothers inlays. Actual size.

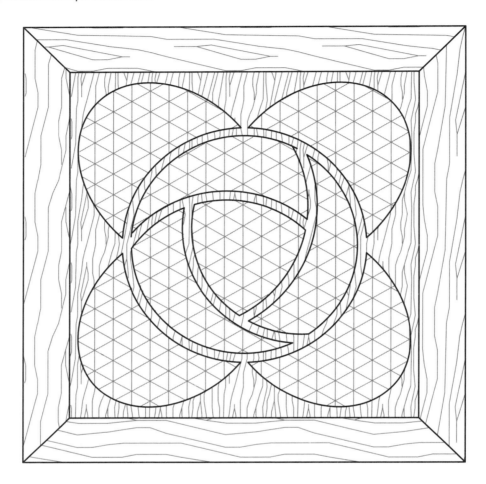

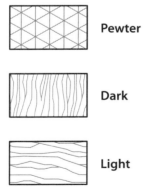

Pewter

Dark

Light

STICKLEY BROTHERS METAL FLORAL

The English roots are again apparent in this small and elegant design. Full size.

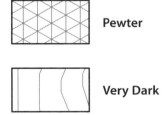

Pewter

Very Dark

STICKLEY BROTHERS VENEER FLORAL

This all-veneer design is from a hexagonal Stickley Brothers table. The drawing is full-size.

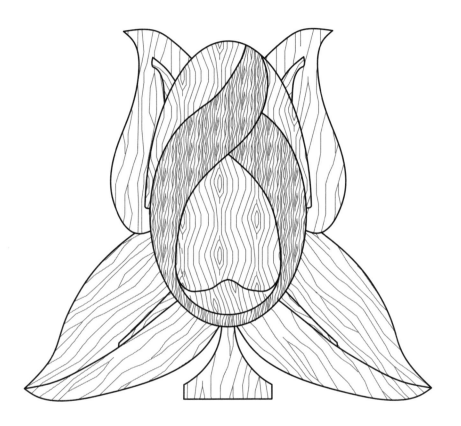

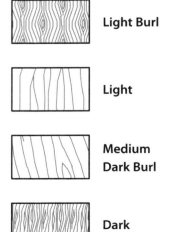

Light Burl

Light

Medium
Dark Burl

Dark

STICKLEY BROTHERS BIRDS

A pair of these designs was on the back panels of the "Balmoral" settle. This drawing is 75% of actual size.

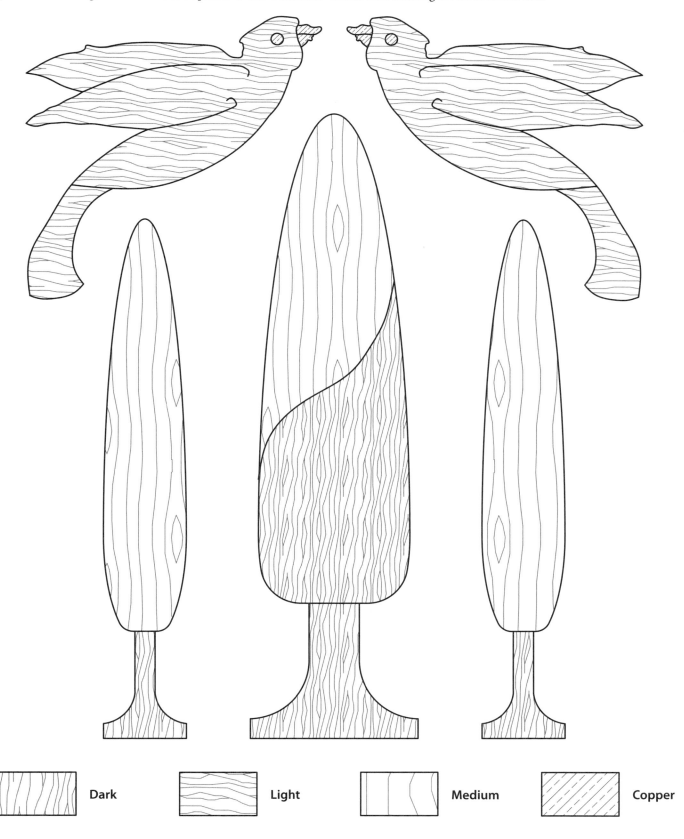

Dark   Light   Medium   Copper

GUSTAV STICKLEY HORIZONTAL V-SHAPED PULLS

SMALL

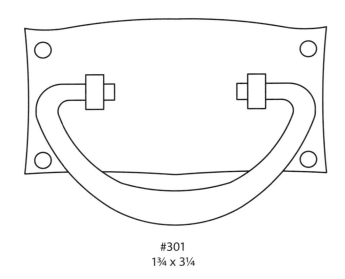

#301
1¾ x 3¼

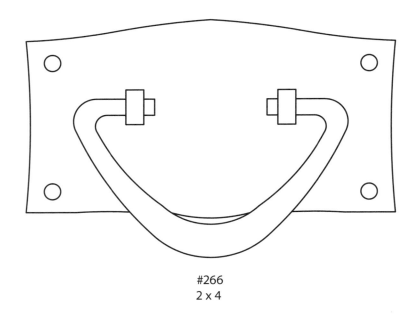

#266
2 x 4

GUSTAV STICKLEY HORIZONTAL V-SHAPED PULL

LARGE

These V-shaped pulls were the most common drawer pulls used in Craftsman furniture, along with the matching door pull (#267) on page 315. Small pan-head screws, patinated to match the hardware, are used for fastening. On pieces with several drawers, the same-size pull would be used on every drawer.

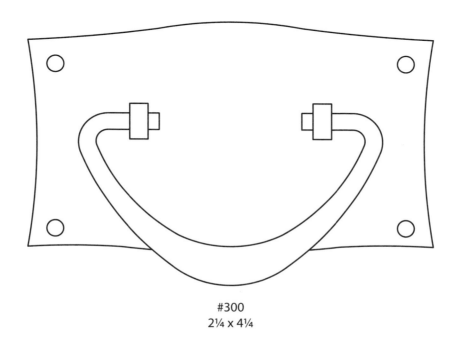

#300
2¼ x 4¼

GUSTAV STICKLEY VERTICAL O-SHAPED PULLS

These O-shaped pulls were another common type, usually seen without the keyholes. On pieces with graduated drawers, the back plates of the pulls would be the same height as the drawer fronts, giving the appearance of a continuous metal band on the finished piece.

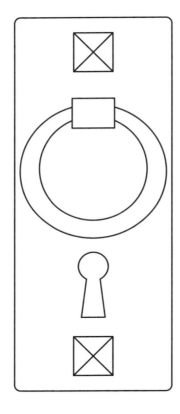

#27
1⅝ x 4

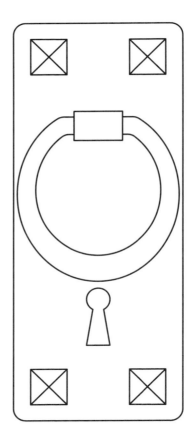

#54
1¾ x 4¼

GUSTAV STICKLEY V-SHAPED AND O-SHAPED PULLS

The pull on the right is fastened with pyramid-head screws, which are still available from several reproduction hardware suppliers. The holes should be tapped with a regular screw of the same or slightly smaller size, so that the pyramid-head screw may be more easily driven in.

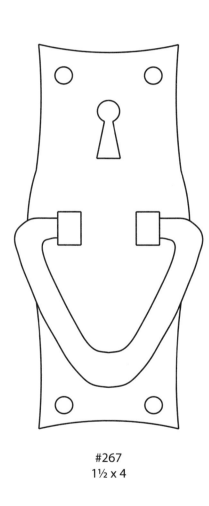

#267
1½ x 4

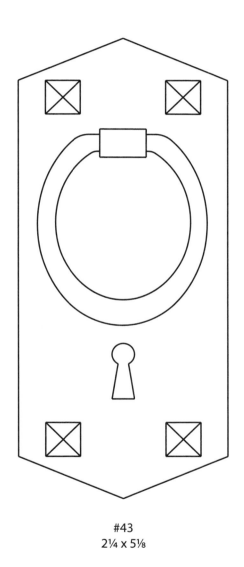

#43
2¼ x 5⅛

GUSTAV STICKLEY—EARLY PULLS WITH METAL PYRAMID KNOBS

These pulls both have a pyramid shaped knob, as seen in the side view at the bottom of the page. These knobs could be forged, but the originals were cast in sand. Reproduction pulls are available, though they are usually cast in bronze rather than copper. These could be used with a hammered back plate if a close reproduction, rather than an exact one, is acceptable.

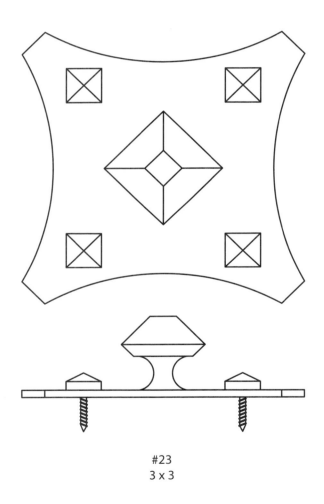

#23
3 x 3

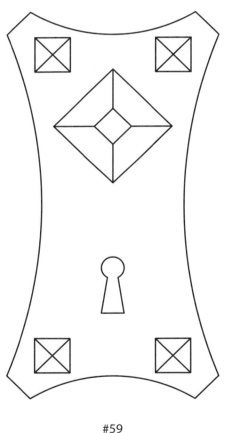

#59
2¼ x 4¼

GUSTAV STICKLEY STRAP PULL AND ESCUTCHEONS

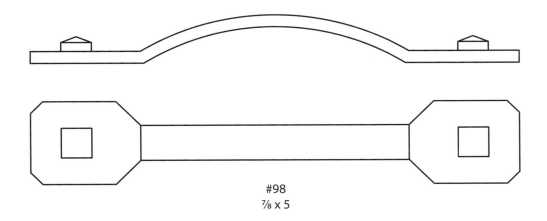

#98
⁷⁄₈ x 5

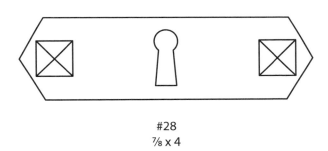

#28
⁷⁄₈ x 4

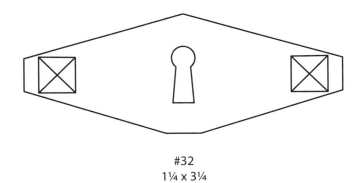

#32
1¼ x 3¼

GUSTAV STICKLEY HORIZONTAL O-SHAPED PULLS

The O-shaped bails are simple to forge around the horn of a small anvil, with the final bend placing the end of the bail into the hole of the bail holder.

The ends should be reduced in diameter to fit in the hole, which goes completely through the holder.

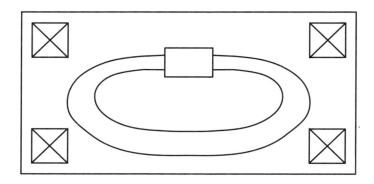

#38
1¾ x 3½

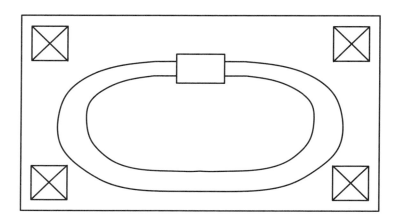

#24
2⅛ x 3¾

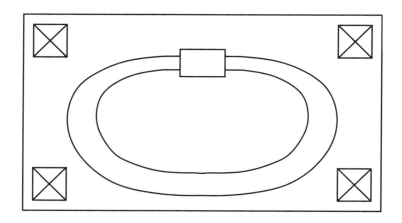

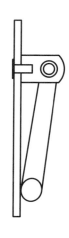

#31
2¼ x 4

GUSTAV STICKLEY HINGES AND HINGE STRAPS

Hinge straps (shown here at ½ actual size) could either include a hinge, or be simply a strap applied to the face of the door, the edge against a common butt hinge. It is simpler to form the strap without the hinge, and to use commercially available butts.

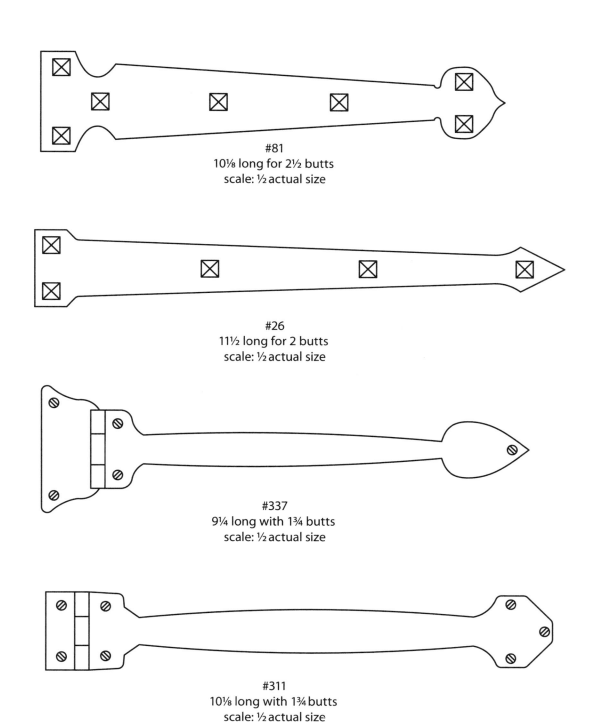

#81
10⅛ long for 2½ butts
scale: ½ actual size

#26
11½ long for 2 butts
scale: ½ actual size

#337
9¼ long with 1¾ butts
scale: ½ actual size

#311
10⅛ long with 1¾ butts
scale: ½ actual size

GUSTAV STICKLEY GRADUATED
O-SHAPED PULLS

The rectangle inside the perimeter, in line with the pyramid screws, is
a narrow groove in the hammered copper.

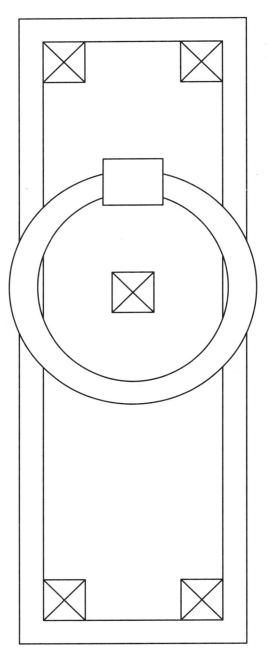

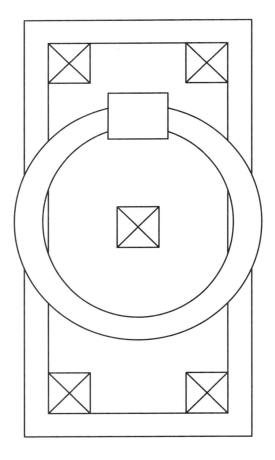

#907
2⅜ x 4½

#906
2⅜ x 6¾

GUSTAV STICKLEY GRADUATED O-SHAPED PULLS

Dressers with graduated drawers, such as the Harvey Ellis designed No. 913 (page 187), often had pulls that matched the heights of each drawer.

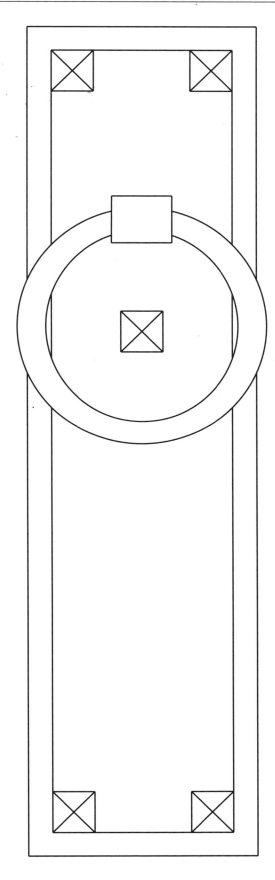

#905
2⅜ x 8⅞

GUSTAV STICKLEY U-SHAPED PULLS
SMALL AND MEDIUM

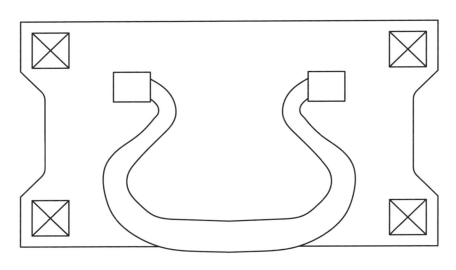

#171
2⅜ x 4¼

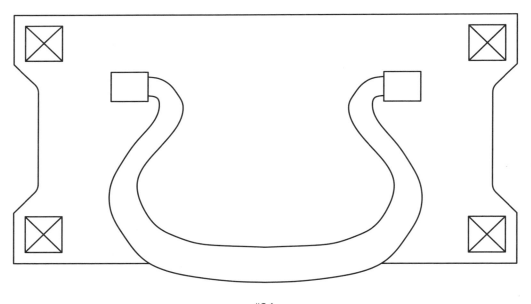

#34
2¾ x 5⅜ ·

GUSTAV STICKLEY U-SHAPED PULLS

LARGE

The U-shaped pulls were not as common as the V-shaped and O-shaped pulls, appearing in the *Hand-Wrought Metal Catalog* of 1905, but not on the production furniture.

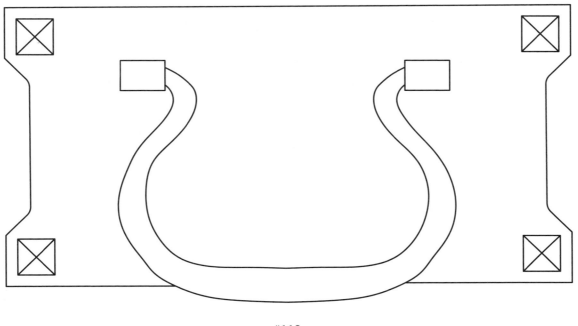

#118
3 x 5¾

Endnotes

1. Gustav Stickley. *Craftsman Homes*, pg. 158–159.

2. David M. Cathers. *Furniture of the American Arts & Crafts Movement.* New York, N.Y.: New American Library, 1981.

3. Cleota Reed. "For the Glory and the Good of Art: Irene Sargent & The Craftsman." *Style 1900,* Volume 14, No. 4, November 2001.

4. Barry Sanders. "Harvey Ellis: Architect, Painter, Furniture Designer." *Art & Antiques,* January–February 1981.

5. *Western Architect.* Volume III, February 1904.

6. Claude Bragdon. "Harvey Ellis: A Portrait Sketch." *The Architectural Review,* Volume XV, No. 12, December 1908.

7. Bragdon, 1908.

8. Bragdon, 1908.

9. Claude Bragdon. *Merely Players.* New York, N.Y.: Alfred A. Knopf, 1929; Cosimo Classics, 1995.

10. Reed, 2001.

11. Gustav Stickley, ed. *The Craftsman,* Volume IV, Number 4. July 1903.

12. *1910 Craftsman Furniture* catalog, pg. 8

13. Cathers, pg. 89.

14. "Structure and Ornament in the Craftsman Workshops." *The Craftsman,* January 1904, Vol. IV, No. 4.

15. Cathers, p. 241.

16. Gustav Stickley, ed. *The Craftsman,* July 1903.

17. *American Cabinet Maker and Upholsterer.* September 13, 1902.

18. David Cathers. "Gustav Stickley, George H. Jones, and the Making of Inlaid Craftsman Furniture." *Style 1900,* Volume 13, Number 1, February 2000.

19. Reed, 2001.

20. Gorden, Hugh M.G. "Harvey Ellis, Designer and Draughtsman," The Architectural Review, December 12, 1908.

21. Gustav Stickley, ed. *The Craftsman.* February 1904.

22. Gustav Stickley, ed. *The Craftsman.* January 1904.

23. Gustav Stickley, ed. "Metal Work." *The Craftsman.* October 1907.

Bibliography

Cathers, David M. *Furniture of the American Arts And Crafts Movement.* Eau
Claire, Wis.: Turn of the Century Editions, The Parchment Press, 1996

Hoadley, R. Bruce. *Understanding Wood.* Newtown, Conn.: The Taunton Press, 1982, revised 2001,

Johnson, Bruce. *The Official Identification and Price Guide to Arts and Crafts.* The House
   of Collectibles, 1988.

Jones, Bernard. *The Complete Woodworker.* Berkeley, Calif.: Ten Speed Press, 1998.

Joyce, Ernest. *The Encyclopedia of Furniture Making.* New York, N.Y.: Sterling Publishers, 1987.

Smith, Mary Ann. *Gustav Stickley, the Craftsman.* Mineola, N.Y.: Dover Publications, 1992.

Stickley, Gustav. *Making Authentic Craftsman Furniture.* Mineola, N.Y.: Dover Publications, 1986.

_____. *Craftsman Homes.* Mineola, N.Y.: Dover Publications, 1979.

REPRODUCTIONS OF ORIGINAL FURNITURE MANUFACTURER'S CATALOGS:

Stickley Craftsman Furniture Catalogs. (Catalog of Craftsman Furniture made by Gustav Stickley at the Craftsman Workshops, Eastwood N.Y. 1910.) Mineola, N.Y.: Dover Publications, 1979.

The Work of L. & J. G. Stickley, Fayetteville, N.Y. circa 1914.

Gray, Stephen, and Edwards, Robert, editors. *Collected Works of Gustav Stickley.* (Catalog 1904, retail plates 1907, articles, and illustrations from "The Craftsman" various dates, 1901-1914.) Eau Claire, Wis.: Turn of the Century Editions, The Parchment Press, 1981.

Davidoff, Donald, and Zarrow, Robert L., editors. *Early L. & J. G. Stickley Furniture.* (1906-1909 Catalog, retail plates circa 1909.) Mineola, N.Y.: Dover Publications, 1992.

Limbert Arts And Crafts Furniture, The Complete 1903 Catalog. Mineola, N.Y.: Dover Publications, 1992.

Roycroft Furniture Catalog, 1906. Mineola, N.Y.: Dover Publications, 1994.

The 1912 And 1915 Gustav Stickley Craftsman Furniture Catalogs. Mineola, N.Y.: Dover Publications, 1991.

Index

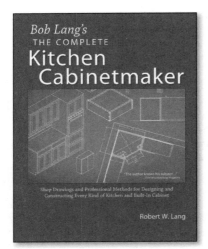

Bob Lang's The Complete Kitchen Cabinet Maker

Shop Drawings and Professional Methods for Designing and Constructing Every Kind of Kitchen and Built-In Cabinet

By Robert W. Lang

This extensive guide details how to approach the complex job of designing and making traditional and contemporary built-in cabinets.

ISBN: 978-1-892836-22-9
$ 22.95 • 224 Pages

Shop Drawings for Craftsman Interiors

Cabinets, Moldings & Built-Ins for Every Room in the Home

By Robert W. Lang

This comprehensive book is for decorators, homeowners, carpenters, and woodworkers who wish to create interiors of the iconic Craftsman movement.

ISBN: 978-1-892836-16-8
$ 24.95 • 224 Pages

Shop Drawings for Greene & Greene Furniture

23 American Arts and Crafts Masterpieces

By Robert W. Lang

Presented in this book, for the first time as working shop drawings, are 23 Greene & Greene furniture pieces, which are widely recognized as the finest expression of the American Arts & Crafts movement.

ISBN: 978-1-892836-29-8
$ 22.95 • 160 Pages

Large-format Plans for Craftsman Furniture

Please visit www.craftsmanplans.com, home of authentic detailed drawings of early 20th century American furniture as originally manufactured by Gustav Stickley, L. & L.G. Stickley, Charles Limbert & Roycroft. The plans are researched and drawn by Robert W. Lang, author of Shop Drawings for Craftsman Furniture, More Shop Drawings for Craftsman Furniture, & Shop Drawings for Craftsman Interiors. *Plans are rendered in AutoCAD and printed in 24" x 36" format. Each set of plans includes a detailed Bill of Materials.*

Visit the author's blog at readwatchdo.com.